3-9-77

3-9-77

International Trade Policy:
Agriculture and Development

International Trade Policy: Agriculture and Development

Vernon L. Sorenson
Professor in Agricultural Economics
Michigan State University

1975
MSU International
Business and Economic Studies

Division of Research
Graduate School of Business Administration
Michigan State University

ISBN: 0-87744-127-8
Library of Congress Catalog Card Number: 74-620204

To
Marilyn

Contents

List of Tables

xi

List of Figures

Preface

This book is intended for classroom use. My approach is to deal with trade and policy issues in a global framework rather than within the limited scope of U.S. self-interest. Such an approach involves study of the relationship of trade to efficient use of resources, the role of trade in economic development, and the implications for the domestic objectives of countries involved in international trade.

Detailed knowledge about international commodity markets, international conditions, and the policies of participating nations is not likely to be available to any one individual. However, I have written the volume in the belief that the scope and depth of coverage is sufficient to produce a core of material and ideas that will be useful to the individual reader as well as provide a framework and format for the teacher who wishes to prepare organized classroom material. For the individual reader who wishes to explore a particular topic beyond its coverage here, I have included a bibliography to provide a starting point for further research.

On completion of a task such as this, gratitude is due many people. Lawrence Witt, Nicholas Luyks, and Bruce Huff all reviewed a partial early draft and made many useful suggestions. John McKeon and Robert Stevens provided helpful comments on a later draft. I am also indebted to several persons in the Department of Agricultural Economics at Michigan State University for their assistance in typing, preparing footnotes, editing, and handling other questions of format and completeness.

Most of all, I want to express appreciation to the students with whom I have had many hours of discussion in and outside the classroom. They have played a central role both as stimulators and critics of the thoughts and issues on which this volume is based. Without their interest and curiosity this project would not have been started.

Introduction

During the post–World War II period, problems of international commercial conflict have centered increasingly on agriculture and the role of trade in development. Major economic, institutional, and political changes have occurred that have both changed market organization and increased political stress. The most ambitious attempt to negotiate international trade rules — the Kennedy Round — resulted in little measurable progress toward solving the world's agricultural or commodity trade problems. Three United Nations conferences on trade and development (UNCTAD) had limited success in finding solutions to the trade problems of less advanced countries. The task of effective policy formation to lessen confusion in trading relationships and to reduce conflict in commodity markets continues to confront the trading countries of the world. There are many reasons for the current status of disorder, conflict, and difficulty in arriving at mutually agreeable international policy for agriculture, but two factors are of dominant importance.

One of these is the network of policies formulated by individual nations. All advanced countries have established domestic policies aimed at varying degrees of protection for their agriculture, and many of these policies interfere with the orderly flow of international trade in agricultural products. While it is more usual to condemn the accompanying import restrictions needed to implement these policies, exporters are no less guilty of influencing trade by placing commodities onto markets at prices and in quantities quite different from those which would exist in the absence of domestic income programs for agriculture. In the less developed countries, domestic programs (often implemented through marketing boards) seek to exploit agriculture in the interest of foreign exchange savings and economic development. Other policies aimed at import substitution diminish total trading volume and, in combination with export marketing programs, influence trading prices and quantities in international markets.

A second problem encountered in formulating trade policy for agriculture arises from the great differences among countries in technical, economic, and institutional conditions surrounding agricultural production as well as the differing importance of agriculture in trade of individual nations. The United States is by a wide margin the world's largest exporter of agricultural products and raw materials. But these exports in total generate no more than about 2 percent of gross national product. This is in sharp contrast to smaller countries, such as the Netherlands, Ireland, Denmark, and others, with much smaller total volumes of trade, but with agricultural exports representing between 10 and 15 percent of the gross national product.

Among advanced nations there are wide variations in resource bases and conditions surrounding agricultural production. Less densely populated countries such as Canada, Australia, and the United States rely on extensive land areas and relatively large, low cost farms to establish their positions in world markets. Smaller industrial countries such as the Netherlands and Denmark enter export markets with intensively produced livestock products achieved at a relatively low cost. Among the major net importing countries — the United Kingdom, West Germany, and Japan — wide variations in production exist, but all have high population-to-land ratios and inadequate land bases, even with high output per hectare.

Among the less developed countries there are wide differences, both in the extent to which domestic production fulfills domestic needs and in the kind and degree of specialization involved in production that enters world markets. In the more static and least advanced countries, agriculture tends to be organized on a local subsistence basis. Participation in international markets (where it exists) is limited to one or two specialized products, and production and exporting often are controlled by outsiders. Some developing countries have begun or are seeking a more broadly oriented participation in international markets, as exporters, importers, or both. Plans to develop both agriculture and industry with a view toward expanded domestic output and effective participation in international markets have been instituted by many countries. Differences in the degree of structural adaptation of agriculture to modern technology and a general excess of labor in agriculture create wide variations in production costs among countries. In some cases these differences prevent adaptation of output to market requirements. This fact, along with excess commitment of total resources in some countries and widely differing demand conditions, has accentuated the conflict between national and international policy goals and objectives. Overcoming these differences to reconcile the varying interests and problems faced by different countries and groups of countries creates numerous problems in arriving at a policy framework that can be subscribed to by all or even most countries.

This study is an attempt to analyze conditions in international agricultural markets and some of the underlying phenomena that influence international trade and policy. It is tempting to start with an assessment of the conflict between domestic price or income policy and trade policy. I have chosen not to do so because it could overemphasize the immediate problem of conflict and overlook the causes behind the conflict. Only the nature of the conflict, not its causes, can be understood by looking solely and directly at existing policies and programs.

Consequently, the first three chapters attempt to lay the groundwork for discussion of policy issues. This is done by looking briefly at the historical and environmental conditions that influence commodity trade and policy, by sketching postwar development in trade, and by analyzing the economic foundations that influence trade and competitive positions in international agricultural markets.

The remaining chapters deal directly with policy issues. The first part of the policy discussion emphasizes trade problems among advanced countries, and the latter part of the book concentrates on issues and problems facing developing nations. This separation is not entirely satisfactory because the issues involved are often closely interrelated. Policies in advanced countries frequently have as much effect on the trading position of the less advanced as they do on trade among themselves. Yet differences between advanced and developing countries in economic condition and policy objectives and methods are clearly great, and they need to be looked at as separate although clearly interrelated problems.

1

Setting and Background

Much of what we believe to be possible as well as good or bad about trading relationships today is rooted in the events, conditions, and economic and political thought of past eras. The cumulative conditions that influence today's trading problems largely began with the Industrial Revolution. Specialization and mechanization meant lower prices for many goods. Because of lower production costs, business firms developed surpluses, and increased profits were possible. The development of an industrial structure created the need for and the possibility of trading economies extending beyond local exchange. A need developed for expanded markets and increased sources of raw materials. This in turn led to a major reorganization of social and economic structures within more advanced countries, particularly the United Kingdom, and the expansion of trade on an intercountry basis.

The Emergence of Trade Policy

The first policy issue to gain ascendancy in the newly formed nation states of the eighteenth and nineteenth century was the question of the ultimate source of national wealth. The first practical men to develop a solution were known as *mercantilists*. The scope of mercantilist economic doctrine is illustrated by the following quotation:

> All commodities found in a country, which cannot be used in their natural state, should be worked up within the country . . . . Attention

should be given to the population, that it may be as large as the
country can support . . . . Gold and silver once in the country are
under no circumstances to be taken out for any purpose . . . . The
inhabitants should make every effort to get along with their domestic
products . . . . [Foreign commodities] should be obtained not for gold
or silver, but in exchange for other domestic wares . . . and should be
imported in unfinished form, and worked up within the country . . . .
Opportunities should be sought night and day for selling the
country's superfluous goods to these foreigners in manufactured
form . . . . No importation should be allowed under any circumstances of which there is a sufficient supply of suitable quality at
home.[1]

A wide range of policies was implemented to serve these mercantilist
goals. Many forms of trade restrictions, licenses, duties, tariffs, export
subsidies, and an extensive regulation (planning) of domestic economic
activity became the foundation of national policy. Directing commercial policy toward the end of national wealth with a major emphasis on
state control of international commerce as the vehicle for increasing
wealth dominated early development of international trade policy.

But as with all extreme positions, a reaction set in. During the late
1700s, the methods and aims of mercantilism increasingly were questioned. The notion that prosperity and growth would be augmented by
giving free play to the selfish motives of individuals began to emerge.
The writings of Adam Smith produced an analytical undergirding for
the doctrine that the wealth of nations and economic growth are
enhanced through the efforts of individuals seeking their own ends
through the market mechanism, and with minimum direction by government. While Smith was concerned primarily with the creation of
wealth, economists who followed him were interested mainly in the
distribution of wealth in the form of rents, profits, and wages and in the
formation of market prices through the interplay of supply and demand. They built on Smith's concepts to achieve a systematic analysis of
market adjustment. Being men concerned with practical affairs of the
day as they existed in England, it was natural for them to turn to
questions of international trade. While it was obvious that there were
some differences between domestic commerce and international trade
— in such matters as factor mobility, money, banking, the settling of
accounts, and national policy and economic life[2] — a great virtue of the
self-regulating market analysis was that it could be transferred directly
into the analysis of international markets. Armed with this analytical
framework, the classical economists developed three concepts in trade
analysis.[3]

The most renowned of these is the theory of comparative advantage. The argument demonstrated that absolute cost differentials were not necessary to create trade and that countries could gain from trade with each other despite general differences in production cost levels. Comparative advantage is thus a welfare theory which argues the good of expanded trade and also demonstrates how trade is possible despite basic differences among the economies of different nations.

A second major concept, the price-specie flow theory of payments, was developed to argue and demonstrate the automatic nature of the adjustment of trade and payments among nations. Stated in its simplest form, if a nation is receiving more gold in exchange for export sales than can be absorbed domestically at full employment equilibrium, prices will rise, export sales in turn will decline, and gold will flow out. A nation in a deficit trade position will lose gold, prices will decline, its commodities will become more attractive in international markets, exports will expand, and there will be a compensating inflow of gold. In this manner prices will fluctuate automatically to maintain an equilibrium adjustment among countries. This was, of course, a long-term equilibrium argument, and it overlooked short-term disequilibrium problems and the question of how trade is financed.

The third major idea used reciprocal demand to explain international values. This theory argues that countries will offer goods in international markets and demand goods from international markets in relationship to domestic demand and production conditions and that each nation will share in trade in relationship to its competitive efficiency.

Each of these notions was conducive to arguing the case for free trade as a welfare maximizing system and for limited government intervention to facilitate the orderly conduct of commercial affairs. These arguments were supported by the institutions and circumstances of the times. The United Kingdom was rapidly emerging as the dominant world economic power. London became the financial center of the world, and British institutions developed the mechanisms for international clearing of payments and for international lending and investment. Industrial capacity both in Great Britain and Western Europe was expanding rapidly, and a complementarity developed in the export of capital and manufactured goods and the import of raw materials and food. This complementarity was implemented through a rapid expansion of colonial empires. In the case of Great Britain, close ties with North America and Asia emerged, and new institutions, such as the East India Company and the Hudson Bay Company, were established to implement the physical and financial activities required for the expansion of international trade.

Along with these institutional developments, major technological advances, particularly those associated with improved transportation and communication, further stimulated the growth of trade. The pushing of railroads westward in the United States and eastward in Russia opened vast new areas to agricultural production and mining. These, along with production mechanization, such as the reaper in agriculture, reduced costs and greatly increased the scale of complementarity between vast overseas agricultural regions and the concentrated industrializing European countries. Overall, these factors increased the base for expansion of world markets and led to the commercial revolution of the nineteenth century. Its success depended upon the establishment of an appropriate philosophical framework to guide economic organization and policy and upon numerous institutional and technical developments unique to the times and highly complementary in their effect.[4]

Classical economics justified drastic changes in the institutions of mercantilism. Under British leadership, a strong move toward economic liberalization began in the early 1800s. The first major step came within the United Kingdom through the repeal of the Corn Laws in 1846, thus ending the world's first major price support program for agricultural commodities. This event occurred under the political pressures of a developing mass consumer society and culminated in a victory of consumer over property interests (or of individual over property rights). The Corn Laws originally were passed through the power of the landed aristocrats in an effort to protect their income. With their repeal, the power of the aristocracy was broken, and agriculture was left essentially at the mercy of markets. Thus the most important factor in the free trade movement was the unilateral abolition of Great Britain's trade restrictions.

Following this internal commitment to economic liberalism and to competitive domestic economic organization, the British sought worldwide liberalization through trading agreements, principally with other major European powers. These agreements, although bilateral, were interpreted to mean that any liberalization achieved would be extended to all trading nations. The most-favored-nation principle was applied. The most important of these agreements was made with France in 1860, and it led to a chain of others that created a widespread European free trade movement over the next decade. As indicated by the following statement, during this period trade liberalization for agricultural products proceeded further than for industrial products.

> By 1860 Britain had abolished duties not only on grain but on almost all other agricultural imports, leaving only a few revenue duties. France practically removed agricultural protection in the 1860 treaty, and in 1861 abolished her sliding scale of grain duties. Farmers in Germany were still interested mainly in exporting grain and therefore wanted free trade: the Zollverein's duties on grain had been abolished in 1853. In Italy the moderate Piedmontese duties formed the basis of the tariff for the unified kingdom, and after treaties with France and other countries, agriculture was protected only by low duties on grains. Belgium in 1871 decreed free entry for the main foodstuffs. The Netherlands dropped its grain duties in 1862. In most other countries agricultural trade was free or nearly so.[5]

Dissent and Divergence from Free Trade

The arguments for free trade that emerged from the classical economists never received unqualified international acceptance. The British free trade policy lasted until about the 1930s, but aberrations appeared on the Continent and in the United States almost as soon as the original agreements were signed.

The most important immediate cause of the movement toward protectionism on the Continent was agricultural competition from the United States and Russia, but the groundwork had been well laid by an economic doctrine developed in Germany, primarily by Frederick List.[6] List did not dispute the conclusion that free trade would optimize resource use if equilibrium adjustment were achieved, but he argued that accumulating wealth for economic development required protection. He advocated, among other things, customs unions of individual states, arguing that economic policy should be aimed at strengthening the state. He proposed incorporating border states into Germany to achieve a wider market and generally urged adoption of policies aimed at self-sufficient nationalism and development through protection.

His ideas portrayed a nationalistic approach which never has been abandoned by some nations. A few countries refused to adopt List's ideas, and the differences between the two categories condition trading relationships to this day. Denmark and the Netherlands resisted protection and currently are efficient trading nations and highly competitive in world agricultural markets. Other countries which followed the German lead and implemented protectionist policies continue to adhere to them. Furthermore, it should not be forgotten that the initial arguments for regionalism and a European customs union were established on the Continent as a part of the List doctrine.

A second major aberration in the free trade policy promoted by Great Britain occurred in the United States, which in its earliest era was basically protectionistic. By 1840 the United States had developed a substantial system of tariff protection with justification centered in the infant industry concept and more broadly on the need for protection to promote economic development. A period of tariff liberalization during the 1840s and 1850s occurred in response to British leadership, and for a time the United States joined the free trade movement. But the absence of southern states from the Congress, pressures from emerging northern industrial states, and revenue needs for the Civil War opened a new era of protectionism. From the 1860s until 1929, high levels of protection persisted, with modest upward or downward movements depending largely upon the outlook of the political party in office. It cannot be asserted that the United States was a major contributor to the free trade philosophy of the nineteenth century. Although protectionist, its position could be tolerated because of the limited scope of its international economic activity. From a commercial point of view the United States was still a small country.

Nineteenth-century trade liberalization thus was based on British dominance, institutions, and leadership. This era ended with World War I. Thereafter, all of Europe was impoverished and required heavy foreign purchases that placed a major strain on the balance of payments. Monetary depreciation and economic collapse ultimately resulted. Furthermore, the political map of postwar Europe largely had been redrawn. Countries began to seek self-sufficiency and designed trade impediments toward that goal. A second major element of change was the rise of the United States and Japan as major industrial producers as a result of wartime requirements. Consequently, their actions, particularly those of the United States, had a much greater impact upon international commercial policy. However, this effect was not recognized in the United States, which continued to pursue protectionist policies. The United States had changed from a raw material exporter and importer of capital to an industrial nation and, in fact, became the major source of import goods to reconstruct Europe. It had become a major creditor nation, but, unfortunately, protectionism placed major obstacles in the way of repayment. Because the country failed to recognize the requirements of being a world banker, its policies had a major and heavy impact on the collapse of trade and economic stagnation in the 1930s.

The role of economic and policy developments in the United States was crucial. As stated by Dudley Dillard:

During the 1920's the state of international trade, especially after the return to the gold standard, depended on a large and continuing volume of long-term loans from the United States. Although a heavy international debt structure was built up, the adjustments in underlying economic conditions needed to liquidate these debts did not develop. Beginning in 1928 the volume of new long-term loans available from the United States began to dwindle and after the New York stock exchange crash in 1929 virtually ceased altogether. The early victims were the countries producing primary products (foodstuffs and raw materials), the prices of which fell precipitously between 1929 and 1932.

In order to meet their balance-of-payments deficits the agricultural countries threw wave after wave of products on the world market for whatever price they could get. They cut down on imports wherever possible and pushed their exports into tumbling world markets, each time causing further declines. The real burden of debts increased enormously in consequence of the fall in prices. In addition to the severe blow to international trade from the Hawley-Smoot Tariff of 1930, the dollar shortage was accentuated because a sharp fall in incomes in the United States reduced imports of commodities and kept American would-be tourists to Europe and elsewhere at home.[7]

A combination of circumstances led to the most comprehensive of all breakdowns in international commercial relationships — the collapse of the international financial mechanism. Great Britain was forced off the gold standard in the 1930s. Despite its shifting position in world affairs, the United States was concerned largely with domestic matters and failed to assume any of the responsibility for international market mechanisms that previously had rested with the British. The world was left with no effective mechanism for international transactions, and trade restrictions expanded rapidly, including exchange controls, bilateral barter arrangements, and other protective devices. In toto these controls destroyed the basis for multilateral free trade developed during the nineteenth century. The era of liberalism in trade policy ended, possibly inevitably so, since all the institutional and complementary relationships upon which this liberalization was built were completely altered, and a new set of conditions had arisen.

While, on the one hand, the interwar period can be viewed as the breakdown of an old trading system, on the other it can be seen as the period of gestation for modern issues and problems in international commercial relationships. Just as nineteenth-century philosophy grew out of the social and economic turmoil caused by the Industrial Revolution in the world's leading industrial country, modern conditions grew out of the social and economic turmoil created by the Great Depression and consequent changes in domestic economic organization within

individual countries. Highly significant in this process was the growth
of large-scale business and powerful labor unions. Both businessmen
and labor leaders began to assume control of their economic destinies.
This development, in turn, disrupted the adjustment process both
within and among countries.

A second major postdepression feature was the development of
protection for agriculture in most advanced countries. Agriculture was
the largest industry which could not develop its own economic power
through organization or expansion in size of enterprise or combine.
This development had a major impact on international commodity
flows, affected worldwide production patterns, and had the secondary
effect of generating greater degrees of self-sufficiency. In particular,
protection impeded exports from less developed countries which could
have been used to purchase industrial imports. According to present
spokesmen for developing countries, protectionism helped induce a
wave of import subsititution industries that in many cases are inefficient and currently represent one of the basic conditions affecting
relationships between advanced and less developed nations.

A third interwar occurrence that strongly influenced current international commercial problems was the development in economic doctrine. Centered largely around the early writings of J. M. Keynes,
criticism of the automatic adjustment mechanism began to develop.

Keynes's repudiation of the philosophy of laissez-faire was stated as
follows:

> Let us clear from the ground the metaphysical or general principles
> upon which, from time to time, *laissez-faire* has been founded. It is *not*
> true that individuals possess a prescriptive "natural liberty" in their
> economic activities. There is *no* "compact" conferring perpetual rights
> on those who Have or on those who Acquire. The world is *not* so
> governed from above that private and social interest always coincide.
> It is *not* so managed here below that in practice they coincide. It is *not* a
> correct deduction from the Principles of Economics that enlightened
> self-interest always operates in the public interest. Nor is it true that
> self-interest generally *is* enlightened; more often individuals acting
> separately to promote their own ends are too ignorant or too weak to
> attain even these. Experience does *not* show that individuals, when
> they make up a social unit, are always less clear-sighted than when
> they act separately.[8]

Thus began the argument for the need to formulate government
economic policy through monetary and fiscal devices for the stabilization of employment at a high level and the achievement of society's
other economic aims. Governments, Keynes argued, should take responsibility for the welfare of the nation and pursue positive policies of

economic management. Obviously this doctrine was not consistent with the automatic adjustment mechanism postulated by the classical economist. Keynes's arguments began to affect the outlook and actions taken by governments. Keynesian economics, at this stage, has been applied internally in virtually all countries.

Over the past few decades, the world has changed both in business and labor organization and in the responsibility that governments feel for pursuing national economic policies of full employment and growth. Each of these changes adds rigidities in economic organization and policies counter to the international adjustment mechanism that operated more or less automatically during the nineteenth century. Actions by business and labor to achieve private ends and policies by governments to achieve domestic goals have taken precedence over policies to maintain international equilibrium.

The Issues in Modern Perspective

This brief background of past developments indicates a number of factors that have been important in the past and will continue to be so in the future. One of these, as evidenced by the breakdown during the 1930s, is the central importance of an effectively operating international monetary system. An adequate international monetary system must satisfy at least two conditions.

First, sufficient international liquidity should be provided, which is to say the system should include enough reserves to permit international trading and should allow for expansion of reserves in relation to expansion in volume of international trade. In international as well as in domestic commerce, a sufficient amount of money, in this case internationally acceptable, must be available to handle the volume of business conducted.

Second, the system should be arranged so that adjustments to overcome balance-of-payments difficulties can be accomplished. From about the mid-nineteenth century until World War I the gold standard provided stable exchange rates and a pattern of adjustments that permitted trade to flow among nations on the basis of price differences. In its simplest version the adjustment process operated as follows: If an individual country bought more than it sold in international markets, the difference was paid for in gold. As gold was the basis of money, the country's money supply therefore was reduced. A reduced supply of money reduced the amount available for domestic expenditure. Domestic incomes and prices for domestic goods declined relative to prices of import goods, and the flow of international trade corrected itself automatically. If exports exceeded imports, gold flowed into the country and increased the money supply relative to goods. Prices rose, the price of import goods declined relative to exports, and a reverse correction of the trade balance occurred. Gold served as a common international standard of value, and commodity prices fluctuated relative to it. International equilibrium and stable exchange rates were maintained. Commodity trade flows, in turn, adjusted to shifts in prices resulting from a balance-of-payments disequilibrium, but this meant that international stability was maintained at the expense of instability in the domestic economies of individual trading nations. The internal prices and incomes of each country were influenced by external conditions; the system worked effectively only when individual countries were willing to subject their internal economy to the dictates of an external equilibrium.

This kind of international monetary system is no longer adequate for several reasons. Business organization has changed, and prices and incomes are no longer flexible in most countries. Powerful labor unions and large-scale business organizations will not accept price fluctuation, and they have the power to prevent it. Most important, however, is the fact that governments have undertaken to maintain full employment, stability, and acceptable rates of economic growth. From the viewpoint of public policy it is no longer possible to permit domestic economies to experience either recession or inflation in the interest of international equilibrium.

In the absence of an automatic system of adjustment or of adequate natural growth in an acceptable international standard of exchange, effective internationl cooperation in maintaining a system of exchange is a necessity. The conflict between the maintenance of domestic policy objectives and international equilibrium must be overcome, however. The overall issue of national versus international policy is not restricted to agriculture and commodity trade, but is a general policy problem. Furthermore, the adequacy of the international monetary system will affect international commodity trade problems directly. In addition to their influence on general economic policy, balance-of-payments pressures can influence policies to promote self-sufficiency and at minimum can influence attitudes toward removal of trade restrictions. Monetary problems thus may have an important facilitating or inhibiting influence on the solution of international agricultural and commodity trade problems.

A second overall issue in trade and trade policy is derived from the two important aspects of gains from trade. These are the gains from specialization according to comparative advantage and those from the contribution of trade to the process of economic development. Both in the writings of economists and in the actions of policy makers this issue has been debated, theorized about, and acted upon with opposing points of view throughout most of the history of international commerce. It remains a major issue today.

The principle of comparative advantage argues that at any point in time each country should produce those products for which it has the lowest relative production cost and should export some of these in return for products in which it has a comparative cost disadvantage. In this way, the world's resources will be used most efficiently, and maximum world output will be achieved. A major question arises, however, as to whether policies aimed at achieving maximum adjustment to comparative advantage will achieve *only* that: Will they lead to maximum output from a given bundle of resources, or will conditions arise that encourage economic growth? Will movement toward comparative advantage enhance, retard, or be neutral as a factor in achieving economic growth?

Over time, trade policy has included elements of both a search for comparative advantage and for economic growth. Seeking the former has become identified with a free trade policy, and seeking the latter tends to have been associated with trade regulation. The essence of the mercantilist doctrine and policy was to regulate external trade in order to achieve maximum development of the nation state. Great Britain's growth was maximized, it was believed, by comparative advantage adjustment to free trade. Nations with less absolute advantage than the United Kingdom challenge this view. German writers and German policy led the way toward general protection to achieve the gains of growth, and U.S. protectionism rested heavily upon the argument that development could be speeded by protection of infant industries. As we will see in chapter 7, some modern economists advance the argument that there is no conflict between achieving the gains from comparative advantage through a free market and maximum diffusion of economic growth. Others take an opposite view. Each argument has affected policy over time and continues to do so today.

Policy in recent periods follows this dichotomy. The general principles developed as guidelines for trade policy in the General Agreement on Tariffs and Trade (GATT) emphasize the concepts of free trade and, implicitly, a trade policy aimed at achieving the gains from com-

parative advantage. On the other hand, the basic program presented by the United Nations Conference on Trade and Development
(UNCTAD) emphasizes the need for market organization and trade
rules that will contribute most to development of the world's poor
countries.

As a practical matter, theoretical and historical evidence can be
found to support either argument as a welfare maximizing and growth
inducing trade policy. While economists often conclude that the burden of proof lies with those who argue that any system other than free
trade and maximum exploitation of comparative advantage is best, this
position recently has been challenged through the theorem of second
best. This argument states that unless all the conditions for free trade
exist there is no basis for contending that the best outcome is achieved
by moving one element of policy in that direction. Clearly many conditions in the real world do not and cannot be changed to create a free
market both within and among trading countries.

Furthermore, the beliefs and policy motivations of individual nations diverge widely from the free trade norm. Many advanced countries endorse movement toward liberal trading relations, but on a
controlled basis. In agriculture, in particular, many nations support
some form of organization for international markets. The European
Economic Community (EEC) urges world market organization for
most major commodities, and the United Kingdom implemented several commodity and regional trading arrangements during the 1960s.
Less developed countries call for extensive development of marketing
agreements on commodities of interest to them. U.S. policy since 1934
has been based on the search for multilateral reduction in trade barriers on a worldwide basis. To this date the United States has not
accepted the proposition that greater organization of international
markets is needed. Beyond this, its leadership position in international
commercial affairs has been seriously impaired by strong internal
pressures for increased protection. Can the world continue to move
toward more liberal trading arrangements? If so, under what system —
free or organized markets? How can arrangements be negotiated or
developed and implemented? All of these are open questions.

A third continuing and major conditioning factor in establishing
order in agricultural markets and in formulating policy stems from
changes and realignments in the international political and institutional system within which trade takes place and policy must be formulated. Much of our intellectual and institutional foundation for dealing
with international commercial policy is based upon strong Anglo-

Saxon leadership and dealings by these countries with other individual nations.[9] But nothing similar to the hegemony of British leadership during the nineteenth century nor the more circumscribed dominance of the United States during the post–World War II years until the mid-1960s exists today. Nor is it likely that comparable dominance will exist in the near future. At one level, commodity trade and policy have been influenced strongly throughout the postwar period by the division of the world into the two basic camps — communist and noncommunist. This occurence has been accompanied by a postwar dissolution of colonial empires and the establishment of regional groups of nations or spheres of interest both within and outside the communist world. The most dramatic and far reaching of these has been the formation of the European Economic Community. Also of major importance has been Great Britain's retreat from a policy of generalized liberal trade to one of special relations with Commonwealth countries and regional associations within Europe. Initially these relationships were handled through the European Free Trade Association and now through membership in the EEC. These changes in Europe plus several efforts at regional association by less developed countries have reached the point of a "movement" that has, and will continue to, profoundly influenced trading patterns and policy issues. In addition, the emergence of numerous developing countries from colonial status has been followed by their emergence in UNCTAD as a cohesive force, and their views on trading policy diverge greatly from those of advanced Western nations.

Among the world's three gross groups — communist, advanced free world, and developing countries — each has quite different interests and motivations. Within each of these larger categories, regional groupings also have developed with varying consequences. The most important overall effect is that offsetting forces for policy negotiation have been established. Viewed in the historical perspective that major progress toward trade liberalization has been achieved only when a single country has achieved dominant leadership, it is clear that today's challenge is for reassessment and vision if progress is to continue.

Summary

These, then, are the broader contexts within which the problems of international trade and trade policy for agriculture must be viewed. Historical lines of development have created situations and attitudes that impinge heavily upon both the willingness and ability of policy makers to innovate and change. Furthermore, solutions to trade problems for agriculture will be difficult to achieve unless the mechanisms of exchange, finance, and payment operate effectively. Many of the different approaches to trade policy centered around the objectives sought. These differences involve the question of the relative role of efficiency and comparative advantage versus economic growth and beliefs about what kinds of policies best serve these ends in the real world. Finally, the nature of world organization and political interrelationships between countries and among groups of countries is a pervading condition that will influence progress in achieving solutions to trade policy problems.

2

Postwar Trends and Emergence
Of Trade Problems

A well-organized market is one that guides resource use according to relative production costs and demand, where price variations between different selling points are related to transfer costs, and where restrictive practices by large business organizations or by government are not too great. By these criteria, there are major deviations in international trade and distribution as well as in levels of production. These deviations, plus inherent characteristics of consumption and production of agricultural products, create major problems related to prices, trade, volume, and resource allocation for traded commodities. Before we take up these problems, a description of international trade flows and recent changes will be helpful.

Commodity Trade Patterns

Through time, agricultural products and raw materials have played an important part in international commercial exchange. For much of the nineteenth century and even during the early part of the twentieth, this trade tended to center on the industrializing countries of Western Europe. They were the major importers, their principal supplying regions being Eastern Europe, their colonies, and North America. Trade grew rapidly during much of the nineteenth century, and the complementarity between industrialized Europe and outlying areas through commodity imports and capital exports developed into a commercial "revolution" comparable in scope to the Industrial Revolution. Throughout the nineteenth century and prior to World War II, trading patterns and the commodity composition of trade remained relatively stable. The quantity index of total exports (1913 = 100) increased from 30 in 1876 to 121 in 1937, while the index of food exports increased from 33 to 133 during the same period.[1] Foodstuffs represented an average of 25 percent of all commodity imports in the period 1925–1927 and 24 percent for the period 1936–1938.[2] Since the 1930s, and particularly during the 1950s and 1960s, major changes in trading patterns have occurred. One such is the declining share of agricultural products and raw materials in total commodity trade (Table 1).

This change can be viewed in two ways. First, it can be argued that it is an inevitable result of increasing industrialization which, in turn, leads to an increasing proportion of trade in manufactured products. A supporting argument for this conclusion has been developed by Alfred Maizels.[3] Since 1900, two trends have emerged. Until 1950 there was a tendency for advanced countries to rely increasingly on domestic output of industrial products. During the 1950s this trend reversed itself, and a rapid expansion in industrial trade occurred. Maizels's hypothesis is that this is based on the search, in countries with high living standards, for an increasing variety of goods and that, as a result, there is reason to expect the expanding trade in industrial products to continue. To this argument we should add that the process of industrialization in smaller advanced countries requires international markets for achieving scale and production economies, improved efficiency, and continued rapid economic growth. Viewed in this perspective, and considering the positive policies in some countries (such as Germany, Italy, and Japan) to use exports as major vehicles of economic growth, it is not surprising that industrial trade has expanded more rapidly than trade in primary products, nor is there reason to expect or want this trend to be reversed. Rapidly expanding industrial trade contributes to consumer welfare and can be viewed as an engine for the promotion of economic growth for the participating nations.

This argument strongly contradicts a viewpoint held by some analysts who emphasize the historical complementarity between industrial exports from advanced to less developed countries in return for primary products. While conceding that exports have been important

Table 1. Total Trade and Trade in Agricultural Products for Selected Years, in Billions of U.S. Dollars

Exporting region	Total world imports						
	1955	1960–1964	1965–1969	1970	1971	1972	1973
Developed:							
Total exports	60.5	98.3	155.9	224.7	250.7	297.7	407.0
Agricultural[1]	13.5	20.3	26.8	32.6	36.7	45.9	71.0
Percentage agricultural	22	21	17	14	15	15	17
Less developed:							
Total exports	23.7	30.1	41.9	55.0	60.6	72.1	102.5
Agricultural[1]	13.5	14.4	16.5	18.8	18.7	22.3	32.0
Percentage agricultural	57	48	39	34	31	31	31
Central plan:							
Total exports	9.3	17.4	25.3	33.0	35.9	42.6	57.4
Agricultural[1]	3.0	4.3	5.7	5.2	5.8	6.4	9.0
Percentage agricultural	33	23	22	16	16	15	16
World:							
Total exports	93.5	145.8	223.1	312.7	347.2	412.4	566.9
Agricultural[1]	30.0	39.0	49.0	56.6	61.2	74.6	112.0
Percentage agricultural	32	27	22	18	18	18	20

SOURCE: Arthur Mackie, "Patterns of World Agriculture Trade," in *U.S. Trade Policy* (Ames: Iowa State University Press, 1973). Data for 1972 and 1973 provided by the U.S. Department of Agriculture.

[1] Including SITC sections 0, 1, 2, and 4; excluding division 24, 25, 27, and 28 of Section 2.

to growth in industrial countries, they argue that, in the long run, industrial trade cannot continue to grow relative to trade in primary products. In part, the rapid growth in industrial trade beginning in the early 1950s is viewed as an aberration related to the 1930s. A high degree of protective nationalism coupled with the worldwide depression resulted in a massive decline in trade and an artificial distortion in trading patterns among industrial countries. Once this situation is corrected, the rate of growth in industrial and primary product trade will normalize, and each will move toward a historically stable share of total world markets.

The argument is presented that a readjustment to older patterns must occur or, in the long run, a serious impediment to economic growth will develop in industrial countries (and by implication in the less advanced). Any extended deterioration in the buying power of developing nations, either through lag in growth of quantities exported or through declining prices and deterioration in terms of trade, will reduce purchases of industrial products with direct consequences for rates of economic growth. The central implication of this argument is that a long-term normal relationship exists between trade in industrial products and raw materials, both in price and quantity, and that deviations from this norm will and should be righted.

This argument has declining validity. The trading system of the nineteenth century no longer needs to provide the basis for operation of international specialization. It is evident that many of the trading relations and economic conditions of individual countries have changed in the post–World War II period and that projections and normative valuations based on the past must be viewed with skepticism. *A priori*, there is no reason to assume that industrial trade among advanced countries cannot thrive largely independent of the exchange of industrial goods and raw materials between rich and poor nations. Among advanced countries, comparative advantage and demand preferences lead to specialization in various industrial and agricultural products. These are exchanged for both the industrial and agricultural products from other countries, and no norm exists for the comparative amounts of industrial and agricultural products. Less developed countries continue to participate in trade largely on the basis of exchanging agricultural products and raw materials for industrial products, but they need to seek ways of breaking this pattern and entering trade on the more diversified basis existing among industrial nations.

Recent Changes in Commodity Trade

Along with changes in the ratio of agricultural commodities to total trade, a number of adjustments have occurred within agricultural markets. A recent series of studies by the U.S. Department of Agriculture covering the period 1951–1965 and supplementary data for 1972 indicate a number of important shifts. These are shown in Table 2. The index of all major commodity groups has increased by more than 100 percent during this period, except for tropical beverages and textile fibers. These two categories have a direct effect on the export earnings of many less developed countries. The commodities that fared best in

Table 2. *Change in World Commodity Exports for Selected Years, in Thousands of Metric Tons*

Commodity	Exports				
	1951	1965	Index 1951=100	1972	Index 1951=100
Total grains	46,911	102,116	217.6	130,888	279.0
Wheat and flour	28,377	56,350	198.6	63,832	224.9
Rice	4,978	7,463	149.9	7,554	151.7
Feed grains	13,556	38,303	282.6	59,502	438.9
Tropical beverages	3,045	4,828	158.5	5,474	179.8
Coffee	1,901	2,815	148.0	3,490	183.6
Cocoa and tea	1,144	2,013	175.9	1,984	173.4
Oilseeds and oil nuts	4,747	9,864	207.8	15,128	318.7
Animal oils and fats	982	2,620	266.8	2,304	234.6
Vegetable oils	1,766	3,863	218.7	6,248	353.8
Oil equivalent of seeds	1,999	3,381	169.1	6,576	329.0
Oilseeds	5,016	12,248	244.1	23,915	476.8
Sugar, fruits, and vegetables, total	19,766	44,605	225.7	49,036	248.1
Sugar	10,542	18,476	175.3	22,304	211.6
Fruits and vegetables	9,224	26,129	283.2	26,732	289.8
Textile fibers, total	4,506	6,075	134.8	5,421	120.3
Cotton	2,612	3,778	144.6	3,892	149.0
Other	1,894	2,297	121.3	1,529	80.7
Animal products, total	3,510	8,584	244.5	10,161	289.5
Meat	2,030	5,148	253.6	6,576	323.9
Dairy products	1,480	3,436	232.2	3,585	242.2

SOURCE: U.S. Department of Agriculture, Foreign Economic Reports Nos. 42–47, *World Trade in Selected Agriculture Commodities 1951–65* for all commodities except animal products. These are based on data from the *FAO Yearbook 1953* and *1969*. Data for 1972 provided by the U.S. Department of Agriculture.

relative terms were feed grains, meat, dairy products, oilseeds, and fruits and vegetables. The importance of these changes cannot be evaluated fully without comparable series of export unit values, and these are not readily available for aggregates of commodities.

Contrary to the results suggested in an evaluation of commodity trends from 1913 to 1953, where the main conclusion reported by one study was that "tropical foodstuffs fared better than agricultural products from temperate zones in terms of export earnings,"[4] the opposite conclusion emerges from recent data. Products from tropical areas have the slowest growth rate in quantities traded.

Regional Trade Patterns

Behind these aggregate quantities and changes a number of important regional patterns emerge. Recent overall changes among noncommunist regions are shown in Table 3. In terms of total quantities traded, grains continue to be the most important category and wheat the single most important traded item. The regional flow of grain trade has changed materially. North America continues to be the largest exporting region, but a recent reversal has begun. The dominance of Europe as an import area has diminished slightly because of major increases in imports in Japan, communist countries, and noncommunist Asia. It is, of course, important to remember that imports into Asia have been influenced by the green revolution and that a major portion of the imports into South Asia were under United States PL 480 programs. Hence, two unusual elements have influenced the level of Asian imports. Overall, however, it is true that Asia has moved toward substantially greater net deficits when measured in terms of normal crop years and commercial purchases. In viewing the total shift in export and import trade, while North America remains the "bread basket" of the world — a position it attained in the immediate postwar period — that position has diminished, and the worldwide base of trade, particularly in wheat, has expanded substantially.

A number of shifts have occurred in other commodities. In tropical beverages, at least, two important trends have operated: Imports of tropical products into Western Europe have expanded relatively rapidly, while those in North America have expanded slowly and have declined relatively as a percentage of total world imports. The major shift among exporting nations has been that Africa has rapidly increased its exports, reaching a near par with South America as a world

Table 3. Exports and Imports of Agricultural Products by Regions for Selected Years

Region	Exports				Imports			
	1956 (Value, billions of U.S. dollars)	1972 (Value, billions of U.S. dollars)	1956 (Percentage of total)	1972 (Percentage of total)	1956 (Value, billions of U.S. dollars)	1972 (Value, billions of U.S. dollars)	1956 (Percentage of total)	1972 (Percentage of total)
North America	6.60	12.95	29.5	19.1	6.29	12.94	23.1	19.4
Japan	.26	1.12	1.1	1.6	1.62	5.11	6.0	7.6
Western Europe	6.30	24.76	28.2	36.5	16.33	35.33	60.1	52.9
Australia, New Zealand, South Africa	2.25	6.48	10.0	9.5	.26	.85	1.0	1.3
Total advanced countries	15.41	45.31	68.8	66.7	24.50	54.23	90.2	81.2
Latin America	3.23	9.70	14.4	14.4	.49	2.66	1.8	4.0
Africa	.73	4.77	3.3	7.1	.36	2.60	1.3	3.9
Asia (noncommunist)	3.02	8.03	13.5	11.8	1.81	7.27	6.7	10.9
Total less developed countries	6.98	22.50	31.2	33.3	2.66	12.53	9.8	18.8
Free world total	22.39	67.81	100.0	100.0	27.16	66.76	100.0	100.0

SOURCE: United Nations trade statistics. Data for 1972 provided by the U.S. Department of Agriculture.

supplier. In the case of oils and oilseeds, the most important changes are in the expansion of exports from North America and the increase in purchases by Western Europe and Japan. The data in Table 3 do not indicate the full extent of this shift. The most spectacular single change has been a major increase in exports of soybeans from the United States, primarily to Western Europe and Japan. As is true of expansion in feed grain trade, this phenomenon is associated with economic growth, improved income levels, and increased consumption of live-stock products in these areas.

A third change related to economic growth and rising income levels in advanced countries is an increase in trade of livestock products, particularly meat. Europe and Japan are deficient in beef and have expanded import levels, and in recent years the United States has become a substantial beef importer. U.S. imports are not the result of a general insufficiency of resources or lack of the farm organization needed for beef production; rather, they fill a specific need. Domestic production of lower quality meat useful for processing has not kept pace with demand, and an import gap has developed. This gap likely will continue to expand in the future and could be increased greatly if dairy herd numbers decline, reducing domestic supplies of lower qual-ity beef.

In fruits and vegetables, the dominant pattern has been a continued increase in net imports by Europe, Japan, and North America, but with a much slower rate of growth in the latter. Japan has moved from a minor to a major buyer on world markets. The expansion in European trade reflects diverging patterns. Sugar imports into Europe remained virtually unchanged for the 1951–1970 period, indicating that domes-tic production has expanded sufficiently to offset expansion in de-mand. Major increases in imports have occurred for fresh fruit, vege-tables, and nuts.

In the case of textiles and fibers, Latin America, Africa, and Asia continue to be the major net exporters in a slowly expanding market.

Overall Changes and Their Meaning

It is clear from the foregoing that important shifts have occurred in trading patterns since the early 1950s. In some cases these accentuate changes indicated by analyses of earlier periods, and some previous trends have been reduced or even reversed.

The data in Tables 2 and 3 are not impressive in themselves, but when evaluated it is clear that they represent major shifts in world trade patterns. The five most important of these are noted below.

First, a major new dimension in agricultural trade has been added through the rapid expansion of commerce in feed grain and oilseeds. This represents trade that, with the exception of Argentina, is largely among advanced countries and is a direct reflection of rapid income growth and the upgrading of diets in advanced countries.

Second, a major increase in imports has occurred in Asia, due to rapid population expansion in relation to output.

Third, Africa has emerged as an important exporter, particularly of tropical beverages. Important increases also have occurred in sugar, fruits, vegetables, oilseeds, and oil nuts. Much of the expansion has been in shipments to Western Europe and reflects growing demand in that area. While there is no evidence that this rise is directly caused by the relationship of the European Economic Community with overseas territories, it does reflect a degree of regionalization of north-south trade patterns that could become more important in the future, especially if supported by policies that lead in this direction.

Fourth, Latin America continues to be an important exporter of traditional commodities, although it has lost position relative to Africa. It is, however, the only underdeveloped area to make major inroads into world grain and livestock markets. The two most important elements of this change are an increase in trade within the area in food grain and external shipments of beef and feed grain, largely to Europe.

Finally, a significant broadening of the base of food grain trade has occurred. Imports into Europe, Asia, and communist countries have expanded, but in each case this has been accompanied by significant increases in exports from some countries in these areas. The most important change is the manifold increase in Western Europe's grain exports, primarily wheat.

A full explanation of the causes of these shifts could not be developed without extensive statistical analysis, yet there are forces and phenomena that obviously have had a strong impact on trade developments. As previously implied, one is the very rapid rate of economic growth in countries whose per capita income ranged from about $600–$1,200 per year in the mid-1950s, primarily the Western European countries and Japan. Expansion in incomes from that range to higher levels has been accompanied by rapid shifts in diets, particularly increases in the consumption of livestock products. This shift has led to imports of large amounts of meat as well as feed grains to support domestic livestock industries. A second important demand factor is population growth, which has been a dominant force and explains much of the flow of grain from advanced to developing countries.

Technological improvements have had a major effect on production. Through the mid- to late 1960s these were reflected in the expansion of export capacity in North America and other traditional exporting countries and an expansion of production in Europe.

National policies of self-sufficiency, particularly in Europe, and the effect of price supports on output stimulation in the United States have been important causes of shifts in trade patterns. Furthermore, certain political and institutional factors have been relevant. The most important of these has been the establishment of regional trading groups, a policy of both communist and free world countries.

Finally, in looking at trading patterns for agricultural products, the question of future prospects is important. Experience, even since 1965, indicates that change will continue. The Soviet Union, for example, moved from a net exporter to a major net importer in the mid-1960s, regained self-sufficiency, but again required major imports in the early 1970s. The development of new varieties of wheat and rice meant that some less developed countries, particularly in Asia, reached self-sufficiency and for a time even became exporters. Other eventualities, such as the Eastern European nations becoming major importers of feed grain, are distinct possibilities, depending largely upon political decisions. Furthermore, the consumption of tropical products in most communist countries is very low and could be expanded substantially if markets were opened.

One stable trend is the growth of demand for high resource using products in countries that reach and continue to move above an annual per capita income level of about $600 per year. This fact would suggest that the international markets for livestock products and feed grains will continue to expand and represent an increasingly important element of total international commodity trade.

Organization of International Markets

The general nature of international agricultural markets is shown in Table 4, from which a number of important characteristics emerge. Approximately 49 percent of all agricultural trade occurs among advanced free world countries; they account for 61 percent of total exports and 73 percent of total imports. Communist countries account

Table 4. Percentage Distribution of World Total and Agricultural Exports for Selected Years

Exporting region	Importing region											
	Developed			Less developed			Central plan			World		
	1955	1970	1972	1955	1970	1972	1955	1970	1972	1955	1970	1972
Developed												
Total exports	45	55	57	18	13	13	2	3	3	65	70	73
Agricultural	35	47	49	8	9	9	2	2	3	45	58	61
Less developed												
Total exports	18	13	12	6	3	3	1	1	1	25	17	16
Agricultural	35	22	20	8	5	5	2	4	3	45	31	28
Central plan												
Total exports	2	3	3	1	1	1	7	7	6	10	13	11
Agricultural	3	4	4	1	2	2	7	5	5	10	11	11
World												
Total exports	65	71	72	25	18	18	10	11	10	100	100	100
Agricultural	73	73	73	17	16	16	11	11	11	100	100	100

SOURCE: Arthur Mackie, "Patterns of World Agriculture Trade," in *U.S. Trade Policy* (Ames: Iowa State University Press, 1973). Data for 1972 provided by the U.S. Department of Agriculture.

Chapter 2

for only a small percentage of agricultural trade, and most of this is among themselves. Developed country imports from less advanced nations greatly exceed exports to them, which represents an important part of the total foreign earnings available to the less developed.

While the general trade flow is diverse, in its simplest form it can be viewed as a system centering around the trade needs of advanced nations. The principal import areas are Japan, Western Europe, and North America. The major advanced country exporters are individual European nations, North America, Australia, and New Zealand. In addition, the advanced trade with the less developed largely as importers of tropical products and raw materials. Recent export of food grain to developing countries has been largely on a concessional basis. Trade with communist nations also has been mostly food grain required to overcome deficiencies which, although important in recent years, may prove to be temporary.

Importance of Commodity Trade in Foreign Exchange Earnings

From the viewpoint of importing countries, a great variation exists in the extent of reliance on imports both for human consumption and as raw material for industrial production. Commodity exports, in turn, vary greatly among countries, both in their contribution to gross national product and as income for agricultural producers. From the viewpoint of structural balance and policy issues, probably the most relevant measures of differences among countries and regions are the degree to which commodity exports contribute to the foreign exchange earnings and, for individual countries, the extent to which commodity exports are concentrated in one or a few specific commodities. Agricultural products and raw materials are the major source of exchange earnings of developing regions. This general pattern of export specialization is further accentuated in many individual countries, where one or a few commodities dominate exports. Some examples are shown in Table 5.

Trade Problems and Policy Issues

Having reviewed the major patterns and recent changes in international markets, we need to ask whether these data can be interpreted in any qualitative sense. The answer clearly is negative. No optimum level

Table 5. Commodity Concentration in the Export Trade of Developing Countries, 1965

Country	Percentage share of commodities in total export earnings	Three commodities as percentage share of total export earnings
Libya	Petroleum 99, oilseeds 1	100
Venezuela	Petroleum 93, iron ore 5, coffee 1	99
Mauritius	Sugar 96, tea 2	98
Cuba	Sugar 86, nickel and oxide 6, tobacco 5	97
Iran	Petroleum 90, cotton 4, hides and skins 1	95
Sierra Leone	Diamonds 64, iron ore 19, oilseeds 10	93
Senegal	Oilseeds and vegetable oils 79, phosphate 8, fish 4	91
Rwanda	Coffee 52, tin 36, pyrethrum 2	90
Congo (Brazz.)	Timber 44, diamonds 43, oilseeds and vegetable oils 3	90
Chad	Cotton 77, livestock 8, petroleum 4	89
Uganda	Coffee 48, cotton 27, copper 13	88
Uruguay	Wool 47, meat 32, hides 8	87
Dahomey	Oilseeds and vegetable oils 78, cotton 5, coffee 3	86
Ghana	Cocoa beans 66, timber 12, diamonds 7	85
Niger	Oilseeds and vegetable oils 64, livestock 16, pulses 5	85
Guinea	Alumina and bauxite 65, coffee 10, bananas 8	83
Viet Nam	Rubber 73, tea 6, oilseeds and vegetable oils 2	81
Malawi	Tobacco 38, tea 28, oilseeds and vegetable oils 15	81
Bolivia	Tin 72, lead 4, silver 4	80
Somalia	Bananas 46, livestock 28, hides and skins 6	80
Nigeria	Oilseeds and vegetable oils 37, petroleum 26, cocoa beans 16	79
Jamaica	Alumina and bauxite 47, sugar 23, bananas 8	78
Upper Volta	Livestock 58, oilseeds and vegetable oils 12, cotton 7	77
Indonesia	Rubber 30, petroleum 38, oilseeds and vegetable oils 7	75
Dominican Rep.	Sugar 49, bauxite and concrete 9, coffee 6	74
Afghanistan	Fruits and nuts 34, karakul skins 23, cotton 16	73
Laos	Tin 61, coffee 5, teak 5	71

Table 5 — *Continued*

Costa Rica	Coffee 42, bananas 25, sugar 4	71
Mali	Livestock 33, fish 20, oilseeds and vegetable oils 17	70
Pakistan	Jute and products 51, cotton 12, rice 5	68
Honduras	Bananas 42, coffee 18, timber 8	68
Cameroon	Cocoa beans 23, coffee 23, aluminum 17	63

SOURCE: Derived from United Nations, *International Trade Yearbook, 1965*; IMF, *International Financial Statistics*; and IBRD economic reports. Published in IMF, IBRD Joint Staff Study, *The Problem of Stabilization of Prices of Primary Products* (Washington, D.C.: 1969).

NOTE: Underlining indicates that more than 50 percent of total exports is derived from one commodity or closely related commodity group.

or trade pattern can be specified; hence, trade data do not in themselves indicate the nature of trade policy problems. In chapter 1 a number of general criteria for analysis of trade problems and policies were stated. While these can serve as guides, we must be more specific in defining economic and political conditions that represent impediments to ends desired by specific countries or groups of countries and, as such, define the nature of international trade problems in agriculture. This can best be done by looking separately at problems among advanced countries and problems facing the less developed.

Problems and Issues among
Advanced Countries

The most important questions concerning agricultural trade among advanced countries are those that arise from the conflict between international objectives and domestic policies. The commodities traded consist largely of temperate zone products, but because of rapidly improving agricultural technology and protective policies, agricultural production in total has expanded rapidly, and major market imbalances exist. The central objective of agricultural policy in all nations is income-protection for farmers, and, with the exception of smaller countries where agricultural exports represent an important share of gross national product, emphasis has been placed on accommodation of agricultural policy to internal economic, political, and social requirements.

The problems (and conditions that have created them) are not the same in all areas. Japan, in particular, represents a unique case. Postwar agricultural policy has focused on expanding output of basic food requirements, particularly rice and fruits and vegetables. Japan's position as a major importer of temperate zone agricultural products is of relatively recent origin and is based on rising incomes and a rapidly expanding demand for higher quality and different foods, particularly wheat and livestock products. Because of limited land the basis for developing a major feed grain/livestock industry does not exist, and these commodities are imported. Imports have expanded rapidly, and conflict with major exporting areas has been minimal, which lack does not reflect an absence of domestic support programs. Farms are small, and price support, state trading, and import controls are comprehensive.[5] Rather, the lack of conflict is based on the separation between Japan's domestic agricultural economy and major export interests in the United States, the leader among temperate product exporters. The

United States's basic interest has centered on grain and other field crop exports, not on major products produced in Japan.

The most complex issue in trade of temperate zone products is that related to Western Europe.[6] Recent changes in food consumption and agricultural production have resulted in surpluses for some products, while others are in short supply. This situation has altered import requirements and caused expansion of export sales and increased use of export subsidies on international markets for some commodities.

Recent expansion in consumption has been most marked in livestock products other than milk and in fruits, vegetables, and sugar, with annual increases on the order of 2–3 percent for most of these products. Consumption levels, however, vary widely within Europe, and the potential for future expansion, in response to both income and price variation, differs greatly by regions. In Northern Europe, consumption of some commodities is approaching North American levels, and income elasticities of demand are relatively low and declining. In Southern Europe, potential for expanded consumption of some products with a stong response to both higher income and lower price appears to exist.

Changes in consumption have been accompanied by relatively rapid rates of expansion in output for most commodities. The index of total agricultural output increased about 3 percent per year during the 1950s and 1960s. Coupled with the fact that per capita consumption levels are now relatively high for many food products and rates of increase in consumption have declined, it is unlikely that this rate of increase in aggregate output can be absorbed in the future.

Trade problems in North America, although somewhat less diverse, are equally acute. They arise from essentially the same causes. Market imbalances reflect both rapid improvement in technology and the effect of domestic price programs. Expansion in capacity to produce has far exceeded domestic market absorption, and accumulation of surplus stocks has been a part of the North American agricultural scene for many years. This accumulation has led to a continuing search for expanded export outlets, and major international actions have been undertaken in this pursuit. These have included market development export subsidy, and food aid programs, intensive policy bargaining, and strong pressures on "protective" countries to liberalize import restraints against temperate zone agricultural products.

As indicated, trade policy in all advanced countries is closely tied to agricultural income policy. The effort to maintain or increase incomes in agriculture is implemented largely through direct price supports, which in turn interfere with agricultural trade. Virtually all commodities receive some form of market protection in most countries. Price supports and supplementary measures have led to widely different price levels among nations. The degree of price distortion that has been created is illustrated by the case of wheat, as shown in Table 6. Other products have similar price patterns. These distortions reflect the levels of support given to agriculture and are a source of conflict between exporters and importers.

These price differentials reflect cost conditions in agriculture and the level of support needed to maintain incomes in some specified relation to nonfarm incomes.

Adjustment to international conditions by advanced countries has been exacerbated by rapid and differential rates of change in the technology of agriculture. As a result major price distortions exist, and conflict of interest between exporters and importers has increased. In the total complex of trade among advanced countries the policies that have the greatest impact are those of Western Europe and North America, the major trading areas where both exports and imports are important. In most of these countries per capita agricultural income is well below other areas of the economy, and with continued rapid general economic growth this problem tends to be perpetuated.[7] The

Table 6. *Wheat: Selected Price Data*

Country	Price in U.S. dollars per bushel 1963–1964	Ratio of support prices to import value, 1962
Denmark	1.58	92
United Kingdom	1.63	97
Ireland	1.83	105
France	1.94	111
Greece	2.01	118
Netherlands	2.09	112
Austria	2.12	124
Belgium	2.12	123
Italy	2.20	129
Sweden	2.30	129
Spain	2.30	121
Portugal	2.34	137
Germany	2.38	139
Norway	3.20	187
Switzerland	3.68	215
Finland	4.22	204

SOURCE: *FAO Developments in Agricultural Price Stabilization and Support Policies 1959–1964*, CCP 65/5, 22 March 1965.

income question is relative, not absolute, and agricultural income must improve continually to keep up. Problems of trade conflict are directly related to internal market adjustment and domestic policies and effectively cannot be dealt with separately. Few countries, however, are willing to subject their domestic policies to international negotiation, and little progress has been made in coordinating domestic agricultural and trade policies.

Problems and Issues Facing
Less Developed Countries

The driving force behind the issues raised by developing countries is their search for expanded markets and greater foreign exchange earnings to aid economic development. The problems faced in achieving these goals have been stated both in broad and narrow terms.

In the broadest sense, it has been argued that many of the problems facing these nations were ushered in by the Great Depression and the accompanying shift of world order.[8] The depression led to a major decline in commodity exports by less developed countries, and without exports, purchases of needed industrial products were impossible. Hence, a policy of import substitution, sometimes at very high cost, was introduced. In addition, the shift in the weight of world economic activity from Europe to North America is looked upon as having had a major effect on underdeveloped countries. This point has been stated as follows:

> The United States displaced the United Kingdom as the leading dynamic centre. This was more than a mere change of hegemony; it had a far-reaching influence on the rest of the world. The enormous natural resources of the vast territory of the United States and the resolutely protectionist policy it pursued from the start of its development were apparent in the steady decline in its import coefficient. In 1929 on the eve of the world depression, this coefficient was barely five percent of total income, and the restrictive measures resulting from the depression reduced it still further. In 1939, at the beginning of the Second World War, it had fallen to 3.2 percent.[9]

While there is no doubt that a major shift in the center of world economic activity did occur, it is less clear that this in itself has had a major impact on the growth rate of markets available to less developed countries. During the 1930s, the effects of the worldwide depression probably far outweighed structural shifts in world economic activity. Nonetheless, and viewed over time, it is clear that growth in exports of raw materials from less developed nations has been slower than for industrial exports and even agricultural products from advanced countries. The extent of this difference in recent years is indicated in Table 7.

Table 7. *Selected Indexes of Quantity and Unit Value of Exports of Agricultural Products (1957–1959 = 100)*

	1956	1960	1965	1970
Total value of exports				
All products	98	107	135	160
Food and feedstuffs	94	108	158	199
Beverages and tobacco	103	98	109	138
Agricultural raw materials	104	111	103	95
Unit value				
All products	105	98	101	103
Food and feedstuffs	104	96	104	112
Beverages and tobacco	103	89	90	101
Agricultural raw materials	114	108	94	86

SOURCE: Food and Agriculture Organization, *The State of Food and Agriculture 1971* (Rome: FAO, 1972), pp. 15 and 17.

In part this pattern is due to the inherent characteristics of the demand for products that developing countries sell. For example, one reason for low demand is that advanced countries generally have modest population growth rates. This has been particularly true of Western Europe and Japan as well as Eastern European communist countries. Furthermore, the income elasticities of demand for many products exported by less developed countries tend to be relatively low and probably decline rapidly as income levels increase.

In addition, with the exception of livestock products, price elasticities are low for most agricultural products, creating severe pressure on price even with modest amounts of market oversupply. In the case of products subject to short-term fluctuations in output, considerable short-term variation in prices arises, and for tree crops such as coffee, long delayed and persistent price declines can be generated.

Another major problem enters the picture in the case of agricultural raw products: synthetic substitutes. A recent study by the Food and Agriculture Organization (FAO) states this problem as follows:

> One of the main threats to the exchange earnings of developing countries in recent years has come from competition of synthetics with agricultural raw materials, principally cotton, wool, jute and allied

fibers, hard fibers (mainly abaca) and rubber. In the period 1959–61, world exports of these products were valued at about U.S. $5,600 million, equivalent to 24 percent of the total value of world agricultural trade. Moreover, more than half (55 percent) of the total originated in developing countries, where they accounted for 30 percent of total exports of agricultural products.

The overwhelming item in the developed countries' exports of agricultural raw materials is wool, the bulk of the trade in which originates from Australia, New Zealand and South Africa, and United States, cotton. Otherwise the trade consists essentially of a flow from developing to developed countries.

The world output of synthetic materials is heavily concentrated in developed countries (the United States, western Europe and Japan) and centrally planned countries.

The location of synthetic industries in the main agricultural raw material importing countries is, of course, basically inimical to an expansion of the trade in the natural products. However, the establishment of such industries is usually inspired by technical, rather than autarchic, considerations except insofar as the synthetic products are competing among themselves. It is but one facet of the general process of technological evolution which is affecting the demand for agricultural raw materials in many different ways.[10]

This statement is unequivocal, but as pointed out by Lawrence Witt, the case is not that clear-cut.

First, these new synthetics provide certain qualities which create new uses for end products, carpets in places not previously carpeted, a more extensive use of soft drinks, wider use of foam rubber cushions, etc. Thus, synthetics displace much less than the equivalent amounts of natural commodity.

Second, in some cases, synthetics and natural products are being combined to create commodities more pleasing to consumers. Such joint products may enhance the sales opportunities, creating a larger demand for the final products, as has occurred recently in fibers.

Third, the price patterns are modified by the existence of a close substitute. The price elasticity of demand for the natural product is increased, thus reducing the probable range of price movements.[11]

A likely balance between these two positions is that the inroads synthetics have made are important, but they have not had the impact indicated by direct comparison of data on relative utilization. It also is probably safe to suggest that competition from synthetic substitutes will continue to be a major factor displacing raw materials and, increasingly, food items.

Another important factor influencing expansion of less developed country exports is the policies followed by advanced nations. In viewing this problem, a functional breakdown of traded commodities into temperate, tropical, and temperate tropical commodities can be made. Tropical commodities are produced almost exclusively in less advanced areas and do not compete with producers in advanced countries. In consequence, import restrictions are more limited, but are present. Many European countries have retained rather substantial internal taxes on some of these commodities. Often this is a carryover of consumption taxes for government revenue established when these items were judged as taxable luxuries. Although their importance as revenue sources is now small, some still persist. Communist countries, under state trading, place generally severe limitations on these imports.

More important are the effects of price support and self-sufficiency programs in advanced countries on temperate-tropical products, such as sugar. The EEC, for example, is more than self-sufficient in sugar, and the domestic proportion of U.S. consumption has increased in recent years. Other commodities where domestic protection and border restrictions have been of consequence to exports of less developed countries include vegetable oils, cotton, fruits, vegetables, rice, and peanuts. Also, the major temperate zone products cannot be left out of the picture. Some exports of grain and livestock products come from less developed countries, particularly South America. In the future, this flow, or at least its potential, may be greater, and the effect of advanced country restrictions will be more important.

Another element of advanced country protection is a tariff structure that discriminates against processed and semiprocessed products, as is illustrated in the following numerical example.

	Price	Tariff	Percent
Raw product	1.00	10¢	10
Processed product	1.50	20¢	13
Value added in processing	.50	10¢	20

The tariff rate on the finished product is only moderately higher if computed on product price, but the marginal tariff on value added in processing is very large, in this case double the rate on the raw material. This tariff structure not only restricts trade but also inhibits growth of processing industries in less advanced countries.

Impediments to export expansion used by developing nations slow the rate of expansion in export earnings and cause price fluctuations which, in turn, create uncertainties in programming export expansion as a part of development plans. The effect varies considerably among commodities and countries. The trade position of individual nations is related to domestic conditions and policies as well as external conditions. A recent study by Barend DeVries indicates there is a great deal of variation in the trade position of individual countries measured in terms of export expansion relative to growth in world markets. While recognizing that external factors are important determinants of overall market growth, he concludes that within a given set of external conditions "differences (among countries) are of such magnitude that their causes deserve continued and careful study. They also suggest that the economic policies and basic economic factors in the exporting countries may have an impact on the development of their exports."[12]

Summary

Over time, agricultural products have been an important component of international commercial trade. Various shifts in the commodity composition have occurred, and regional patterns of trade have changed. They are likely to continue to change. Economic forces, institutional change, and policy developments are contributing factors. Traditional trade relationships based on the exchange of industrial products for agricultural commodities and raw materials no longer dominate international commercial exchange, although this pattern still prevails between the industrialized and the less developed.

Policy conflicts among industrial countries arise out of domestic price support policies. These policies and protection levels, in turn, are determined largely by economic and structural conditions that influence cost and income levels in the agriculture of each country. Trade policy problems facing the less developed stem, in part, from restrictive import policies in industrial countries, and also from slow market growth, the inroads substitutes have made, and economic and policy conditions within developing nations. The overriding objective of the less developed is to expand exports and provide foreign exchange needed to import capital and technology for development.

The issues and problems surrounding international agricultural markets are thus diverse and complex. We have looked at trade trends, overall market organization, and policy issues and problems in this chapter. We now turn to questions of comparative advantage and factors that influence differences among countries in cost and, hence, price support and their ability to compete in international markets.

3

The Economics of Commodity Trade

One of the questions that concerns agricultural economists is whether the economic tools developed over time to analyze comparative advantage and competitive cost have any relevance in today's world. The question is asked in two ways. The first is economic-analytical and seeks answers to specific problems. For example, what is the long-range competitive position of an individual nation, or, even more broadly in the light of world food needs, how can requirements be met most efficiently and with the greatest economy in total resource use? The second approach relates to the value of trade theory as a guide for policy. Comparative advantage and its logical end point — a policy of free trade — generally is accepted as the foundation for an international policy that will lead to the best of all worlds. But as T. W. Schultz asks, "why are most of less developed countries foregoing many of the gains to be had from international specialization and trade?"[1] We might further inquire as to why advanced countries have moved to a point of limited trade barriers on industrial products, permitting forces of comparative advantage to operate, but consistently refuse to do so in agriculture. In the past, agricultural economists have sought answers to these questions from general economists with varying results.[2] Opinions exist both that the relevancy of present analytical tools is substantial and that it is minimal.

International trade theory in its pure form employs traditional tools of economics and can be applied to both internal market adjustment and regional competitive structures. But when applied to international commerce, a number of special kinds of conditions should be recognized. There are differences in countries' legal-economic environments. Exchange between individuals and regions within a nation usually is carried on under a common set of legal rules concerning taxation, credit and acquisition of capital, licensing, and the like, but these institutions and requirements differ among countries. Second, the general sociopolitical environment that embodies unwritten codes of conduct defining habit, business customs, and the social institutions that affect commercial activity vary greatly. These, along with variations in resource mobility, problems of information and communication, problems of arranging transactions and financing, different languages, different currencies, and different overall economic objectives and policies, lead to the need for a special study of international trade even though the basic or pure economic concepts apply as they do to transactions internally within any economy.

Despite the many items that obscure the relation between theory and reality, an acquaintance with theory is necessary to gain insight into factors that create differences in the existing and potential competitive cost relationships among countries. The main purpose of this chapter is to provide an analytical foundation for policy analysis in the chapters that follow. It is useful to begin this process by reviewing the principal assumptions that lie behind theory of international trade. This is followed by discussion of the main theoretical concepts that have been formulated to explain comparative advantage and by an assessment of the factors that create differences among countries in relative costs and trade position for agricultural products.

Basic Elements of Trade Theory

The basic assumption of trade theory, as with any other market theory, is that individuals are economically rational and will seek to maximize gains. Consumers will allocate expenditures to achieve the greatest possible utility, and resources will be employed by producers to equate marginal productivity of all inputs in all uses and, hence, maximize the total product of the economy. But because of the special characteristics of international trade, a number of additional assumptions are required.

One of these is that all exchange prices are flexible and that money is neutral in affecting economic activity. Neutrality of money implies that an acceptable international standard of value and exchange is available in sufficient quantity and that problems of currency and money do not affect the flow of trade or interfere with the free interaction of supply and demand.

A second category of assumptions has to do with resources and the basis for production. Initially, both the quantities of factors available and the technology employed in their use remain fixed. This means that an increase in wage rates will not bring forth additional supplies of labor, nor will increased interest rates call forth more capital. The assumption most unique to international trade theory is that complete resource mobility exists within countries, but that no mobility exists among countries. Furthermore, full employment is assumed to exist, so that if a nation expands the output of one commodity, it can do so only if the output of another commodity declines.

Another important assumption is that income distribution, tastes, and preferences are given and do not change in response to availability of internationally traded goods.

Finally, trade theory abstracts from problems or impediments to trade that arise from transport costs, lack of information, poor communications, or other difficulties that will hinder or affect the transfer of goods among countries.

Within this framework of assumptions, trade theory has sought to explain (1) the basis for international production adjustment and division of labor, or who should produce and trade what goods; (2) the process whereby international accounts are settled, and how prices are established; and (3) the welfare effects or the gains from trade and, in turn, the consequences of artificial restraints on the free play of supply and demand through international markets. The theory that seeks to deal with this basic core of questions has been refined over time to deal with a number of related questions regarding the effects of specific policies, the factor price effects of trade, and, very important in more recent analysis, the effect of economic growth on trade.

The initial statement of comparative costs was developed by classical economists who sought primarily to explain the gains from trade and establish the basis for a free trade policy. Comparative advantage was founded on the assumption that costs were related only to the "real" input of labor. If other inputs were used, their amount was assumed to: (1) be either small and insignificant; (2) be spread evenly over labor and used always in fixed proportions with labor; or (3) represent stored-up labor and thus be accounted for in labor costs. This analysis implies a single input production function. With this assumption, the input-output possibilities and relative cost for two commodities in two countries can be expressed through input-output diagrams, as shown in Figure 1.

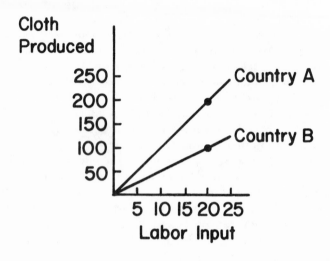

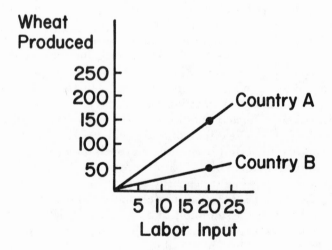

Figure 1. Production Functions Implied by Two Country–Two Commodity Analysis of Comparative Advantage

In Figure 1, output of cloth per unit of labor in country A is double that in country B, but output of wheat per unit of labor in country A is three times that in country B. Furthermore, this relative productivity ratio in the two commodities exists at all levels of output since, with a single homogeneous input, production functions will be linear. Each additional unit of labor produces the same additional amount of goods at all levels of input use.

This kind of production relationship has important consequences for trade analysis that can be illustrated through the relationship between production possibilities in each country as shown in Figure 2.

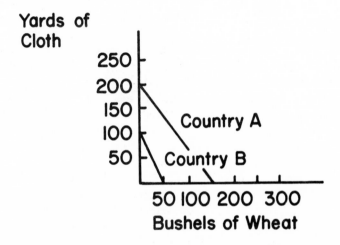

Figure 2. Production Possibilities with Constant Opportunity Costs

The transformation relationship between commodities is linear, and for each country the slope of the transformation line indicates the price relationship between commodities. Under the assumed conditions of perfect competition and full employment, country B can increase cloth production one unit by giving up .5 units of wheat, or it can increase wheat output .5 units by giving up one unit of cloth. This represents the exchange ratio between the two commodities if labor is shifted from the production of one commodity to the other. Country A, on the other hand, can exchange wheat and cloth in a ratio of one cloth for .75 wheat. The basis for trade is in establishing an exchange ratio for the two commodities between the two countries, somewhere between the ratios in each individual country. Thus, if country A desires more cloth and can obtain one unit from country B for .60 units of wheat (to obtain one unit of cloth country A must give up .75 units of wheat in a domestic trade-off), then country B can obtain .60 units of wheat for one unit of cloth. (Country B can obtain only .5 units of wheat by shifting domestic resource use to give up one unit of cloth.) Clearly, both countries gain from trade, and the principle of comparative advantage and gains from trade is established. With linear transformation in production there is no theoretical reason exchange should stop before each country is completely specialized in production of the commodity in which its comparative advantage lies. This problem was handled by classical economists through reciprocal demand analysis and more recently through the introduction of indifference curves.[3]

The essence of the production analysis presented here is that countries can gain by trading if relative production costs differ among them and that this difference is caused by variations in technical input-output ratios. While no attempt was made by classical economists to explain the reason for differences in resource productivity in the technical input-output sense, clearly this is the foundation of this initial attempt to explain the basis for differences in comparative costs. In other words, trade is based on relative differences in input-output relations.

The next stage in the development of trade theory accepts the same basic idea — that comparative cost differences are related to differences in input-output relations — but argues that analysis based on real labor costs is inadequate. A series of changes in the analysis developed the following arguments.[4] First, it is necessary to introduce money values and measure costs in monetary terms. The importance of this step can be indicated with a simple numerical example.

Production of Wheat with Twenty Days of Labor

	Bushels	Wage per day	Cost per bushel
Country A	200	$2.00	$.50
Country B	150	$1.00	$.33

It is apparent in this case that if labor is the only cost, real costs are lower in country A, but that money costs are higher and product price will be higher. It is also necessary to recognize that other inputs impinge on costs, and these all must be priced and included in establishing relative cost relationships.

A second argument of postclassical economists is that, for a number of reasons, the typical condition in production is diminishing rather than constant returns. Viewed in terms of national production possibilities, this situation is related to differences in the quality of inputs, variations in the extent to which inputs are specific or specialized in usage, and the fact that fixity of resource use may arise from obstacles to mobility, such as transfer costs plus legal and social impediments to movement. Typically, opportunity costs will increase, and production possibility curves will take the form shown in Figure 3. As in earlier theory no effort was made to specify why relative costs differ among countries. Furthermore, it was argued that the nature of the input mix was not important in explaining comparative costs. The significant issue is the shape of the production possibility curve and the opportunity cost of giving up production of one commodity to gain addition of another. With diminishing returns, this opportunity cost would change with each shift in production.

This improvement in analysis, while still failing to explain differences among nations in costs, had important implications for trade

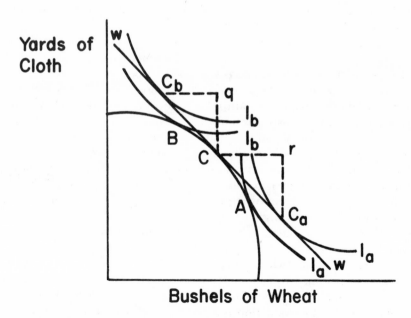

Yards of Cloth

Bushels of Wheat

Figure 3. Trade with Identical Production Possibilities but Different Demand

analysis. Trade still depends upon differences in price ratios among
countries, and specialization still should occur, but not completely.
Since each international transaction will affect domestic price ratios, an
equilibrium and identical price (assuming no impediments to trade)
will be arrived at between trading partners. This process is illustrated in
Figure 3.

In Figure 3 the point of domestic production is illustrated at points
A and *B* for each country, and domestic price ratios are indicated by the
slope of the price line through these points. Since the shape of the
production possibilities curve is identical for each country, the difference in equilibrium points is due to differences in demand as illustrated
by the indifference (I_a and I_b) curves. If trade occurs, a single international price will be established somewhere between the domestic prices
in each country. Trade will occur, and each country also will have
moved to a higher consumption at points C_a and C_b. The quantities
traded are indicated by the triangles. Country A imports C, r of wheat
and exports C_a, r of cloth. Country B imports C, q of cloth and exports
C_b, q of wheat. A new international price ratio equal to the slope of line
ww is established. Because diminishing returns exist and the domestic
prices of commodities shift as trade occurs, complete specialization is
not implied.

A more recent addition to trade theory has been an effort to explain
the basis for differences in relative production costs and the basis for
change in those costs. Emphasis is placed upon differences in the
relative endowment of factors of production among countries as the
principal determinant of a country's production possibilities curve and
hence comparative costs position.

The analysis demonstrates that differences in factor endowment
will cause differences in production possibilities if two products use
factors in different proportions and if these differences are the same or
similar in both countries. Precise geometric illustration of the effects of
differences in factor endowment requires a number of assumptions
and is developed through Edgeworth box diagrams.[5] We will limit
ourselves here to illustration of the consequence of differences in
factor endowment and general discussion of the line of reasoning used.
If we stay with our two country–two commodity analysis (cloth and
wheat) and assume two factors (labor and capital) in each country, it is
necessary that one commodity be labor intensive and the other be
capital intensive in production and that this be true in both countries. If
the ratio of capital to labor in cloth production is greater than in wheat
production in country B, this same condition must hold true in country

A in order to achieve a theoretical demonstration of the effect of different factor endowments. If these conditions prevail, the country that has the greatest amount of capital relative to labor will have a comparative advantage in production of the capital-intensive good (cloth), and the country with the greatest relative supply of labor will have a comparative advantage in production of the labor-intensive good (wheat). If we assume that country B has the greatest relative (not necessarily absolute) supply of capital and country A has the greatest relative supply of labor, the production possibility curves would be shaped in relation to one another as in Figure 4.

As shown, the indifference curves are identical in each country, and the equilibrium production with no trade in country B is point B and in country A, point A. But if allowed to trade, each country can move to a higher indifference curve at point C. To do this, country B will export C, q of cloth and will import B_1, q of wheat. Country A will import A_1, r of cloth and export C, r of wheat. The reason for trade in this case is the difference in the production possibilities in each country, and the

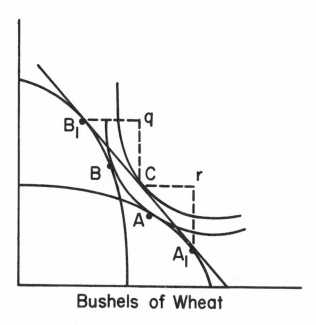

Figure 4. Trade with Different Production Possibilities and Same Demand

reason for that difference lies in differences in factor endowment. Country A has more labor relative to capital and can produce more wheat relative to cloth, and the opposite condition prevails in country B. Greater specialization occurs with trade in that country B moves to further specialization in cloth from point B to B_1, and country A moves to greater specialization in wheat from A to A_1.

Trade and Economic Growth

The most recent important extension of trade theory is that emphasized by H. G. Johnson in his study of trade and economic growth.[6] He analyzes the effect of changes in factor endowment and improvements in technology on consumption and production and, in turn, translates this into its effect on increases and decreases in the growing countries' demand for imports. The question is whether a given change in relative resource availabilities or technologies will be biased for or against trade or neutral in its effect. A change is defined as *neutral* if it alters the country's demand for its import product in the same proportion as it alters its demand for its export product. A protrade biased change would increase demand for the import product by a greater proportion than for the export product, and the opposite would occur with an antitrade biased change. The number of possible combinations of change may be large. Growth may occur through an increase in the available supply of labor (population growth) or capital and through technological improvement. Furthermore, each kind of change may have different relative effects on the comsumption of the country's import or export good as well as on the production of its import or export good.

Despite the multiplicity of possible outcomes, a few clear generalizations emerge. An increase in technology or capital with an implied increase in income will increase consumption of a good with high income elasticity of demand. If the country is an exporter of this good, the change will be antitrade biased; if it is an importer, it will be protrade biased. But if the change increases production by a greater amount than demand, the net production and consumption effect will be antitrade biased. An increase in labor supply (population growth) will increase consumption of necessities (for example, basic food commodities) and will be protrade biased if the country is an importer of these and antitrade biased if it is an exporter. It is apparent that the consumption and production effect may be either complementary or offsetting depending upon the nature of the change and the preexisting comparative cost positions among countries.

This argument is suggestive of a number of changes that have occurred over time and provides an important addition to theory. The analysis of trade and growth to some degree ties together the main lines of thought previously developed. The most significant notion provided by the classical economists is that technical input-output ratios are an important determinant of comparative costs. Later, the effect of factor prices, factor qualities, specificity in use, and fixity were introduced. The Heckscher-Ohlin version of trade theory adds the notion that factor endowment influences comparative costs. In analyzing reasons for change in comparative costs, Johnson blends all these previous notions and, in particular, deals both with factor endowment and technical efficiency in explaining change in comparative cost and trade.

But despite its basic relevance, trade theory does not provide a fully operational basis for analyzing the competitive position or the reasons for change in competitive position of agriculture in different countries. The conditions that differentiate agriculture among nations are not reducible to a few well-specified concepts. To do this we need to add to what underlies the nature of input-output ratios, namely, prices, levels of resource availability and attempt to move closer to reality for evaluation. A first step in this process is to recognize that the assumptions used in theory lead to results that specify a general equilibrium in the sense that all resources are employed in their most "efficient" use, all firms employ the best available technology and are of optimum scale, and complete adjustment to efficient production under competitive conditions exists. It thus is long-run general equilibrium analysis. The best a theory with these assumptions can do is provide broad guidelines and suggest variables to be taken into account in attempting more pragmatic analysis.

A Partial Equilibrium Framework

A more applied or manageable approach to trade analysis involves the following questions: (1) What are demand levels, and how are they likely to change? (2) What are supply levels and absolute cost relations among countries, and how will they likely change? (3) What trade patterns will likely follow from these conditions, or would follow if artificial restraints were absent? Analysis can be done only in a partial equilibrium framework which seeks to evaluate such things as demand

and supply relations, incomes, technology and business organization, and how trade has or will shift over time in response to changes in these variables. The partial equilibrium analysis implied in this kind of framework is illustrated in Figure 5.

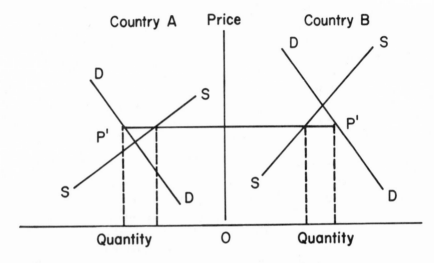

Figure 5. Commodity Supply-Demand and Trade

Country B in this illustration is the higher cost country and can both increase consumption and lower consumer costs through trade. It is apparent also that imports reduce price to producers in the importing country, and herein lies much of the source of international conflict surrounding agricultural trade policy. Furthermore, if one were to tilt either or both the demand and supply curves of each country to a more nearly vertical (inelastic) position, the price effect of trade would be intensified. This again is a characteristic that influences the issues and degree of conflict in international agricultural markets.

The position of the supply curves is determined by underlying conditions such as factor endowment and level of technology and industry organization. The position of the demand curve is influenced by population, level and distribution of income, tastes and preferences, and other factors. If the supply curve of the importing country shifts outward more rapidly than demand, trade is reduced. If this occurs in the exporting country, trade is expanded. The opposite would occur if demand curves shift more rapidly than supply curves.

It is important to keep in mind that comparative cost positions, viewed in terms of supply curves, need not be inconsistent with comparative cost viewed in the more complex framework of production possibilities curves, provided that the assumptions used in the analysis of production possibilities apply. If this were true, supply curves would have a shape and position consistent with precisely defined comparative costs. On the other hand, in the supply-demand analysis, attention is focused on price quantity relations as they exist. Both the shape and location of the supply curve may be influenced by various kinds of rigidities, market imperfections, and policies that in reality influence a country's competitive position. But even where this is the case, meaningful definition, quantification, and measurement of supply-demand relationships are feasible, and analytically they are a great deal more operational than production possibility and indifference curves.

Multiple Commodity Relationships

In moving out of the world of abstraction, a second step is to recognize that trading is a multiple commodity–multiple country phenomenon and that comparative advantage, viewed from the perspective of two countries, each with two commodities, has limited application. Evaluation of a country's position for many commodities in a trading mix of many countries is difficult, but the nature of the realtionships involved can be illustrated in Table 8.

Three kinds of questions can be asked relative to this table. The first is the commodity question, or which country is the lowest cost producer of a given commodity? This is indicated by the columns. Second, there is a question of internal ordering for each country, or, for any given country, what is the relative cost among products? This is indicated by the rows. Third, combining these two, does the country have a general

Table 8. *Money Cost of Production with a Given Resource Bundle*

Country	Product				
	A	*B*	*C*	*D*	. . . *etc.*
1	22	20	18	16	
2	20	22	18	20	
3	16	23	20	22	
4	24	11	13	15	
etc.					

cost advantage or disadvantage? In the above example, country 4 has a cost advantage in all commodities except A. Country 4 easily could represent the U.S. world competitive cost position in dairy products (A), corn (B), soybeans (C), and barley (D). Country 3, on the other hand, could represent certain European countries that are low cost producers of dairy products but high cost producers of field crops.

The Bases for Cost Differences

The numerical illustration in Table 8 is still simplified. The significant question is whether an operational framework for evaluating cost differences and shifts in cost positions can be developed, using both understandable and measureable categories of factors that influence a country's trading position.

Trading position in agricultural products for any individual nation should be viewed in terms of demand conditions as well as capacity to produce and enterprise costs. Demand will vary primarily with population and level of income. More people simply require more food, but income levels have a great bearing on the quality and kind of food used.

The extent to which requirements for specific commodities can be met domestically will be determined by basic resource availabilities, including land, labor, and capital, as well as the degree to which output increasing technology has been adopted. In addition, the cost at which specific commodities can be produced will depend on how production is technically organized and what prices apply to the inputs used. Minimum average costs may be low in a given country relative to another, but supply curves may be positioned such that demand cannot be filled due to resource restrictions relative to demand, or, alternatively, surpluses may arise at less than full resource utilization. Trading position and comparative costs thus are influenced by an interrelated mix of factors that simultaneously affect the capacity to produce and enterprise costs. These factors can be designated broadly as (1) aggregate natural and resource endowment, (2) farm and business organization and technology, and (3) price factors. They further can be specified in sufficient detail and clarity to become a useful basis for intercountry comparisons of relative productive capacity and cost positions and suggest the basis for evaluating existing trade position and possible future shifts. The following classification of factors involved in determining productive capacity and agricultural cost structures is a useful starting point.

I. Natural and Resource Endowment
    A. Natural endowment
        1. Climate and topography
        2. Land area and quality
    B. Capital
        1. Level and rate of accumulation
        2. Capital markets and relative availability to
            agriculture
    C. Labor
        1. Population and labor supply
        2. Labor quality and capacity in agriculture
II. Farm and Business Level Conditions
    A. Technology and its use
        1. Labor saving
        2. Output increasing
        3. Land saving
    B. Farm size and organization
        1. Land limitations
        2. Capital limitations
        3. Managerial capacities or limitations
    C. Supporting institutions
        1. Product markets
        2. Input markets
        3. Capital markets
III. Price Factors
    A. Level of economic development, business cycles,
        and opportunity cost for labor
    B. Alternate demand for capital and interest rates
    C. Alternate demand for land and land prices
    D. Price policy and capitalization of land values

The most clearly defined element of aggregate resource base is natural endowment. Tropical products are so designated because they can be produced at low cost only in a tropical climate. But more subtle differences exist. Wheat production is lower cost relative to corn in semiarid areas, but sorghum has an advantage over wheat at very low levels of moisture and on somewhat poorer soils. Glass house production of vegetables, a major recent development in western Holland, is highly dependent upon appropriate weather conditions to achieve low cost output. Within generally similar ecological conditions, endowment of quantity and quality of land is a major factor. The dominant position of North America in world grain and oilseed markets is based on its vast supply of high quality land, but this factor alone is not adequate. Brazil also has vast quantities of good land but does not compete in world markets for land using products.

A large number of additional variations in the importance and degree of utilization or exploitation of natural advantages could be cited. Equally important is the availability of and capacity for utilization of capital and technology. An obvious difference exists between advanced and less developed countries. Capital accumulation and the technological sophistication of the less advanced is, by definition, low. Even among economies at similar levels of development, vast differences exist for at least two reasons. One is whether or not agriculture is organized to use capital and technology effectively. Another is whether effective institutions have been established to channel capital into agriculture. In general, farms with large acreages can absorb cost reducing power and mechanical equipment and yield increasing capital and technology for both land using and land independent types of production. Smaller farms, as measured by acreage, can exploit output and yield increasing technology, but are limited in their ability to use laborsaving technology. In less developed countries, this distinction often is found between plantation and peasant agriculture. Among advanced countries, differences in average farm size significantly affect capital use and cost levels. Population growth rates and general economic structures in less advanced countries are such that employment in agriculture remains high and even increases in absolute amount under conditions where relative increases in capital occur. The dominant characteristic of overall resource use in advanced countries is the high level of capital use relative to land and labor. These general differences in resource use patterns are influenced by levels of economic development, adequacy of education, and the technological sophistication of each society.

In looking at specific differences among countries that are at generally similar levels of development, variation in market systems and availability of inputs, including credit and direct educational services for producers, may be important. The ease with which U.S. farmers have been able to obtain credit, along with its low cost, has provided a definite advantage over even many European farmers where capital, although available, has not been easily channeled into agriculture.

Equally important, extensive expenditures on research and education, both on technical and managerial questions, have been a definite factor in the high productivity ratios achieved in U.S. agriculture. Ultimately, comparative costs rest both on physical productivity ratios and prices. Opportunity costs (interest rates) for capital until recently have been considerably lower in North America than in most other advanced countries, and often farmers in less developed nations face very high interest costs. Labor prices also vary widely among countries. Labor costs in general are related directly to the level of wage rates in alternative employment in advanced countries, where a degree of mobility from agriculture to other pursuits exists. Both hired labor costs and the earnings expectations of farmers are affected. These differences influence general agricultural cost structures as well as relationships among commodities. Despite a relatively efficient dairy industry (in a technical sense), the United States does not appear to be competitive with European producers, largely because of a relatively high wage structure.

A final important cost factor is land. Prices vary widely because of differences in availability and alternative demand and for other reasons. In Germany, a tradition of land ownership and desire for security against wartime conditions have created land prices well above levels of return that normally can be achieved in agriculture even with relatively high prices. Most advanced countries protect agriculture, and this in turn, through capitalization of the gains, creates higher land prices that affect competitive cost structures over time.

Classification of Countries

Differences in resource use and farm organization lead to wide variation in resource productivity (Table 9). At one extreme, U.S. and Canadian agriculture achieve a relatively high value added per worker despite relatively low farm prices. This reflects extensive use of output increasing and labor displacing capital. At the other extreme, output per worker in Turkey is very low, reflecting the general conditons of inadequate capital and technology (as is the case in most of the nonindustrialized world). Between these two extremes exist varying degrees in levels of development and inadequacy in agricultural structure.

Differences in farm organization and the sophistication of support industries and institutions influence the farmer's ability to specialize, the mix of resources used, and his ability to realize economies of scale and to command capital and related technology for low cost efficient

Table 9. *Employment and Value Added in Agriculture, Selected Countries, 1967*

Country	(1) Percentage of active labor force employed in agriculture	(2) No. of workers employed per 100 hectares of arable land and land under permanent crops	(3) Value added per worker in agriculture (dollars)	(4) Value added per hectare of arable land and land under permanent crops (dollars)
Turkey	71.0	36.4	330	120
Spain	29.4	17.5	990	170
Denmark	16.6	13.7	2780	380
Netherlands	8.3	39.7	4010	1590
West Germany	10.6	33.5	1830	620
France	16.6	16.7	2220[1]	370[1]
Italy	24.1	29.9	1600	480
Sweden	10.0	12.2	2020	660
United Kingdom	3.1	10.6	3180	360[1]
Ireland	30.5	9.0	3430	400
Canada	9.0	1.5	4450	80
United States	5.2	2.2	6350	140
Japan	23.1	199.0	930	1850

SOURCES: OECD Agricultural Statistics 1968, OECD National Account Statistics, and FAO *Production Yearbook 1968.* Value added converted to U.S. dollars with exchange rates from IMF, *International Financial Statistics,* vol. 23, no. 9, September 1970.

NOTE: Computations of value added have not been adjusted to account for differences among countries in farm prices.
   [1] 1966

production. The existence of small, inefficient farms in many of the world's industrial countries has a major implication for policy. It simply requires high price levels to support the income of a farm family where an inadequate resource base is available to them. These variations among countries in economic, resource, and institutional conditions influence their trading positions. Among high income countries, three are almost exclusively importers: Japan, West Germany, and the United Kingdom. Each is characterized by limited availability of land relative to population, and each imports large quantities of land using products. These include both food and feed grain and meat produced under land extensive conditions. At the opposite end of the spectrum among advanced countries are Australia, New Zealand, and South Africa, which almost exclusively are agricultural exporters. Their imports consist largely of tropical and semitropical products.

The general picture, however, is one of varying degrees of specialization along lines of comparative advantage where both imports and exports are important. Denmark and the Netherlands, with relatively limited land, have specialized in production of capital-intensive livestock products. Northern European countries and others, such as Switzerland and Austria, with cooler climates or uneven topography produce excess quantities of dairy products but import many other temperate products as well as tropical and semitropical products. Canada, with vast areas of semiarid lands and a northern climate, is strongly specialized as an exporter of wheat, but imports products that are produced best in warmer climates. The United States, with an extensive natural resource base and adequate capital, is a major exporter of a wide variety of temperate zone products, a major importer of tropical products, but also an importer of large quantities of some temperate zone products.

The most important factor creating different comparative enterprise costs among advanced countries, other than basic natural endowment, is farm structure, particularly as it influences labor input relative to land and/or capital. Low cost production can be achieved only if a high ratio of either one or both can be achieved relative to labor and land (for example, broiler factories), but for crop production both land and capital inputs must be high relative to labor. Achieving appropriate resource ratios with predominately small family farms is the principal adjustment problem facing European and Japanese agriculture. On the other hand, the high opportunity cost for labor is the most important problem facing U.S. agriculture in maintaining low costs, especially in relatively high labor using production such as dairy products and certain fruits and vegetables.

Among low income countries, one important element that influences costs and trading position is the natural resource base relative to domestic needs. This is the foundation of export capacity in countries such as Argentina, Brazil, Thailand, and Nigeria. An additional foundation for trade and competitive advantage is low labor costs and production of high labor using products such as sugar. Also, in some cases exports are supported by highly developed export market and supply industries, as in the case of bananas and coffee. Recently the level of production technology has become an important factor. A leading example of a country's extensive use of yield increasing technology to establish an export base has been Taiwan. New varieties of wheat and rice, along with greater use of fertilizer and other inputs, also represent a major application of new technology that will have an impact on the future trading position of a number of developing nations.

Agricultural Trade and Economic Transformation

Of the factors that create differences in costs and production capacity among countries, natural endowment is the only element that cannot be changed over time. But natural endowments can be exploited in different ways. Land can be used intensively or extensively, depending upon the mix of other resources and the technology employed. Furthermore, all livestock enterprises can be divorced from direct dependence on land and made dependent upon the market for inputs. Two dynamic elements have dominated recent change in agriculture in high income countries: additions of capital and improvement in technology.

Farming in advanced countries has become capital intensive in the sense that a greater value of capital than labor inputs is used. Some enterprises (broiler production) have become capital intensive relative to industrial and service industries generally. The transition has occurred at different rates among commodities, and in some commodities at different rates among countries.

Although change has been rapid, and in a broad sense agricultural production throughout the world does reflect comparative advantage, it is also clear that major imperfections are rooted in the internal economic conditions of individual countries. In general, these distortions reflect limitations on the "capacity for transformation" that exists in different degrees in different countries.[7] Essentially there are two kinds of transformation problems in advanced countries: the ability to adjust within agriculture to market conditions and the ability to adjust total resource use in agriculture.

The clearest example of the inability to keep agriculture in line with market conditions is found in Western Europe. In total, Europe is an importer of temperate zone agricultural products, but clearly there is a maladjustment of resource use within agriculture. Massive surpluses of wheat, dairy products, and some other products have arisen, while deficiencies exist in other commodities. But commodity price changes, within reasonable limits, will not reallocate resource use to correct these imbalances. The basic reason for this is a farm structure characterized by many small farms with a high family labor input. This structure requires organizing production to maximize return to land and labor and limits flexibility in adapting enterprises that use land extensively. Expansion in the scale of individual farm units would increase flexibility to adapt output in line with market requirements and permit cost reduction through greater use of labor saving capital and technology.

A second aspect of change in market requirements involves adjusting the overall level of resource use in agriculture. The policy issues involved are at best difficult. First, as long as the potential exists to replace labor with capital and improve productivity and reduce costs, reducing the flow of capital into agriculture would not be wise. Furthermore, a continued flow of new capital and technology is required to replace worn out and obsolescent capital. New, more efficient tractors should replace old ones, and new, higher yielding seed should replace older, lower yielding varieties. In total, individual farm units should not be impeded in their efforts to improve productivity and lower costs, but the number of farm units should not be so great that total output is excessive. In the case of livestock, direct limitation of output is difficult, but production tied to the land can be reduced through retirement of land and associated inputs. This issue goes beyond questions of economics and involves policy related to social and community structure, and it has not been dealt with effectively in individual countries or collectively among countries.

The transformation problems facing less developed nations are quite different. The initial phase of agricultural transformation involves increasing productivity through expansion of capital and improvement in output increasing technology. Change of any kind tends to occur slowly and often is inhibited by social and political conditions. Even if technology is available to increase productivity, the capacity for major structural shifts is limited. It has been argued that farmers in developing countries will respond to price incentives. This implies that they will make marginal adjustments in allocating resources and will adopt new technology when product prices are sufficiently high to warrant the risks involved. But because of the inability of the total economy to absorb major structural shifts in agriculture (especially the release of labor through laborsaving technology), the basic initial problem is to generate yield increasing technology that raises output per unit of land and labor. The capacity for this kind of transformation is basic to improved agricultural productivity in low income countries. As the economy becomes more industrialized, the need for structural transformation becomes increasingly important if agricultural income levels are to be maintained relative to other sectors of the economy and if production costs are to be kept low. This position has been reached in Europe, Japan, and among smaller farms in all advanced countries, evidenced by the fact that even high government price protection no longer can maintain incomes effectively.

Structural change, however, is a slow and difficult process in all countries, and this is particularly true in low income countries that lack absorptive capacity for labor in other sectors and also lack capital for investment in agriculture. Both improvement of agricultural productivity and growth in nonagricultural sectors to permit structural change are needed and hence have been of concern to trade policy makers in developing countries.

Summary

Through time international trade theory has focused on technical input-output ratios, opportunity costs, and factor endowment as the foundation for comparative advantage and for analysis of the gains from trade. Knowledge about each of these areas contributes to understanding economic conditions that influence international agricultural markets and the trading position of individual countries. Trade theory, on the other hand, abstracts from a number of institutional, structural, and policy phenomena that also have a major impact. Trade theory is both general equilibrium and long run in its perspective. Empirical analysis and policy actions rarely can be cast in this perspective, but empirical analysis is important. Less developed countries need research to assess their potential for trade sector development. Analysis is also needed to estimate the effects of both national and international policy actions. Seeking answers to these kinds of questions requires a great deal more insight than is suggested by the static theory of comparative advantage. Changes in international cost position are brought about not only through marginal adjustments in resource use, but also by technological, institutional, and structural change. Policies not only can create marginal change in resource use patterns, but also can affect income distribution and bring about structural shifts in the economy of trading nations. Thus, while trade theory provides useful insights, it does not provide an adequate basis for economic or policy analysis, nor is it an adequate guide for policy formulation.

4

Trade Policy Issues and the Foundation of Policy Conflict

The effects of international trade policy spread broadly and often cut deeply into national economies. Consumer prices can be lowered or raised, business profits enhanced or reduced, and inefficient industries generated or destroyed. Despite the pervasiveness of international trade policy, it is not an area of interest to large numbers of people; its formulation has been left primarily to government and a limited number of pressure groups that have a direct commercial interest. Because the effect of trade policy on consumer and export industries often is indirect and delayed, these groups tend to be inactive in policy formulation. Political pressure tends to arise from those industries seeking protection and is not offset by pressure from organized groups concerned about liberal trade.

Against these pressures, governments have tried to define the ends and means of international economic policy within the framework of some, usually loosely defined, concept of national interest. Defining a trade policy that falls within the national interest is not an easy matter. Numerous basic issues are at stake, including: (1) the effect of trade policy on consumer prices and costs; (2) the need to maintain certain industries in the interest of national security; (3) the effect of trade policy on the balance of payments and economic stability; (4) the effect of trade policy on employment and income distribution; and (5) the effect of trade policy on economic development and growth.

The specific interest of this volume is focused on international policy in relation to commodity markets, but issues in this area cannot be dealt with in isolation from general policy and overall commercial relations. Before proceeding, therefore, we need to look at some of the arguments and issues that have influenced governments in formulating overall trade policy, most of which have carried over into agriculture. These include the arguments for free trade and the arguments, both applied and theoretical, that have tended to counter or offset the free trade philosophy.

Arguments for Free Trade

Arguments for free trade rest explicitly on the concept of comparative advantage and the gains that could be achieved by specialization according to comparative advantage. In its initial development, the theory emphasized that gains be achieved within an economy through specialized use of labor. This reasoning later was extended to argue that sufficient specialization would lead to the development of large-scale production and achievement of economies through scale, as well as permit the use of machines, power, and other inputs that would further enhance production and national income. In a dynamic sense this process would lead to greater societal savings, increased investment, and economic growth. But the degree of possible specialization was limited by the extent of the market, and to overcome this it was necessary to trade.

Development of a theory to support the argument for free international trade required only an extension of the logic associated with the arguments for internal specialization and division of labor. As with domestic analysis, it was argued that this kind of adjustment best could be achieved if international markets were unobstructed by governments and if private entrepreneurs were free to seek their own ends. International specialization would result in maximum efficiency in resource use; hence, overall welfare would be greater if free trade existed. This position implicitly assumes that the international market system will work to equate prices everywhere to marginal costs and will result in the same return to inputs in all pursuits. Marginal production costs thus will be equal to marginal social value. Optimum efficiency would exist in the sense that no change could increase the total product to make anyone better off without making someone else worse off. In essence, the free trade argument says that resources will adjust internationally as well as nationally so that marginal value products for land, labor, and capital will be equal in all uses, and the result will be optimum welfare for the world in total.

The question of whether the free trade argument is an adequate guide to policy decisions reduces to whether or not the international price system can work adequately if not restricted. The discussion of this latter question centers around a number of considerations.

Do monopolies, oligopolies, or private international arrangements inhibit adjustments to price changes? The principal culprits cited here are big business organizations and labor unions that have economic power in the market. If prolonged or significant power exists to manipulate prices or wages to the advantage of one group and to the disadvantage of another, it can be argued that the price system will not work fully to allocate resource use, and the theory is not a fully applicable guide to policy.

Is there an inherent tendency for the terms of trade to turn against any particular producer group? The Prebisch-Singer thesis argues that, over time, there is an inherent tendency for terms of trade to turn against the producers of raw materials. While empirical evidence neither substantiates nor refutes this assertion, the question remains relevant. In recent years theoretical developments in production economics and applied research indicate that there is an inherent tendency for overinvestment in agriculture, a finding which supports the argument that unfavorable terms of trade will persist for producers of agricultural commodities. If this is the case, it represents a malfunctioning of the price system, and the free trade argument is even more dubious as a guide to policy.

Can disguised unemployment exist in a free trade economy? Arguments vary. Some assert that this is a perpetual condition, especially in less developed countries; others assert that no disguised unemployment exists and that, in fact, the marginal adjustments, particularly of agriculture in less developed countries, are precisely honed, and shifting labor will affect production in relation to its marginal productivity. The difference between these points of view may be partly definitional. Those who assert that unemployment exists can cite evidence that large numbers of workers have moved out of agriculture in some economies, while output and productivity of agriculture have increased. This is not a clear argument, of course, because while these workers were moving out, additional capital and new technology were moving in. Hence a substitution effect exists representing no measure of underemployment. Those who argue that underemployment is nonexistent assert that, with given technology and methods, labor cannot be withdrawn from agriculture without affecting production. Furthermore, there is a question of defining disguised underemployment. Does underemployment exist only if marginal product is zero, or is there underemployment if marginal product in agriculture is less than alternative earning opportunities in other areas of endeavor? The conclusions can vary depending upon the assumption used in analyzing the situation. If underemployment (by some accepted definition) exists, this would indicate that market adjustment is not complete and that free trade, as a guide for policy decisions, would fall short of maximizing output and welfare.

The most pervasive question in analyzing the applicability of free trade as a policy guide may be the implications of external economies and diseconomies. In theory, free trade can allocate resources and bring forth production in accordance with market demands. But if there are major costs or benefits not registered in the market, a further and severe limitation as a policy guide will exist. Externalities may take many forms, both positive and negative. We are all familiar with the pollution of rivers and lakes resulting from industrial development and with smoke and smog effects in cities. These costs to society are negative externalities and do not in any way respond to the effects of price. On the positive side, activities undertaken in response to price incentives may result in the upgrading and improvement of the labor force through on-the-job training and may create institutions that are beneficial to society beyond what can be measured in the market. On balance, the positive and negative effects seldom are equal; in fact, if they exist at all, a justification for policy intervention that reduces the negative and increases the positive effects would exist.

A final important issue in the free trade discussions is whether or not free trade will have a substantial secondary expansion effect on the economy. This impact may occur through the effect on development of expanded infrastructure or through expansion in related intermediary industries that would arise if adjustment to or away from comparative advantage occurs. An important argument made by some less developed countries is that their export sector, based on traditional commodities, is isolated from the general economy. Expansion of exports in this situation will not lead to development or to secondary expansion in other industries. Diversification of exports, including more processed goods and manufactures, on the other hand, can lead to a number of benefits, including stimulation of more broadly based raw materials production and the general development of infrastructure needed in a more diversified and dynamic economy. The policy issue is whether these kinds of changes are likely to occur under free trade or whether planning and interference by government is required. Most less developed countries appear to believe the latter.

Throughout its development, the free trade argument also has ignored two very important questions. First, it says nothing about what represents an appropriate income distribution within which production and trade should develop. Second, it says nothing about the effects of the patterns of asset ownership. Free trade theory raises no question about and has no concern for economic justice; it is merely an efficiency argument with these aspects taken as given. Just as an individual economy can be organized efficiently to produce in accordance with the demands of a few wealthy and many poor individuals or families, so the world can be organized to produce in line with the requirements of a few wealthy and many poor nations. In fact, it might be noted that the only two countries to have led major campaigns for free trade are the United Kingdom, during the nineteenth century, and the United States, during the post–World War II period. In each case these nations had dominant wealth relative to their trading partners.

In summary, the discussion of the applicability of free trade doctrine as a policy guide in international agricultural markets has asked whether the price system will work well enough to ensure that movement in the direction of a free market is a logical policy stance. The discussion by economists has not led to any consistent conclusions,[1] nor has it been supported by a great deal of empirical inquiry. Only in the area of the terms of trade argument has any specific research been done, and this has been limited to data from advanced countries. The terms of trade argument, however, recently has been used largely in relationship to its implications for the trading position of less advanced countries, and here no empirical evidence has been forthcoming.

The questions turn on whether the assumptions used in postulating the free trade argument are sufficiently valid to ensure that the market will perform as it is expected. Equally competent economists argue different sides of the issue. In part, different answers can arise depending on whether the concern is with short-term, partial equilibrium analysis or with long-term, general equilibrium analysis. Although free trade may be an untenable policy in a short-run context, the doctrine and the concepts of comparative advantage upon which it is based clearly have relevance to countries seeking long-range economic development. How an economy achieves long-term dynamic comparative advantage as opposed to simple expansion in trade of a limited range of commodities based on an existing (static) comparative advantage is a major policy question

Arguments for Trade Restrictions

Almost as long as there has been a doctrine of free trade there have been arguments and pressures against it. These have come from both national and individual or interest groups. In general, the nationalist arguments tend to be noneconomic and center around questions of defense and maintenance of a level of self-sufficiency in production of individual commodities, of a diversity of production to guard against emergency situations, and of certain essential industries needed in case of war or embargo. Economic arguments tend to emphasize the welfare of individual groups within the economy and also contain an important element of national welfare related to general economic balance and monetary problems and economic development. These latter arguments tend to fall into three general categories: (1) protection to offset a competitive disadvantage; (2) trade restrictions to protect monetary flows and balance of payments; and (3) protection to accelerate economic expansion.

The imagination shown by groups interested in protection to counter competitive disadvantage has been almost unlimited. A wide range of specific reasons for protection has evolved. It has been stated that protection is needed against the unfair competition of large industrial corporations in foreign countries. This argument has been used in the United States, and at the present time it is being used in Europe in an effort to offset the power of U.S. corporations. Probably the most familiar argument is the need for protection against low wage countries, the reasoning being that these nations have an unfair competitive advantage, particularly in the production of high labor input goods, and that in countries with high wages and living standards this disadvantage cannot be overcome.

Probably the most complete argument ever developed is based on the notion that tariffs should be used to offset differences in production costs in each country which has a cost disadvantage. This kind of tariff principle, of course, obviates any kind of international competitive organization. If other countries retaliate, the result would be tariff protection that completely offsets relative cost differentials among nations. If initiated in a multicountry context, it would produce reciprocal tariffs equal to the difference between the highest and lowest cost country for all commodities, and trade would be eliminated. These and other arguments have been developed by interest groups and tend to ignore relative advantage and disadvantage among industries.[2] They are short-run arguments in the sense that they do not visualize an employment adjustment into low cost industries which, in turn, can export.

A second major category of arguments for protection includes those associated with the need to control monetary flows and the balance of payments. These have some early precedent, but they are primarily an outgrowth of changes which took place during the inter-war and post–World War II period. The most extensive use of restrictions for balance-of-payments reasons occurred in Europe during the post–World War II period, when most European countries adopted strict exchange control. In addition, many less developed nations maintained various forms of protection and control to protect their balance-of-payments positions. The need for this kind of protection is closely related to the development of national economic policies aimed at full employment and growth, and it is liable to be a part of international economic policy for a long time to come. Most countries no longer are willing to maintain international balance by permitting alternate periods of inflation and depression (inherent in the payments mechanism of the nineteenth century). The arguments postulated by J. M. Keynes relating both to the need for national economic policy and the secondary role of international adjustment were the forerunners of the extensive use of protection for balance-of-payments purposes.

A third major set of arguments for protection are those centered around the need to accelerate economic expansion. These have taken the form of the home market argument, or the need for protected expansion in order to provide large domestic markets for the expansion of individual industries. The result has been to favor protection to encourage the immigration of investment capital. Protection would improve earnings levels and attract capital, which would accelerate economic expansion. If domestic production is increased, levels of employment from domestic sources are expanded, reducing the need for goods from import sources.

The most universally used justification for protection to increase growth is the infant industry argument. This idea originated early in the United States and maintained that new industries should be protected from competition from mature overseas industries whose principal advantage arose from the fact that they were there first. It is grounded in the notion that once industries are underway they will become operationally more efficient, and with expansion in size they can gain the advantages of scale economies and reach low cost production that will be fully competitive with foreign industries. This argument has a degree of validity and has operated to stimulate industrial development in the United States and other countries that have faced competition from developed industry in more advanced nations. While the infant industry argument generally is accepted as valid where the basic conditions for development of competitive industries exist, it also can serve to perpetuate and maintain inefficient production that otherwise could not compete with foreign producers.

It is clear from the foregoing that trade policy involves a number of fundamental questions concerning the economic ends of policy.[3] One of these is whether policy should be implemented to seek structural change within and among countries, or whether marginal adjustment through the market will best achieve this kind of change. Free trade implies that adjustments will occur marginally among countries as a natural result of market processes, whereas the infant industry argument, for example, implies that basic structural change involving the development of an industry in one country at the expense of another is a legitimate policy end.

A second major issue involves the relationship between efficiency and equity in economic policy. An economy is judged more or less efficient to the extent that it is adjusted to the marginal conditions of economic theory, making it impossible to have one person better off without making another worse off. On the other hand, many of the arguments for restriction are based on equity criteria. Policies are sought to change income distribution through protection that improves the lot of one group relative to another. The income argument has been the foundation for agricultural policy and protection both at the domestic and international levels.

A third basic issue is the conflict between national policy and its objectives versus the attainment of international equilibrium. In its most general aspect this question centers around contemporary governmental acceptance of the responsibility to maintain and promote full employment and domestic stability in contrast to the nineteenth century, when it was argued that international equilibrium should be maintained even at the expense of periodic fluctuations in the national economies of individual countries. The current approach has led to a degree of international disequilibrium, manifested in monetary and fiscal problems, and to the need for greater international cooperation to maintain stability.

Trade Policy and Agricultural Policy

Since about 1930, and particularly during the post–World War II period, the concept of protection for agriculture has broadened. Defending agriculture from foreign competition has given way to the more general notion that agriculture needs protection because of inherent characteristics. This more general approach is justified in two ways: (1) Inelastic demand and supply result in price instability from which farmers must be protected, and (2) slow growth in demand, along with an inability of farmers to adjust output requirements due to advancing technology and excess commitment of resources in agriculture, leads to a need for price and income maintenance over time. With this change in perspective, agricultural protection left the realm of solely international policy and became a matter of domestic policy as well.

Both the differences in interpretation of what is an adequate income for farmers and the differences in cost levels in agriculture have resulted in wide variation in the level of agricultural protection among industrial countries. Governments are required to use various kinds of tariffs, quotas, levies, sanitary regulations, and other restrictions to prevent imports or to subsidize exports. The net result is that the international commercial market is very badly organized and seems to operate with no consistent set of rules.

The essence of the problem in international agricultural markets is the extent to which governments, through income support programs, cause major distortions in prices, production, consumption, and trade flows. Many of the policies in effect today have evolved from developments begun in the 1930s aimed at relieving severely depressed agricultural conditions. Protection was strengthened during World War II and the postwar period through programs designed to expand food production and relieve shortages. Since approximately 1950, the objectives of agricultural policy in most countries have shifted to income protection for agriculture along with other general objectives, such as improving agriculture's contribution to the economy, maintaining the family farm, and maintaining the general rural economy of the country. While these general goals are relatively consistent among countries, there is considerable variation in the specific content of agricultural programs based both on interpretation of general objectives and on the methods and approaches in implementing agricultural policy. A brief review of some of these differences follows to indicate variation among countries.

Objectives and Methods in
Agricultural Market Policy

Stabilizing income and maintaining an acceptable level of income in agriculture is an objective of the legislation of virtually all nations. Most countries seek some form of "fair," "proper," "equitable," or parity income, but define these levels in different ways. In West Germany, for example, an adequate income for farmers included in the Green Plan farm sampling program was for years interpreted as comparable to that of nonagricultural workers in rural areas. Green Plan farms are somewhat larger than the average for all of West Germany, but are relatively small in comparison to the commercial agriculture of most exporting countries.

In Sweden, for a long period of time beginning in the 1950s, an adequate income was interpreted to mean achieving a labor income on farms of approximately 15 hectares equal to certain classes of rural area nonfarm workers. Two things are important in the Swedish formula: The return to capital and land in farming is excluded prior to computing the acceptable level of agricultural income, and the computation is based on relatively small farms where the labor input from family sources alone normally would be relatively high. These guidelines for income and the number of small-scale farms have resulted in relatively high agricultural prices both in Sweden and West Germany.

Most other nations, particularly the agricultural exporters, have interpreted an acceptable income level in a less precise fashion and with lower prices. Price support in the United States has been based on a parity formula that has changed over time. Considerable administrative discretion has been permitted in setting price levels depending upon supply-demand and market conditions. Most smaller export countries, including the Netherlands, Denmark, and Ireland, as well as Canada, Australia, and New Zealand have developed relatively limited price support programs. Their approach to agricultural policy has been guided by the necessity to compete effectively in international markets and by limitations on government resources to support prices and subsidize exports.

Another important underlying objective that influences agricultural policy is the interpretation of the role of agriculture in terms of its general contribution to a nation's economy. Most countries seek improvement in the productivity of agriculture and the provision of a sufficient or abundant supply of food relative to basic land resources.

Achieving low cost production has been a central objective of farm leaders as well as public officials in the United States. European countries, in general, have placed more emphasis on expanding the total volume of output as a result of wartime shortages, although in recent years this policy has been questioned. A major recent issue in British agricultural policy, for example, has been the degree of self-sufficiency that should be sought and the commodity compositions that can be produced to best advantage. Other countries have sought specific self-sufficiency goals. Sweden has established a goal of approximately 85 percent, and Switzerland has established a goal of maintaining as high a level of self-sufficiency as is feasible, even at the expense of relatively high farm prices.

A major pressure on international markets has been created by the production goals of both exporting and importing countries. All exporters view the international market as a source of earnings for farmers, and for some of the smaller export countries it becomes a major component in the total GNP of the nation. In the case of Ireland, Denmark, and the Netherlands, the contribution of agricultural exports to total GNP ranges between 10 and 15 percent, and policies must be oriented toward protecting and expanding export markets. Importing countries are equally guilty of disrupting international markets through their policies of output expansion and import substitution.

A third element that has influenced agricultural policy is the objective of maintaining the family farm and rural social structure. Again, differences among countries in specific ends sought are important. With the exception of the United Kingdom, until very recently most European countries oriented their policies toward maintaining the agricultural structure that had developed over time. Even recently, as technology has changed and the basis for expanding farm size and shifting the input mix away from labor and toward more capital has become possible, the concept of farm adjustment has been toward creating viable farms, not efficient farms in line with technological potential. This development has occurred partly because the task involved in moving from existing agricultural structures to large-scale, efficient farms is massive and extremely expensive, but it also is associated with a philosophical outlook related to rural community development. This attitude is based on historical tradition and on the fact that during recent and past wartime periods the importance of large rural settlements has been demonstrated.

Outside Europe, the focus on farm organization follows two interesting patterns. The Japanese have instituted no program to restructure agriculture into larger units, but look toward maintenance of small-scale, highly intensive units with farmers receiving part of their income from nonfarm employment. In export countries with larger land areas, the general concept of farm organization is that structural change should keep pace with technological possibilities, and farm size should expand at least to the maximum that can be handled within the framework of the family farm system. In addition, there is no official action to inhibit the development of very large farms or to establish an outside maximum on the acceptable size of family farms. In Europe, on the other hand, family farms of 100 hectares or more are not encouraged.

In addition to differences in interpreting objectives, the level of protection is influenced by the methods used to set prices. With the exception of the United Kingdom and more recently the United States, where deficiency payments have been used, most countries use some direct price support mechanism. Two general methods are used in fixing the level of protection: (1) some type of automatic formula and (2) direct negotiation and consultation with farm organizations. In some countries, farm prices are adjusted annually, and at times more often, in response to a change in wage levels. This kind of indexing is characteristic of the Scandinavian countries and, as would be expected, has created an inflationary bias. Rises in farm prices in relation to wage rates require rises in wage rates in relationship to food costs. A more loosely defined automatic formulation has been that used in the United States, where a considerable degree of administrative discretion is permitted in determining annual support levels. The results in each case have been quite different.

As with formula pricing, direct negotiation and consultation with farm organizations also can produce widely varying results, depending largely on the extent of power held by the organizations. In Germany, the greater bargaining power over time appears to have rested with farm organizations, and the bargaining process resulted in the establishment of relatively high price levels. The United Kingdom, on the other hand, had an annual review with farmers prior to establishing each year's program, but the weight of government in negotiation appears to have been stronger. Government seems to have protected itself from excessively high support levels and excessive treasury expenditures.

A further variation among countries exists in the scope and conditions for price support coverage. Most European countries provide direct income support programs for 85–100 percent of total production, whereas in the United States, with the most extensive support program of any major exporting country, direct support coverage has never extended beyond about 45 percent of total farm production. Only limited action has been taken to control production. Specific limitation on the production of a few commodities, such as sugar, exists in a number of countries, but the only general program of supply control is that which has been carried on in the United States. The U.S. program has involved both short-term restrictions through direct acreage controls and marketing quotas and the longer term removal of land from production. Only two general programs aimed at reducing production have arisen in Europe during the post–World War II period, and these attempted to use price manipulations to influence output. The French quantum system limited full price supports on grains to a specific percentage of total output, and the British standard quantity system provided full deficiency payments to farmers only within a certain range of a specified total production. If output exceeded the standard quantity, the amount of the deficiency payment gradually was reduced in accordance with the extent of the excess. The effect on total production depended upon the level at which the standard quantity was set each year rather than upon the gradation of payments with a given standard quantity. The common agricultural policy of the EEC has yet to adopt any significant supply control measures (except on sugar); hence, the British standard quantity system soon will be abandoned, as was the French quantum system in the mid-1960s.

Another important distinction in farm programs among countries lies in the different emphasis placed upon the use of producer input subsidies. These subsidies have played an important part in the total support of agriculture in some countries, particularly in Europe. The question of what effect producer subsidies have on total output is rarely raised, but when viewed in the context of an international competitive framework they obviously become important.

Forms of Protection

It is apparent from the above that there are great variations in the objectives of agricultural protection and in the processes used for implementation. The methods used for industrial countries are extremely diverse, but fall into several main categories:[4] those that (1) change market price and thus influence domestic production and consumption; (2) directly influence production only; (3) influence consumption and utilization only; (4) influence imports; and (5) influence exports.

Measures that influence market price are the core of income protection programs in most countries. These programs have the dual effect of stimulating production and inhibiting consumption. The extent of each effect will depend in the short run upon relative demand and supply elasticities and in the long run on the production response of farmers due to increased investment and improved production caused by higher and more stable prices.

Measures that influence production only include income or deficiency payments and input subsidies that raise the net returns for each unit of commodity above those which would prevail in an unprotected market. At present, no country uses direct payments unrelated to the unit price of commodities. Subsidies on inputs or farm costs take many forms, including such things as per unit subsidy on the cost of fertilizer, reduced and subsidized interest rates, grants for capital improvement, subsidies to expand livestock output, and favorable tax treatment. All these tend to encourage production and at the same time reduce costs and improve farm income.

Measures to expand consumption and utilization of home produced products are used less extensively than those that influence supply. They usually are adopted, at least initially, as a necessary action to divert surpluses that have arisen from protection policy. Initial distribution of food under school lunch and welfare programs in the United States fell into that category. This same sequence has arisen in the EEC, where subsidies are being used to increase consumption of dairy products and to divert wheat, dairy products, and sugar into feed use. U.S. policy on food distribution and subsidized consumption clearly has extended to concern with welfare and nutrition improvement, and they no longer are simply components of the system of protection for agriculture.

With the exception of deficiency and direct payments, domestic income programs require import protection and, where surpluses arise, export assistance. These take many specific forms. Tariffs, variable levies, and commodity taxes are the most commonly used forms of import protection. The United States relies heavily on import quotas. State trading, either directly or through assigning a monopoly on imports and exports to a cooperative or some other private organization, is an important control device in a number of countries. In less developed nations, export marketing boards are used extensively.

Direct export subsidies involve payments by government to make up the difference between the domestic support and export price. Indirect subsidies also are used extensively, among them government transport and marketing subsidies, guaranteed credit and low cost loans, and, most important, general tax rebates. This latter subsidy is particularly significant when turnover or value-added taxes are a major source of government revenue. Under this system the final point of taxation for goods produced domestically is the consumer. If the tax is 20 percent, the price of goods is increased by that amount. The tax is added to the price of import goods at the border, but normally is foregone on export goods. Taxation in this form becomes a combination of import protection and export subsidy. The effect of differential taxation is one of the unanswered questions in international commercial policy. As suggested recently in testimony before the Joint Economic Committee of the U.S. Congress, it "probably has produced a world trade pattern rather different from that which would come about under a system which truly neutralizes the international trade effects of differentials in national tax systems."[5]

The Degree of Protection

Measuring the degree and cost of protection for agricultural commodities recently has received increased attention, both from agricultural economists and in policy forums. The recent report of the U.S. Presidential Commission on International Trade and Investment Policy emphasized the importance of this question by stating: "If progress is to be made on lowering international barriers to agricultural trade, it is essential to possess techniques for determining accurately the levels of protection afforded by present policies."[6] The commission recommended an international study that would include systematic analysis of the major effects and costs of agricultural policies.

Measuring the degree and cost of agricultural protection, however, is not a simple task. Two general approaches have been suggested by recent empirical work and in the theory of tariff structures. One is to determine the percentage by which the price received by domestic producers exceeds the price at which the product can be sold or purchased in international markets. The degree of protection is measured as the amount by which producer prices exceed world prices, both in importing and exporting countries. This difference reflects the total combination of steps taken to protect agriculture.

A study by Rachel Dardis and Elmer Learn has designated this kind of measure as the equivalent tariff.[7] The method they used is as follows:

where

P = average price received by producers for all types of sales;
M = marketing margin;
P' = suggested producer price = $P + M$; and
T = import or export unit value (total value of import or exports divided by total quantity of imports or exports),

the degree of protection is defined as equal to $\frac{P-T}{T} \times 100$ = Percentage tariff.

Where marketing margins are also included, the degree of protection equals $\frac{P'-T}{P'} \times 100$.

Dardis and Learn define the ad valorem tariff as equal to $\frac{P-T}{T} \times 100$ or as $\frac{P'-T}{T} \times 100$.

In computing actual tariff rates, they ignore marketing margins for grain products and compute tariff rates based on direct producer price; for livestock products they add a marketing margin to obtain an adjusted producer price. Their analysis uses data for 1959–1961 and covers the United States, Canada, and major Western European countries. In general, they concluded that the degree of protection is higher for most commodities in importing countries, although a positive margin of protection exists for a number of commodities in export countries.

One of their interesting comparisons is between the actual and the equivalent ad valorem tariff for several commodities in Italy, the United Kingdom, and West Germany. These are shown in Table 10. This information provides some measure of the degree to which protection is based on nontariff barriers such as quotas, phyto-sanitary regulations, and trading procedures. The study also indicates something of the variation in the degree of protection among countries.[8]

A shortcoming of this kind of analysis is that it does not provide an indication of the protection afforded farmers through various kinds of input subsidies. To achieve this sort of measurement it is necessary to base an analysis of protection on the concept of the effective tariff level. This involves measuring protection as related to the increase in value added in production as the result of either tariffs or taxes on com-

Table 10. *Comparison of Actual and Equivalent Ad Valorem Tariffs, 1959–1961*

Commodity	Italy	United Kingdom	West Germany
Barley:			
Actual[1]	10	10	0
Equivalent[2]	[3]38	33	[3]43
Wheat:			
Actual[1]	27	0	0
Equivalent[2]	58	4	44
Beef:			
Actual[1]	29	3	20
Equivalent[2]	69	56	70
Pork:			
Actual[1]	18	10	16
Equivalent[2]	30	20	32
Eggs:			
Actual[1]	0	6	5
Equivalent[2]	63	56	61
Milk:			
Actual[1]	30	5	24
Equivalent[2]	166	163	64

SOURCE: Rachel Dardis and Elmer Learn, *Measuring the Degree and Cost of Economic Protection of Agriculture in Selected Countries*, ERS Technical Bulletin #1384 (Washington, D.C.: U.S. Department of Agriculture, 1967), Table 11, page 17.

[1]As of 1 January 1961.

[2]$\frac{P-T}{T}$ 100, where P = producer price (including marketing margin), and T = import price.

[3]Feed barley.

modities, or inputs. Protection thus is defined as the increase in return to the production activity rather than as the increase in the price of a commodity. Nominal protection applies to commodities, whereas effective protection applies to economic activity. The latter is defined by W. M. Cordon as "the percentage increase in value added per unit in an economic activity which is made possible by the tariff structure relative to the situation in the absence of tariffs, but with the same exchange rate."[9]

The formula for computation of effective protection rates is as follows:

where:

v = value added in the absence of protection;

v' = value added with protection;

E = effective protective rate;
P = price of commodity without protection;
C = proportion purchased inputs are of P; and
t = level of tariff or subsidy,

then

$v = P(1-C)$;

$v' = P(1+t) - C$ if protection applies to commodities outputs only;

$v' = P(1+t) - C(1+t)$ if protection applies both to commodities and inputs; and

$\dfrac{v' - v}{v}$ = the effective protective rate.

This formulation normally could not apply to agriculture without modification. Since tariffs rarely, if ever, represent the only form of protection used for any commodity, the t value on commodities cannot be measured directly, but it can be approximated through the formulation used by Dardis and Learn. Where imported inputs are commodities, this same form of approximation is necessary to compute $C(1 + t)$.

A second important variation could arise where t is a negative value. In the case of commodities, this occurs when governments buy from farmers — possibly through marketing boards — at prices below world levels. For inputs this occurs when direct government subsidies reduce input prices to farmers. A negative t value is probably more common than a positive one for some agricultural inputs in most industrial countries. In many cases some inputs (such as fertilizer) would be subsidized and others (such as feed) would be protected. A weighted average protection level would be required. If all inputs are traded inputs, the comparison of domestic with world prices would provide a basis for measuring the protection or subsidy afforded. Even in this case it is conceivable that some input, for example, fertilizer, can be subsidized from high cost protected producing industries and still be provided to farmers at a price near or below import prices from world markets. Import protection would exist but would be offset by subsidies to reduce the cost to farmers. In this case, the net level of protection is determined by offsetting government policies, one of which increases price of inputs and the other of which decreases them.

Another element of effective protection for agriculture is subsidies on nontraded inputs. These could include such items as direct subsidies for capital improvement, improvement of land and water resources, general credit subsidies, and the like, that are often available to farmers. These subsidies influence production and provide general support for the activity of farming. They do not necessarily create shifts in resources from one kind of production to another and cannot be allocated as effective protection to specific commodities. They are, nonetheless, a component of cost which, if reduced, will influence the value added and will affect supply.

The problems of measuring protection to agriculture are great. These include all those associated with measuring nominal tariff levels plus those involved in determining the level of protection or subsidy on agricultural inputs. Effective measurement would add greatly to knowledge needed to refine estimates of the economic effects of agricultural protection and to improve policy formulations. The shortcoming in measuring nominal rates of protection alone is that while these rates indicate the demand effect under alternative policy assumptions and different price levels, they only partially indicate the supply effects. To measure how protection affects supply it is necessary to assess the extent to which protection will attract resources into a particular industry relative to that which might exist in a free market. This extent is more clearly indicated through the effective rate of protection. Unfortunately, because of the complexities involved in measuring either of these forms of protection, existing quantitative estimates are extremely limited.

The Economic and Welfare Effects of Protection

Despite the difficulties encountered in developing quantitative measures of either nominal or effective levels of protection, it is possible to define, and to some extent quantify, the aggregate economic costs and transfers involved in agricultural protectionism.

This kind of measurement employs supply and demand curves and suggests welfare implications based on the concepts of producer and consumer surplus. The general framework for cost and welfare analysis is as indicated in Figure 6.

DD and SS are domestic demand supply curves. W is the world price level, and P_s is the support price. The economic relationships indicated are as follows: At world price levels the domestic supply in the importing country would be equal to Q_1, the quantity demanded would be Q_4. and imports would be the difference, Q_4-Q_1. If prices rise through protection to P_s, then domestic production increases to Q_2, and con-

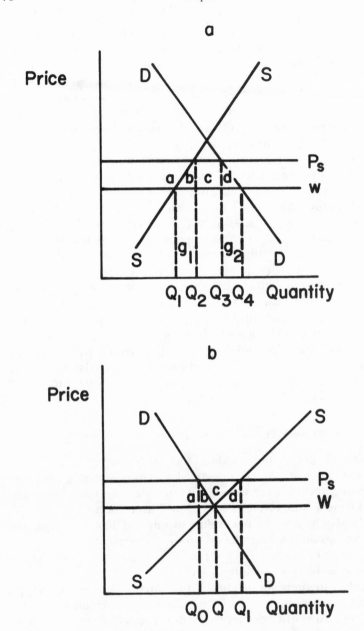

Figure 6: Implication of Protection for an Importing and an Exporting Country

sumption is reduce to Q_3. Imports become the lesser quantity, $Q_3 - Q_2$. The total reduction in consumer surplus is represented by areas a, b, c, and d. If import restrictions are through tariffs or levies, the area c represents a transfer from consumers to government. If import restrictions are in the form of quotas, the area c represents a windfall gain to importers who can buy on world markets at the lower world price and sell domestically at the supported price, and the transfer is from consumers to private trade interests. The transfer from consumer to producer is equal to $a + b$, and the addition to producer surplus is equal to area a. Savings in foreign exchange expenditure also occur equal to areas $g_1 + g_2$. The net economic cost to society from protection is equal to areas b and d. Triangle d represents the loss to consumers which is not represented by gain to other segments of society. Triangle b, on the other hand, is the excess resource cost of gaining the additional quantity, $Q_2 - Q_1$. If this quantity were imported, its valuation on world markets would be equal to the area g_1. Produced domestically, total resource cost is equal to $g_1 + b$, hence the net resource loss from the domestic production is equal to the triangle b.

Figure 6b represents the same kind of analysis for an exporting country where price supports result in surplus production. The analysis of changes in consumer and producer surplus and the net consumer and producer costs involved is the same as those in Figure 6a. The difference arises in the form of income transfer involved. Whereas the basic result of import protection is to transfer income from consumers to producers and government or import industries, the result of protection for an exporting country is the transfer of income from taxpayers through government to producers. The total export subsidy involved in clearing the domestic market is equal to area $b+c+d$. Triangle c is the net consumer cost of protection, and d is the net excess resource cost. Total transfer to producers is $a+b+c+d$, of which a is a transfer from consumers and the remainder is government payment.

The illustrations in Figure 6, both for an importing and an exporting country, assume income protection through price supports. An interesting variation of this analysis occurs if income protection is implemented through deficiency payments. This is illustrated in Figure 7. The principal difference is that deficiency payments do not alter prices to consumers; hence there is no loss to consumers nor direct transfer from consumers to producers or government. The income transfer to producers comes entirely from government and is represented by the per unit payment $P' - P$ times the quantity produced with the deficiency payment Q_1. Producer surplus increases, and the

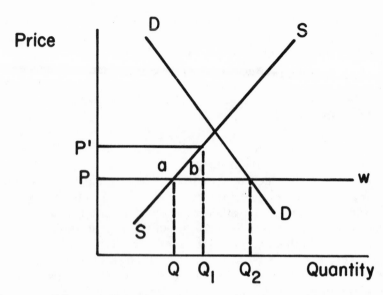

Figure 7: Effect of Deficiency Payments on Production and Trade

net resource cost, represented by triangle b, is the same as with price supports. No transfer occurs from the consumers to producers, and consumption is not reduced through higher prices.

One additional variation of this analysis should be included here. The above model assumes that farmers are producing commodities that move directly into consumption. The analysis should be extended to cover the cost of intermediate goods, primarily feed grains, but also some raw materials that are inputs into different forms of consumer goods. The analysis should be adjusted to avoid double counting.

Figure 8 illustrates protection both on grain used as an input and on livestock as a final product. The difference between price P_1 and P_2 represents the effect of direct protection on livestock and results in the same adjustments and transfers as in Figure 6. The difference between price P_2 and P_3 can be viewed as a compensatory tariff on the final good to offset the additional cost of protected inputs. Price difference $P_3 - P_2$ is determined both by the level of protection on inputs and by their proportion to total costs. Transfers of income from consumers will be determined by the elasticity of demand and the level of total protection, both direct and compensatory, on livestock products. The supply curve for meat will shift upward by the vertical distance $P_3 - P_2$ to offset the

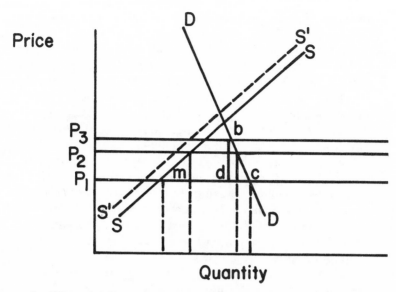

Figure 8: Effect of Protection on Intermediate Goods and Final
Product

higher price of grain caused by protection. The net consumer loss is
equal to the triangle b, c, d. Net resource costs are indicated by area m.
The loss to consumers is the indicated total reduction in consumer
surplus on the final product, and the gain to producers is split between
livestock and grain as shown by the effect of changing price from P_1 to
P_2 and from P_2 to P_3. This accounts jointly for protection in final
product and factor markets. An important case where this analysis is
relevant is protection of feed grain and livestock in the EEC. This
modification in the analysis of protection costs can be quantified and
included in empirical estimating.

Measuring the Cost of Protection

Several efforts have been made to measure the cost of protection,
both for total traded commodities and more recently with specific
application to agriculture. Initially these studies sought simply to define cost as the difference between the amount spent on commodities
subject to tariff as compared with their cost if no import restrictions
had existed.[10] With evolution of the recent theory of effective tariffs, it
has been pointed out that these earlier studies neglected real costs

involved in diversion of resource use and reduced consumption and did not deal with the question of income transfer.

A significant empirical analysis that attempted to account for these economic effects as well as the financial effects of different policies was done by T. E. Josling in his study of the implications of the shift by the United Kingdom from deficiency payment on grains to a grain agreement and variable levies.[11] Josling since has expanded on this work by quantifying the effect of small changes in policy variables and computing the ratio of cost to program benefits in order to measure the efficiency of various methods of income support in achieving objectives sought.[12] The analysis concentrates on policies as a means of obtaining either income transfer or a saving of foreign exchange through import displacement. The policy options included deficiency payments, a variable levy system, a minimum import price system, a combined deficiency payment and variable levy, and a combined deficiency payment and minimum import price.

A sample of the cost estimates obtained for different wheat policies in the United Kingdom is shown in Table 11.

A similar estimate of costs and transfers created by alternative agricultural policies has been completed by Werner Kiene for Austria. His study covers a broad range of commodities and is designed to test contrasting costs of existing policies versus a hypothesized deficiency payment system. His results are shown in Table 12.

The magnitude of demand-supply elasticities crucially affects the outcome of policy alternatives. If both demand and supply are highly elastic, major shifts in consumption and production but only modest income transfers will follow from price changes. With inelastic supply and demand, the consumer and resource costs are minimal relative to the achievement of income transfers. Since it generally is believed that both aggregate demand and aggregate supply for agricultural products are relatively inelastic, the most sensitive outcome of the analysis will be measurement of the extent and direction of income transfers. From the viewpoint of society, this does not represent a real cost. Gale Johnson, however, regards this as a cost of protection and states that "the perspective that permits, perhaps one should say requires, consideration of income transfer as a cost of protection is that taxpayers and consumers are required to make the income transfers, and the income transfers are made for some purpose. Thus, the relationship of the cost of the transfer, and the benefits derived from the purpose or end of the transfer are a legitimate focus of inquiry."[13]

Table 11. *Average and Marginal Cost of Income Transfers to Farmers and Savings in Foreign Exchange Using Various Wheat Policies in the United Kingdom, Including the Effect on Wheat Users*

Cost of each £ transferred to farm income	Deficiency payment (£)	Variable levy (£)
Economic cost		
Average	0.12	0.32
Marginal	0.09	0.26
Budget cost		
Average	1.12	−0.93
Marginal	1.09	−0.51
User cost		
Average	—	2.13
Marginal	—	1.72
Exchange savings		
Average	1.08	0.74
Marginal	0.41	0.23

Cost of each £ of imports displaced	Deficiency payment (£)	Variable levy (£)
Economic cost		
Average	0.11	0.46
Marginal	0.23	1.14
Budget cost		
Average	1.04	−1.35
Marginal	2.68	−2.22
User cost		
Average	—	3.10
Marginal	—	7.39
Income transfer		
Average	0.93	1.36
Marginal	2.34	4.32

SOURCE: T. E. Josling, "A Formal Approach to Agricultural Policy," *Journal of Agricultural Economics* 20 (May 1969): 175–96.

NOTE: Wheat users are processors of wheat products.

The estimates on cost of protection that have been prepared to date have shortcomings. The most important of these is that they are static and in no way suggest the dynamic path of adjustment that might be undertaken by agriculture if differing kinds and levels of income protection programs are adopted. Second, they concentrate exclusively on the direct internal costs for the protecting country. They do

Table 12. *Calculation of Costs of Protection in 1966 as a Percentage of the Change in Producers' Incomes Due to Protection*

Commodity	Change in producers' income in mills of Austrian shillings	Cost as a percentage of the change in producers' surplus	
		Existing policy*	Deficiency payment policy
Wheat	100	5.5	1.2
Rye	60	8.6	1.9
Sugar	1,268	22.5	15.6
Butter	473	15.6	5.2
Cheese	142	4.5	1.8
Pork	942	10.1	1.8
Poultry	143	36.27	10.6
Eggs	256	8.46	3.5
Feed grain livestock sector	1,739	9.7	3.1
All commodities	3,792	14.4	7.4

SOURCE: Werner Kiene, *Welfare Costs of Alternative Agricultural Policies in Austria,* Department of Agricultural Economics, Michigan State University, 1971.
*Direct price support.

not measure any secondary consequences, such as the effect that protection might have on the general economy or the extent to which it will permit secondary reactions by government. A recent paper by Dale Hathaway maintains that one of the principal effects of a liberal trade policy is its use as adjunct to monetary and fiscal policy in efforts to control inflation.[14] Protection, on the other hand, provides leeway for permitting price and wage increases with less concern for the effects of external competition. Hathaway's argument suggests what long has been one of the basic arguments for free trade, namely, that exposure to international markets will have a strong dynamic and competitive effect. This effect becomes increasingly important as governments undertake policies for domestic income and employment stabilization. International competition can establish limits on the actions of government and on other power groups.

External Effects

The above discussion has concentrated on the gains, losses, and income transfers within the protecting country. Clearly, the effects extend beyond. Protection in importing countries increases domestic supply relative to demand and tends to reduce imports. Protection in industrial exporting countries also increases supply relative to demand and tends to increase export availabilities unless effective programs of supply control are implemented. This development has a direct effect on world markets: Other countries find available outlets reduced and prices driven down; within Third World nations the result is a transfer of income from producers to consumers.

There also will be a transfer among countries. The use of export subsidies to dispose of surplus production has a particularly devastating effect in this connection. If, for example, the United States subsidizes wheat on international markets and drives prices to an artificially low level, this benefits importing nations such as Japan and imposes a cost through lower export prices on exporting countries. This kind of transfer is particularly important to less developed nations that rely heavily on agricultural products as a source of foreign exchange earnings. For these, both the loss of world market in importing areas and the artificially reduced prices through export subsidies can impede export earnings severely. As we will see in chapter 8, developing countries argue that the extended effect of this problem is to encourage import substitution industries, leading to high cost agricultural inputs and a deterioration in the competitive position on export commodities.

On the positive side, agricultural protection in industrial nations has led to beneficial effects for less developed countries in at least two ways. One is the availability of food for aid purposes, which is of direct value to consumers and in many cases has been used to promote economic development. Another illustration is the case of U.S. cotton. The U.S. support program through the 1960s maintained high price levels and accumulated substantial stocks that resulted in higher world prices than might have occurred without the program. This permitted the development of cotton production in some developing countries that now can compete successfully in world markets. Other U.S. programs through the mid-1960s have had similar effect, particularly upon grains and, to a lesser extent, tobacco and other minor crops. This effect was built into the programs through accumulation of large storage stocks and through supply control. A transfer from U.S. agricultural producers to those in other countries appears to have arisen in these cases.

In general, the argument that protectionism in industrial nations has been detrimental to less developed countries appears valid. On the other hand, there have been times when the opposite has been true, and foreign exchange earnings were improved and international transfer of production occurred, sometimes with the result that the affected industries in less developed countries have grown up and achieved a permanent advantage in international markets.

Summary

In raising the question of the economic consequences of protection, two things must be kept in mind. First, there is no way of measuring an optimum level of trade, and no quantitative criteria can be established. Second, trade is not an end in itself, but is justified only to the extent that it serves other ends. In a direct and immediate sense, the ends sought through trade can be viewed as the gains in satisfaction available to consumers through imports of lower cost products or products that cannot be produced domestically and, in the case of business firms, the possibility of importing lower cost or nonexistent raw materials. In the case of export industries, trade represents a source of earnings and contributes to the returns to those resources employed in export industries. On the loss side, trade reduces the income in those industries that are displaced or prevented from development by international competition. In an overall sense, and given the assumptions within which trade theory was developed, it is clear that once specialization is attained and all resources are fully employed, the gain to society in total is greatest if free trade exists. Yet, in today's world it is also clear that, given structural and resource rigidities and problems of dynamic adjustment, practical policy cannot be case entirely within the framework of the efficiency criteria assumed in static economic theory. Other criteria, such as the effect of policy on income distribution, structural change, and general economic development, must be taken into account.

5

Postwar Policy Directions:
Advanced Countries

Agricultural trade among advanced countries of the Western world is dominated by temperate zone commodities. Western Europe is the largest trading area and has the most complex problems and greatest market distortions, based both on the organization of its agriculture and its policies. In total, the area is a large net importer of agricultural products. The second largest trading area is North America. Extensive quantities are traded between Canada and the United States, and together they comprise the largest net export area for agricultural products. Of the other major components in the industrial country trading network, Japan is almost exclusively an importer. Australia, New Zealand, and Argentina are primarily exporters.

Viewed in terms of policy issues and current conflicts, primary interest must focus on developments within the North Atlantic area, principally between the United States and the European Economic Community.[1] Market problems and policies in these two areas have led to an almost infinite variety of protection and trade programs. Agricultural policies have been domestically oriented. Many were started for one purpose and evolved to serve another without basic change in program, resulting in commercial conflict centered on agriculture.

EEC Policy: Toward Increased Protection

The EEC agricultural policy is based on objectives and attitudes worked out at the national level by the original six member countries

87

and represents the compromises required in arriving at a common market organization. National policies took shape during the 1930s to offset competition from cheaper foreign sources of supply and were extended during the postwar period to provide incentives to farmers to increase output and overcome war induced food shortages. During this latter period, foreign exchange shortages also provided a motive for increased protection. These objectives have declined in importance, and income protection for farmers and market stability for agriculture have become the dominant ones. Other objectives related to maintaining balanced production, adjusting labor resources in agriculture, improving farm structure, and improving social conditions in rural areas also are included in national measures.

The task of developing a common policy involved enabling agriculture to pass from its individual country's policy framework to a common market competitive structure, as well as solving basic problems facing agriculture in the various member countries. In establishing the framework within which policy was developed, the EEC took a broad approach. The major objectives of its agricultural policy are to: (1) increase agricultural productivity by developing technical progress and ensure the rational development of agricultural production and the optimum utilization of the factors of production, particularly labor; (2) ensure a fair standard of living for the agricultural population, particularly by increasing the individual earnings of persons engaged in agriculture; (3) stabilize markets; (4) guarantee regular supplies; and (5) ensure reasonable prices to consumers.

These general guides have been implemented under three broadly oriented programs: structural policies, market and trade policies, and social policies in the field of agriculture. Social policies imply the incorporation of farmers and rural communities into broader programs aimed at employment generation, security, income during retirement years, and so forth, and do not have specific content insofar as agriculture is concerned. Structural reform in agriculture is interpreted broadly. In addition to the central question of creating larger, more efficient farms to replace small and, in some cases, scattered holdings, structural policy visualizes improving the mobility of agricultural labor and the basis upon which desired capital improvements necessary for individual farm adjustment can be made. Thus, the development of an adequate agricultural credit system and the coordination of markets for inputs, including labor, and agricultural products are included as a part of structural adjustment. Problems of structural reform also are visualized to include questions related to transportation facilities, education, and the development of service industries and infrastructure needed by agriculture. These programs, if implemented, obviously have long-term implications for production costs, quantity and composition of output, and overall welfare of farm people.

The first major action taken by the EEC was to establish a market with a common level of agricultural prices. This was done through (1) progressive elimination of obstacles to trade in agricultural products within the community, (2) establishment of rules governing competition, (3) coordination of a national market organization, and (4) coordination of trade policies among member states and gradual introduction of the system of common external protection. EEC policy has sought to achieve a common policy from closely regulated national markets with widely divergent methods, institutions, and techniques for implementing both internal and trade policies. The stated objectives of EEC policy are comprehensive, but to this point both structural and social policies have been implemented with considerably less vigor than measures aimed directly at income improvement and price stability. This may continue to be the case for some time.

Price Support and Market Policy in the EEC

The common market organization for agricultural products has involved development of common price levels, the elimination of internal trade barriers, and the development of a common external trade barrier. The methods used for protection are summarized in Table 13.

GRAINS. The most closely regulated market under the EEC, as had been the case in preexisting national markets, is that for grains.

French national grain policy involved government price fixing, support purchases, export subsidies, import protection, and a two-price system based upon a quantum procedure that sought to assure farmers one price for quantities needed in the domestic market and the world price for quantities exported. Farmers were required to sell grain at designated points, and prices of products for human consumption were strictly regulated at all market levels, including consumer prices. Completely regulated internal trading and state trading in international markets were in effect.

As a deficit producer, West Germany relied largely on import control through a marketing board to protect domestic prices. For bread grains these were supplemented by percentage requirements for

Table 13. The EEC Market Regulation Scheme

Commodity	Target price	Threshold price	Sluice gate price	Free at frontier price	Import levy	Supplementary levy	Import duty	Provision for market intervention	Provision for export refunds	Quota	Quality standards	Producers organization	Initial date	Date of unification*
								Arrangements						
Grain and grain products	x	x		x	x			x	x				1-8-'62	1-7-'67
Rice and rice products	x¹	x		x	x			x¹	x				1-9-'64	1-9-'67
Pigs and pig meat			x	x	x	x		x²	x				1-8-'62	1-7-'67
Poultry and eggs			x	x	x	x			x				1-8-'62	1-7-'67
Milk and dairy products	x³	x	x⁵	x	x			x⁴	x				1-11-'64	1-4-'68
Beef and veal				x	x		x	x	x	x⁶			1-11-'64	1-4-'68
Sugar and sugar beets	x	x		x	x			x	x	x⁷			1-7-'67	1-7-'68
Oilseeds	x							x	x				1-7-'67	1-7-'67
Olive oil	x	x	x⁸	x	x			x	x				1-11-'66	1-11-'66
Fruit and vegetables								x	x	x⁹	x		1-8-'62	1-7-'68
Wine							x			x¹⁰	x	x	1-8-'62	1-11-'69

SOURCE: Netherlands Agricultural Ministry, *Selected Agri-figures of the EEC* (The Hague: the Ministry, August 1967), p. 47.

*After 1 July 1967 the European Guidance and Guarantee Fund takes full responsibility for financing the common agricultural policy. The income of the fund then will consist of: (1) 90 percent of the proceeds of the levies on imports from outside the community, and (2) direct contributions by national governments on the following scale (in percentages of the required sum in 1967–1968 and 1968–1969): France, 32.0 percent; Italy, 20.3 percent; Belgium, 8.1 percent; West Germany, 31.2 percent; the Netherlands, 8.2 percent; and Luxembourg, 9.2 percent.

¹In France and Italy
²In the case of carcasses, backs, and bellies
³Only in the case of milk
⁴Only in the case of butter
⁵Guide price
⁶Levy free import quotum for frozen beef
⁷Production quotum
⁸Reference price
⁹Import quotum applicable only through a safeguard clause procedure
¹⁰Import quotum

utilization of domestic grains and, where necessary, temporary stock-piling schemes and subsidies for transportation from surplus to deficit regions.

Italian grain prices were fixed each year by the government to apply to deliveries made under compulsory collection arrangements for a given crop quota. Prices on quantities outside the quota were maintained near the quota level through direct control over foreign trade exercised by the government trading monopoly.

Support to grain was implemented in the Netherlands and Belgium through establishing target prices, government purchases, and close control over import and export trade along with domestic use requirements for bread grain.

Methods used at a national level not only involved price protection for income purposes, but also often included strictly regulated state trading in export and import markets. For bread grains, specified use requirements and, in some cases, quota systems for delivery or price differentiation purposes were in effect. These have been supplanted by an EEC system which relies largely on price to direct market flow and production patterns.

Prices are applied internally through a set of target prices that vary among regions in the EEC and are adjusted seasonally to cover storage costs and help assure a more even flow of grain to market. These prices are implemented in two ways. For areas or crops which exceed production requirements, support purchases are made at intervention prices. In the case of deficit crops, price guarantees are assured through computed threshold prices below which grain cannot be imported. Specific import prices are computed for grain, as such, and also for all grain products by considering the value of the grain in the product, a milling margin, and an allowance for protection of the domestic milling industry, as well as the value of by-products.

The basic EEC price structure for grains has been well above world levels; it is based on target prices using Duisburg, Germany, as the principal deficit area. From this point, based on transport and marketing costs, threshold prices are computed for import grains. For internal prices, derived target prices in other EEC areas are computed in relationship to transport costs from Duisburg or points of import. Intervention prices, while somewhat below target prices, are closely related in all areas.

LIVESTOCK PRODUCTS. National measures of protection for most livestock and livestock products existed prior to EEC involvement. The most comprehensive were those applied to dairy products. All countries assured farmers a minimum price level for milk, achieved through a variety of domestic and import and export programs. Belgium, France, West Germany, and the Netherlands implemented domestic purchases of butter and/or other dairy products when necessary to maintain price. Export aids were used in the Netherlands, Belgium, and France whenever necessary to clear markets. Domestic consumption subsidies were used to some extent in Belgium and the Netherlands, while in West Germany a delivery subsidy was paid to dairies for milk delivered by farmers, and both wholesale and retail prices of liquid milk were fixed. Strict import controls were maintained either through quota systems or, as in the case of France and West Germany, through monopoly control of all import and export transactions by a single organization operating under government auspices. Although less comprehensive and varied in method, substantial protection was provided for beef, veal, and pork. France guaranteed minimum prices and exercised quantitative control on imports. When necessary, export assistance was provided. In West Germany, monopoly control over imports and exports was maintained, and storage and stockpiling was undertaken when necessary by a single import and storage agency. Protection in Italy was provided primarily through import quotas, as it was for beef in the Netherlands. Import controls and export aids were operative in Belgium on both meat products and live animals. Because of extensive exports of Dutch pork products and a tendency for international prices to fluctuate independent of Dutch supplies, a comprehensive program was in operation. Farmers and slaughter houses received an agreed price set periodically. If export prices fell below this level, a government allowance covered the difference; if export prices rose above the set level, the government collected an export levy to cover the difference.

Much less comprehensive protection existed for eggs. France provided seasonal minimum prices, with government intervention if necessary, and an equalization tax to offset differences in prices of imported eggs. Belgium had a direct production subsidy through a deficiency payment on eggs delivered, and West Germany provided a direct production subsidy through a payment equal to the differential in cost of feed grain at German prices versus world price levels. It appears that no direct market supports were provided for poultry meat, although it was protected through import regulations in most countries.

For livestock, as in the case for grain, EEC policy swept away a maze of quotas, subsidies, state trading, export programs, and import controls. Prices are relied on exclusively to allocate internal EEC trading and production relationships. These are supplemented by import levies and export subsidies to third countries where necessary.

The internal price for beef is based on a guide price computed to represent a weighted average of the beef price for each country, adjusted for seasonal and quality differences. Direct internal support is provided through intervention purchases between 93 and 96 percent of the guide price. Basic protection from imports is provided by customs duties that apply equally to all member countries. These can be supplemented by import levies whenever import prices plus the customs duty are less than 105 percent of the guide price.

Internal support for dairy product prices follows much the same form as that for beef. A target price is computed to apply equally throughout the EEC, and intervention agencies remove manufactured products, principally butter, from the market when desirable to maintain farm prices for milk. Import levies are computed weekly for 16 different products or product categories. Import levies are set at a level that will protect the target price on milk.

For pork, eggs, and poultry a sluicegate price is computed and an import levy assessed to offset the difference in costs of grain based on internal EEC prices as compared with external prices. A fixed factor allows for differences in production efficiency within the EEC as compared with external sources and provides protection to processed product industries.

Impact of the Common Agricultural Policy

The common agricultural policy has had a number of impacts on internal and external economic relations. Initially, a substantial realignment of farm prices among countries and among commodities occurred. Farm prices in West Germany, especially for grain, declined. Prices in France and the Netherlands tended to move up substantially, while those in Italy and Belgium tended to change somewhat less in the aggregate. Commodity prices were realigned in all countries. Wheat prices increased relative to other grains. Livestock-grain price ratios increased in some areas, but tended to decline in others. Feed grain became more expensive relative to livestock prices, which appears to have had an important effect on feed utilization levels. This has been illustrated dramatically in the Netherlands, where the grain component of mixed feeds declined from about 66 percent in the early 1960s to about 35 percent in 1969.[2] Since feed is a major import, this has had a trade reducing impact.

A number of equity and income transfer issues also are raised by the common agricultural policy. With a leveling out of prices for all the EEC, a result was that prices increased by the greatest amounts in areas which and to farmers who previously had higher than average incomes. Prices in surplus producing areas — generally those with the best agricultural resources — became equalized with those in deficit areas.

Another form of redistribution occurred through effects of the policy on the balance of payments of individual countries and the transfer of income among countries. Net importers send receipts from import duties and levies to a common fund; net exporters, particularly France and the Netherlands, receive payments to cover the difference between domestic and world prices on exported commodities.

The common agricultural policy also has had important production and trade effects. These can be viewed in two contexts: the short-term effect of price response on agricultural production and the direct effect of trade diversion, and the long-term implication for regional shifts in production and improvements in agricultural resource use within the area. Evidence to quantify these effects precisely is difficult to obtain; therefore, we only can infer, except where striking changes have occurred. The output trend in these countries had been strongly upward, and trade among EEC member countries had been increasing sharply prior to implementation of EEC policy. These trends seem to have increased. Over time the extent to which EEC policy will affect agricultural output and trade will depend upon the extent to which it stimulates dynamic adjustment and increased output through technology, shifts in production location, and improved resource use. These kinds of changes can be stimulated by shifts in price relations among commodities and among regions. Since major price shifts of this kind occurred in implementing the common agricultural policy,[3] substantial long-range adjustments in EEC agriculture should be anticipated.

U.K. Policy: Toward Market Organization

A second major dimension of European policy important to world trading relationships has developed in the United Kingdom. For almost a century prior to 1932, agricultural policy in the United Kingdom was based on the concept of free trade. The essence of policy since that time, however, has been a move away from multilateral free trade to controlled relationships with specific countries or controlled trading of specific commodities. The free trade approach first was abandoned in 1932; the British Duties Act established an ad valorem duty rate on virtually all imports, and the Ottawa Agreement provided a tariff preference between the United Kingdom and overseas members of the Commonwealth.[4] The agreement permitted free entry into the British market for virtually all agricultural commodities from Commonwealth countries, but specified a 10 percent tariff on most imports from non-Commonwealth nations.

Immediate postwar British agricultural policy was based on efforts to expand agricultural production. This focus changed in 1954, and while production expansion continues to be a major element in domestic policy, it has been pursued on a more selective basis than during and after World War II.

During the 1960s, the United Kingdom completed trade agreements with the major suppliers of several important commodities. Under the Commonwealth Sugar Agreement of 1961, prices and quotas were established within which approximately 90 percent of British sugar was imported. These imports all came from Commonwealth countries and were handled through the British Sugar Corporation. The agreement is aimed at providing assured supplies for the United Kingdom and at establishing stable prices for British consumers as well as for Commonwealth producing countries. In general, import prices tended to be above world market prices, and, in this sense, the arrangement was a gain for exporters.

A second major agreement, on bacon, was concluded in 1963 as an adjunct to British domestic support policy for hog producers. The agreement, intended to stabilize market prices at a reasonable level, was directly stimulated by low prices during 1961 and 1962, which resulted in heavy Treasury costs for deficiency payments to producers.

A grains agreement was established in 1964 with four principal suppliers: Argentina, Australia, Canada, and the United States. Additional exporters later signed the agreement, and it covered virtually all grain imports coming into the United Kingdom. In conjunction with this, a standard quantity system for domestic deficiency payments on wheat and barley was established. Under this system, when domestic production exceeded the standard quantity, the deficiency payment was reduced on a proportional basis. This method tended to establish a price-quantity relationship for farmers, as shown in Figure 9.

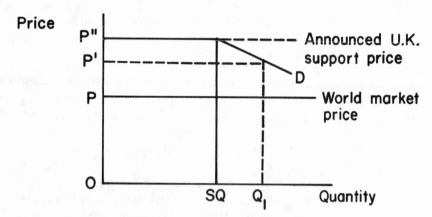

Figure 9: Effect of Standard Quantity on British Farm Prices

SQ represents the standard quantity on which the full announced deficiency payment would be paid. At production beyond SQ, the payment is reduced to lower unit returns to farmers. With production at SQ, gross price to farmers is P'', and at production Q_1 gross price is at P'. This feature was viewed by exporters as a supply control mechanism, and it was assumed in establishing the agreement that U.K. production would be effectively limited (implying certain assumptions about implementation of the program).

As an additional element of the U.K. grain agreement, minimum import prices were provided. Import levies could be applied if signatory exporting countries failed to comply with minimum prices. The minimum import prices were designed primarily to prevent excessively low domestic prices and consequent high Treasury costs for deficiency payments to domestic farmers.

A second element of change in U.K. trade policy during the 1960s was the Commonwealth trade program. Bilateral agreements were signed with New Zealand and Australia wherein the U.K. promised (1) to maintain duty-free entry of all agricultural products, (2) to maintain specified preference margins on agricultural exports from these countries, with the exception of meat, and (3) to admit, without quantity restrictions, most livestock products from these two areas. In addition, a virtual free trade area agreement was concluded with the Republic of Ireland in 1965. The United Kingdom provided duty-free and unrestricted entry for all agricultural products except butter, bacon, cereals covered under broader trade agreements, and main crop potatoes and refined sugar. In return, Ireland agreed to remove all quantity restrictions on U.K. exports and, over a ten-year period, to abolish all existing tariffs. As a major exception either country was allowed to impose quantitative restrictions on imports for the purpose of safeguarding its balance of payments.

Two special features of this latter agreement are of interest. First, the British government agreed to extend its price support system for Irish beef and lambs and to pay the Irish government annually the sum of the equivalent of the average deficiency payment received by U.K. producers on imports from Ireland to maximum quantities of 25,000 and 5,500 tons, respectively. In addition, Britain directly subsidized Irish farmers through price guarantees on Irish feeder stock imported into the United Kingdom.

A final dimension of U.K. trade policy during the 1960s was an effort to become involved in regional integration within Europe. The first stage was the establishment of the European Free Trade Association (EFTA, which, although primarily aimed at coordinating trade in industrial products, nonetheless developed a trade program for agriculture).[5] A large number of bilateral agricultural trade agreements were established which generally set prices and quantities on trade among individual nations and usually provided for a sharing of market growth in importing countries. The principal importing country was the United Kingdom. Another important element in U.K. policy was its application for membership and acceptance into the European Economic Community. British trade policy subsequent to entry was adapted to that existing in the Common Market and incorporated into the relatively strong protectionist framework it implies.

In the overall, postwar policy trends in Britain created a gradual restriction of trade relationships, both through bilateral arrangements and through commodity agreements. Major changes occurred during the 1960s. In commodity agreements, a note of liberalism was retained in that all specified the balance between British domestic production and market access for export producers. Bilateral agreements established exclusive relationships. These were more restrictive than either tariffs or quotas since they completely specified trading patterns and allowed no competitive inroads by other sellers. Finally, with U.K. entry into the EEC this extensive set of trade agreements was abandoned for a more restrictive import policy based on high domestic price and import levies. The concept of regionalization in Europe was greatly expanded.

Enlargement of the EEC

Recent European Economic Community enlargement has involved accession by three countries, the United Kingdom, Denmark, and Ireland, plus special arrangements with certain other European and British Commonwealth countries.[6] The major impact on international markets, however, will stem from the accession by the three European nations.

Changes in agricultural policy vary among countries. In the United Kingdom, agricultural policy since World War II has pointed toward expansion of output, with emphasis shifting to improved structure and productivity in the late 1950s, to import savings, and finally to selective expansion of certain products. Support programs have been based on a system of long-term guarantees. For example, legislation for grain and livestock provided guarantees that the total returns to agriculture would not be less than 97.5 percent of the total during the preceding year and that the level of guarantee for any individual commodity would not be less than 96 percent of the preceding year's level. Price supports covered most major commodities. Guarantee levels among commodities were adjusted over time to encourage desired redirection for expansion of overall output. Beginning in 1971, the deficiency payment system was, in part, replaced by minimum import prices and levies, with the effect that the prices of some foods were increased to consumers.[7] With entry, additional, and in most cases significant, price increases occurred at the farm and consumer levels.

In addition to price guarantees, British agriculture has been supported through a series of input subsidies and capital grants that annually have involved an Exchequer cost nearly as large as the outlays on price guarantees. These grants were for a wide range of purposes including direct fertilizer and lime subsidies, field drainage, water supply grants, grants for improving livestock raising land, direct grants for maintaining hill cattle and sheep and for raising calves, grants for improvement of silos and other farm structures, and direct grants to disadvantaged small farmers. With entry into the EEC, many of these subsidies have been abandoned and others changed in light of costs imposed on the United Kingdom through the EEC price support and structural reform programs.

The main historical focus of Irish agricultural policy had been to increase output, with emphasis on exports of cattle and livestock products. Production expansion was encouraged through a subsidy program on inputs and costs. Price supports existed on most livestock and grain commodities, but support levels were low relative to EEC prices; a significant overall increase in Irish farm prices followed entry. Cattle and milk prices increased substantially both in an absolute sense and relative to grain prices, thus reinforcing a preexisting direction for expansion in Irish agriculture.

Past Danish agricultural policy was aimed at full utilization and continuing improvement of agricultural resources, including production and market industries. Because of heavy reliance on export markets, emphasis was placed on quality production and the development of a highly integrated system of production and marketing. Despite this general emphasis, Denmark found it necessary to enter into specific programs aimed at direct improvement of farm income. These resulted in a system of price supports and variable import levies on grain and a two-price scheme to maintain relatively high prices in the home market for the major livestock products. The major change with accession to the EEC was increased prices for export items, including pork, beef, poultry, and dairy products.

Policy changes in these countries were imposed on agricultural sectors that occupy widely different roles in each economy and sectors in which considerable change in production and trade patterns had occurred in recent years. In the United Kingdom, agriculture is a relatively small component in the total economy and produces only about 60 percent of the total food requirements. In Ireland and Denmark, agriculture is much more important and is a major source of foreign exchange earnings. In both these countries, livestock production predominates.

Conditions influencing output and trade in the 1960s will not persist in the future. With entry, important price shifts have occurred.[8] The effect on trade will be substantial, as was the case with the original six members.

Separating this change from preexisting trends, however, is difficult. A trend toward European self-sufficiency in grain and livestock products has been underway since the early 1960s. This process would have occurred without the formation of the original EEC and probably would have continued for the three new entrants without accession to the EEC, particularly if recent trends in U.K. price policy had continued. This trend, along with growth in output greater than the increase in utilization, will result in diminishing export opportunities for third country suppliers of grain and livestock commodities.

Furthermore, there likely will be some internal diversion of several major products — dairy, meat, and grain — as a result of expansion.

Danish and Irish dairy products and surpluses in the original six will be more than adequate to displace United Kingdom imports. Surpluses of soft wheat in France easily can fill the U.K. deficit, and little if any need be imported from external sources. Imports of hard wheat for mixing purposes will continue. In feed grain, specific deficits will exist in some countries, and imports from third countries, particularly of corn, probably will continue. Overall self-sufficiency and some export surpluses most likely will exist for pork, poultry, and eggs. Accession will encourage beef production in Ireland, and the expanded EEC probably will represent a reduced market for external suppliers. Internal trade in some other commodities, such as sugar and fruits and vegetables, also will occur at the expense of outside suppliers.[9]

U.S. Policy: Toward Greater Rationality

Another major focal point of modern agricultural trade policy involves developments in the United States. Because the United States has played a leadership role in developing Western world trade policy, U.S. agricultural policy must be measured both in the light of domestic agricultural programs and the implications of these programs for deviation from the general U.S. trade policy orientation.

Modern U.S. trade policy began to emerge in the 1930s under the Reciprocal Trade Agreements programs. The initial legislation in 1934 provided authority for a 50 percent reduction in tariff levels from the 1929 base and added three major provisions to U.S. trade policy. First, the agreements expressed the idea, as implied in the title, that the concept of reciprocity must be imbedded in trade negotiations. In other words, if concessions are granted, some should be received; on the other hand, in order to obtain concessions, a nation must expect to make some. Second, the most-favored-nation principle was established. Any agreement with an individual nation automatically will apply to all exporters and importers of the commodity involved. Third, and very important from the viewpoint of implementing the program, bargaining authority was granted to the executive branch of government, requiring no specific congressional approval of trade agreements that were negotiated. The obvious implication of this latter change is that the legislative branch was removed from direct trade negotiations, and the pressures from interest groups were circumvented to a large degree.

Since its initiation in 1934, the Trade Agreements Act has been revised and extended by Congress on several occasions, but the act remained the basic legislation underlying U.S. trade policy until the passage of the Trade Expansion Act in 1962. This act incorporated all the major principles and provisions of the earlier one and further extended the authority of the President to enter into negotiation for reduction of trade barriers. In addition to general authority for a 50 percent reduction of tariffs from the 1 July 1962 level, specific authority was given for complete elimination of tariffs between the United States and the EEC on items for which these two units engaged in 80 percent or more of the trade. Authority was extended to eliminate tariffs on certain commodities produced by less developed countries in cases where the prevailing rate was 5 percent or less. The Trade Expansion Act further enlarged the bargaining basis by creating a cabinet-level interagency trade organization chaired by a special representative of the President. Most important, it introduced one additional principle into trade negotiations. For the first time this legislation recognized the conflict between specific producer interests and the national interest in international commercial policy; it dealt with the effects of tariff reductions on domestic industry and labor. For industries, the legislation provided aid to affected firms in the form of technical assistance, direct loans and guarantees of loans for readjustments, and for tax assistance during a readjustment period. For labor, readjustment allowances, retraining assistance, and relocation allowances were provided.

Overall, it seems fairly clear that the U.S. trade program and U.S. leadership have had a major effect in reducing trade barriers on industrial products. Little was accomplished during the pre–World War II period, in part because of the methods used in approaching negotiation, but largely because of the general state of world conflict. In the postwar period, however, the United States provided leadership in undertaking six rounds of trade negotiations which have had a major effect on the level of trade restrictions for the bulk of world traded industrial commodities. Following an estimated 35 percent across-the-board reduction on industrial trade barriers in the last of these negotiations — the Kennedy Round — industrial tariffs among advanced countries are relatively low and probably not a major factor affecting international trade. The implications of this fact for the general growth of world markets, including agriculture, are difficult to estimate quantitatively, but undoubtedly are of major importance.

In agriculture, the U.S. posture on international trade matters is less consistent. Both import protection and export disposal programs have been important. Each has been built around and has responded to domestic price support programs and the conditions the price support programs have created. Initial legislation for both import protection and export disposal was provided in the Agricultural Adjustment Act of 1935. Section 22 established import quota restrictions on commodities subject to price support, while Section 32 permitted the use of customs receipts for the disposal of surplus farm commodities. Both programs have been strengthened greatly during the post–World War II period. The limited nature of price supports during the 1930s did not result in the need for massive application of either kind of restriction. During the war and postwar years, completely controlled trading due to the war and postwar shortages dominated international relations. Beginning in 1948, however, surpluses began to develop, and major changes were made in U.S. agricultural programs. Legislation was passed that provided for flexibility in support levels from 70 to 90 percent of parity, for some commodities as low as 60 percent. It soon became evident that supply control through price reduction was not effective, at least to the degree that it had a serious impact on total output. Therefore, major programs were introduced aimed at supply control and surplus disposal.

This post-1948 period also saw several important innovations in U.S. trade policy. The Trade Agreement Extension Act of 1948 contained the peril point provision, which required the tariff commission to determine the lowest duty possible that would not result in major damage to any given industry. In addition, the act provided an escape clause that could be invoked if an increase in imports was demonstrated to be responsible to a significant degree for the deterioration in the sales and profits of an industry. These restrictions applied across the board and were used, to some extent, by agriculture and agricultural industries. Furthermore, Section 22 of the Agricultural Adjustment Act of 1935 was strengthened by requiring the President to establish import quotas on price support commodities under certain circumstances, irrespective of existing international agreements. These actions, along with specific commodity legislation to establish sugar quotas, import quotas on dairy products, and the meat import quota bill passed in 1964, along with certain voluntary agreements, customs administration procedures, overseas procurement requirements, buy-American restrictions, and certain national security provisions, constitute a substantial array of import protection for agriculture if implemented to the full degree.

Major shifts occurred in U.S. agricultural and trade programs in the 1960s. High and rigid price supports for major export crops were eliminated. The principal commodities affected were feed grains, cotton, and wheat. The average Commodity Credit Corporation (CCC) loan rates on wheat and cotton dropped drastically, from the 1962 levels of $2.00 per bushel and 32.5 cents per pound to $1.25 per bushel for wheat and 21 cents per pound for cotton.[10] Along with these reductions in loan rates, direct producer payments were made on the proportion of each crop destined for domestic use. To receive these payments farmers had to agree voluntarily to participate in an acreage diversion program designed to reduce surplus stocks and to balance output and total available market outlets. In 1970, the acreage control aspects were shifted from commodity allotments to a program in which each producer could set aside his share of a national land diversion requirement and plant any crop he wished on the remaining acreage.[11]

Another major shift in programs occurred with passage of the Agriculture and Consumer Protection Act of 1973. The most significant elements of change in this legislation are the elimination of the two-price system that prevailed in the 1960s and the institution of a deficiency payment guarantee at one price for the total crop. Loan rates are retained at a low price, but target prices are set above the loan rate. If market prices fall below target, direct income payments are made to farmers equal to the difference between the target and market price. If market prices drop to the loan rate, government acquisitions and accumulation of stocks could again occur.

One effect of these changes has been to reduce the direct conflict between U.S. domestic policy and its export objectives. The lower loan rates eliminated the need for large export payments on wheat and cotton. Also, programs in the 1960s moved toward allowing market forces to operate in determining the overall level of output and its composition. This is illustrated in part in Figure 10.

Price P_0 represents the support level and CCC loan rate that applied prior to the changes during the 1960s. Price P_1 represents unit return to producers from the market, plus the income payment on the domestic proportion of the allotment, quantity Q_2.

Beyond this quantity, each producer received the lower price, P_2. Since each producer received the higher price on only a percentage of his output, decisions on how much to produce were made relative to the lower price, P_2. As indicated in the figure this should, ceteris paribus, reduce output from Q to Q_1 for the farm illustrated. This shift in pricing would tend to exert a downward pressure on output in the short run. With the complementary requirement of acreage restriction being a condition of participation in the income payment program (the

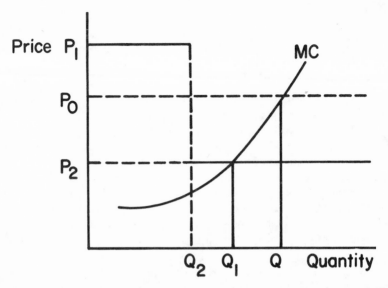

Figure 10:   Supply Effect of Change in U.S. Price Support Programs

unit payment $P_1 - P_2$ on quantity Q_2), the general effect on export crops would be supply reducing relative to previous ones. With the elimination of specific commodity allotments in 1970, farmers could make marginal shifts among commodities to take advantage of perceived profit opportunities.

The Agriculture and Consumer Protection Act of 1973 retained the concept of permitting market prices to drop to the relatively low level indicated by P_2 in Figure 10. Differentiation of domestic and international prices, however, was eliminated, and direct government payments were instituted to increase farmers' returns to the higher level, P_0. This change should tend to increase output in relation to the previous program as illustrated by the quantity Q, Q_1. An important distinction in the approach introduced in 1973 is that government incentives for output expansion have been reintroduced as compared with programs of the 1960s and early 1970s. Both programs, however, reduced the direct conflict between U.S. domestic and international policy objectives as compared with direct price supports.

On major export products, U.S. trade policy has moved to a relatively more defensible position. Programs have separated income support from commodity prices. Export subsidies are nominal, and complementary supply reducing programs are in effect. Since 1970 these have been implemented in such a way that farmers may respond to market conditions and comparative advantage in developing their production plans. The U.S. record on livestock products and a number of minor crops, especially sugar, rice, peanuts, and tobacco, is much less defensible. Protection for these either has increased or stabilized at a relatively high level, and programs for lower protection or change in method of protection are not in sight.

In summary, there was a major U.S. postwar push to liberalize trade, but its position on agriculture has been ambiguous. Through the mid-1960s the United States sought and obtained GATT exceptions and exclusions for agriculture. In the Kennedy Round efforts were made to include agriculture but with little success. Agriculture was difficult for a number of reasons, including internal EEC political problems and conditions in European agriculture. Furthermore, exporters could not agree on price and access arrangements to be sought, and no commitment existed to negotiate domestic agricultural policies.

The major question now is whether the United States can or will provide the leadership for reduction in barriers and liberalization of agricultural trade. In answering this question, it is necessary to recognize a number of new dimensions that will affect future negotiations.

Since the Kennedy Round there has been a weakening of the general multilateral framework that has surrounded postwar negotiations. Further reduction of trade restrictions is becoming more difficult because barriers increasingly are tied up with other social and economic policy. Also, as traditional barriers are reduced, nontariff barriers have become important, and they are difficult both to define and measure.

The United States recently has passed new trade legislation, the Trade Reform Act of 1973, which seems to provide a framework for moving in several directions at once. The act provides authority for new negotiations and a continuation of the program of trade liberalization. It extends presidential authority to negotiate increases or decreases without limit, including nontariff barriers for a period of five years. The act also includes a provision for relief for U.S. industry from disruption caused by "fair" competition. This title liberalizes the criteria (escape clause) for determining that injury to domestic industry is due to imports, expands the kinds of import relief for business (such as orderly marketing agreements), and provides adjustment assistance for labor. This chapter of the act permits increased flexibility in protecting U.S. industry from foreign competition. The bill also revises and strengthens the four preexisting statutes dealing with foreign unfair trade practices. Another section of the bill, entitled "International Trade Policy Management," provides permanent authority to manage trade policy to deal with balance-of-payments problems and inflation.

With this kind of flexibility the future course of U.S. trade policy is difficult to predict. That policy has changed since the Kennedy Round. Pressures for import protection at times have been intense. Policy in the early 1970s has reflected an ad hoc, piecemeal approach, with individual concessions being made to commodity groups along with spectacular actions on monetary questions. Some liberalization occurred during 1973 to curb inflation, but whether this direction will continue is uncertain. The new legislation is sufficiently flexible to permit moving toward greater protection or providing further leadership in seeking trade liberalization. How we move increasingly will be influencd by such imperatives as the overall balance-of-payments position, the effect of trade policy on inflation, and basic import needs such as petroleum and other raw materials. The United States will become increasingly interdependent with other nations, and this will require adaptation of U.S. industry and agriculture to world market conditions. Protection to serve specific commodity interests will become less tolerable. Efforts to achieve further liberalization are the most logical course for future U.S. policy.

Other Countries

The remaining major components of the Western temperate products trading framework are Japan, Canada, Oceania, South Africa, and Argentina. To an increasing degree, individual less developed countries are becoming important exporters, and a number are gaining in importance as importers.

Of the group listed above, Japan is the major importer. A complex set of agricultural and trade policies has been developed with a view toward increasing domestic supplies and controlling imports. Emphasis on self-sufficiency in rice has been overextended, and surpluses have developed. Japan also has encouraged fruit and vegetable production and more recently is seeking to expand livestock output. Protection for agriculture is extensive, but because of its limited resource base, imports are expanding and probably will continue to do so.

The major export countries in the above group maintain increasingly complex agricultural and trade policies. Imports center on products that cannot be produced in each country and to a large extent are unprotected. Policy emphasis has been on improved production and more orderly marketing with a view toward maintaining a competitive position in world markets or toward gaining special access, as in the case of commonwealth preferences and sales agreements with communist countries. In grain, the removal of the U.S. umbrella over world prices in the mid-1960s has created an additional problem for these nations. World trading prices have dropped, and governments have had to assume an additional burden of income support to agriculture. Australia has developed a three-tiered price guarantee system for wheat, and in 1970 Canada undertook a program of incentive payments to farmers to reduce wheat acreage. Argentina has yet to develop major domestic policies that support prices in agriculture. Increasing emphasis, however, is being placed on indirect measures that will improve productivity and expand agricultural output and the export of farm products.

Summary

The agricultural economy of all Western industrial countries is influenced by direct government policies. Emphasis is placed on raising commodity prices to generate improved farm incomes. The extent of governmental intervention varies among countries, but generally is extensive. Despite some lowering of protection levels in the United States, the overall degree of protection in Western industrial countries increased during the 1960s. The most important component of this increase was the change from a national to a common agricultural policy by the six-member EEC. A further increase in protection occurred with the accession of the United Kingdom, Ireland, and Denmark.

Agricultural policies in industrial countries have resulted in a series of programs and actions that constrain and distort trade in agricultural products. Domestic demand and supply imbalance and disequilibrium in the agriculture of individual countries is transmitted to international markets through a wide variety of techniques that protect against lower cost imports and subsidize sales on world markets. As indicated in chapter 4, the extent of this protection is difficult to measure, and the welfare and income transfer effects are not easily defined. The most visible trade consequences have been the import substitution effect of expanded output in many importing countries and the development of exportable surpluses in others. Production and consumption in importing areas develop such that imports become increasingly marginal in relation to total needs. Agricultural protectionism becomes a major factor in restricting trade and distorting patterns of world resource use.

The behavior of both exporters and importers contributes to disequilibrium in international markets. Only coordinated action among nations in both categories will resolve the conflicts that have arisen through independent steps taken by individual countries. This cooperation has not yet occurred, although the situation has led to various attempts to offset the production-consumption imbalances and reduce international conflict. These will be examined in chapter 6.

6

The Search for Solutions

An easy solution sometimes is suggested for problems of international commercial conflict in agriculture. It is reasoned that conflict arises because governments have chosen to protect domestic agriculture and largely disregard international effects. The logical solution is to eliminate domestic protection or, at a minimum, reduce it drastically, and international harmony will follow. Production in the long run will move to areas of low cost, and trade will be determined by comparative advantage.

The issue, of course, is not that simple. Domestic programs in all countries have been developed to offset problems that reflect basic economic conditions surrounding agricultural production. These are: "(1) a relatively low price elasticity for farm products; (2) a relatively slow growth in demand for farm products; (3) a high degree of uncertainty regarding future economic and technical change, together with rapid output-increasing changes; (4) the competitive structure of the industry which inhibits its ability to handle adjustment problems; and (5) asset fixity in agriculture so that resources committed to producing farm products continue in production despite earnings which may fall well below the expected earnings and acquisition costs."[1]

Beyond the recognition of these inherent economic conditions there are historical considerations involved in most protection programs. The central objectives of protection have moved in the last 40 years from primary concern with eliminating poverty in rural areas, to

109

growth and development objectives related to expanded food production, to issues centered on equity and income.

Recent emphasis on domestic objectives and programs tailored largely to income improvement through price supports has resulted in a number of problems. The most important of these has been to destroy the domestic and international equilibrium between supply and demand. Some programs, particularly those undertaken unilaterally by individual countries that affect international markets, have increased conflict and have had a negative rather than a positive international effect although they may have reduced domestic problems.

Such consequences have led to programs in individual countries aimed at correcting the resulting market imbalances, including subsidized consumption, export disposal, and, in the United States, supply control. The other major approach taken, although to a limited extent in agriculture, has been through international negotiations to reduce trade barriers and force the adaptation of domestic programs to international market pressures. The extent of action and degree of success of these various efforts have varied among countries, but in the aggregate they have not succeeded in eliminating conflict among industrial nations.

Domestic Demand Expansion

Programs to expand domestic consumption of farm products are of two kinds: those providing a direct subsidy to increase human consumption and those providing a subsidy that will divert products into a secondary use. The former type has been of greatest importance to the United States, the latter to Europe. Efforts to increase consumption in the United States have emphasized school lunch, milk, and institutional feeding programs. Methods include either providing direct cash grants or selling food at reduced prices through low cost meals. The effect sought is to increase total food consumption by expanding real income or by lowering prices to expand total sales.

The net effectiveness of such programs is difficult to measure. Food stamp or subsidy program purchases will displace those that would have been made in any event. Many foods that come under such programs have both a very low income elasticity (sometimes negative) and a low price elasticity of demand. Therefore, the total expenditure required from public funds to subsidize either income or prices will greatly exceed the additional expenditure for food that can be induced. This approach is an extremely inefficient way of dealing with agricultural surplus disposal. A study at the University of Minnesota, which tested both the effects of income increases and price reduction, concluded that public expenditure would be very high relative to increases in consumption. Both programs could aid in reducing nutritional deficiencies in low income families and well may be justified on nutritional grounds,[2] but they are inefficient in dealing with agricultural surpluses. For the most part, efforts have been made in the United States to abandon this method. Domestic consumption subsidies no longer are viewed as important vehicles for dealing with surplus agricultural production.

The European approach has concentrated on subsidizing commodities so they can be diverted to livestock use. The elasticity relevant to this case, below a certain threshold level, is related to the marginal value product of the commodity in livestock production. Price response below a threshold level is likely to be relatively high on such items as wheat, sugar, and even dairy products that can be disposed of as livestock feed. Per unit subsidies, however, are relatively high, and to date greater emphasis appears to have been placed on disposing of surpluses in external markets.

Supply Control

Supply control has been used primarily in North America, especially in the United States. Limited and sometimes informal programs are used in certain other countries.[3] In Canada, for example, several provincial marketing boards extend controls over quantity and quality of commodities marketed. A number of countries have sugar quotas, and in the Netherlands producer marketing organizations maintained a regulatory system on fruits and vegetables. For minor commodities in a number of countries, compulsory membership in producer marketing organizations places production under strict production and marketing regulations.

Direct control in the United States has taken two forms. The first concerns specific commodities. Prior to 1970 producers were required to restrict their plantings to specified acreages in order to participate in price support loan programs. Concentration was on feed grain, wheat, rice, cotton, tobacco, and peanuts. Participation was voluntary in the sense that no mandatory compliance was required, but coercive in the sense that eligibility for price support was contingent upon compliance.

Commodity oriented programs were revised in 1970 to require that a total acreage be set aside rather than to restrict acreages of individual commodities. Within the remaining acres, each farmer is free to plant any crop or combination of crops he deems most profitable and desirable. This plan has the major advantage of eliminating the farmer's need to maintain base allotments of specific crops, and it permits him to plant the single crop or combination of crops deemed most profitable. In the aggregate, overall cost levels should be reduced by encouraging movement of specific crops into areas of greatest comparative advantage. Acreage restrictions on major crops were abandoned entirely in 1974, although provision remains in farm legislation for their reinstitution if needed, a not unlikely prospect if price support levels are raised materially.

A second program in the United States has been aimed at longer term land retirement. Compensation is paid to farmers who take land out of production for a number of years and place it into conservation use that does not add to agricultural commodity supply.

The total amount of land kept out of production for selected years under both programs is shown in Table 14.

The net effect of these programs on reducing supplies is not completely clear. The amount of acreage removed is not a good indication, since farmers tend to take their lowest yielding acreages out of production and to comply more readily in low productivity than in high productivity regions. Furthermore, it is argued that the reduction in acreage *per se* will induce farmers to substitute other input for land, maintaining production even in the face of reduced acreages. This argument may be partially fallacious. Higher prices through support and the elimination of risk through announcement of prices prior to planting might induce higher levels of fertilization and use of other variable inputs. This would occur to some degree without a reduction in land area. The argument in one case rests on the concept that farmers will add variable inputs until marginal value product equals marginal factor cost, and with higher product prices this will result in expanded use of variable inputs. The other argument rests on the concept that farmers seek to maintain a given level of income and will extend the use of one input to offset the loss of another to retain a satisfactory output and income level. It is difficult to say which of these arguments is more valid. The fact remains that U.S. farmers have expanded their use of capital and purchased inputs during periods of supply control. Whether this has occurred at a more rapid rate than without supply control never can be proven. Change has been equally

Table 14. *Cropland Acreage Withheld from Production under Specified Programs, United States, 1956–1972, in Millions of Acres*

Year	Acreage reserve	Conservation reserve	Feed grain	Program Wheat	Cotton	Cropland conversion	Cropland adjustment[1]	Total[2]
1956	12.2	1.4					13.6	
1957	21.4	6.4						27.8
1958	17.2	9.9						27.1
1959		22.5						22.5
1960		28.7						28.7
1961		28.5	25.2					53.7
1962		25.8	28.2	10.7				64.7
1963		24.3	24.5	7.2		0.1		56.1
1964		17.4	32.4	5.1	0.5[3]	.1		55.5
1965		14.0	34.8	7.2	1.0[3]	.4		57.4
1966		13.3	34.7	8.3	4.6	.4	2.0	63.3
1967		11.0	20.3		4.9	.6	4.0	40.8
1968		9.2	32.4		3.3	.5	3.9	49.3
1969		3.4	39.1	11.1		.5	3.9	58.0
1970		.1	37.4	15.7		[4]	3.8	57.1
1971		[4]	18.2	13.5	2.1	[4]	3.3	37.2
1972[5]		[4]	37.4[5]	20.4[5]	2.0[5]	[4]	2.8	62.7

SOURCE: U.S. Department of Agriculture, *Agricultural Statistics*, 1972.
[1]State detail is available in *Agricultural Statistics*, 1968.
[2]Total diverted, including acreage devoted to substitute crops.
[3]Not required to be put to conserving uses.
[4]Less than 50,000 acres.
[5]Based on 1972 intended enrollment.

rapid in many countries where no acreage restrictions have been in effect. It is probable that much of the change in U.S. technology and resource use that occurred with supply control would have taken place in any event. If this is true, acreage controls have been effective in reducing production.

Another issue concerns whether or not price programs can influence supply. If a positive and reversible supply elasticity exists for most commodities, and if farmers are not forced into a "treadmill phenomenon" by changes in price,[4] there are a number of additional programs that might have some effect on dampening output expansion. These include the standard quantity system used in the United Kingdom; the class price system for milk used in the United Kingdom and the United States; a Canadian system whereby support for pigs, milk, and eggs is limited to specified quantities for each producer; and programs which differentiate between the price paid for fruits and vegetables for fresh consumption and processing. In total, however, these kinds of restraints on output expansion have been limited in most countries, and the dominant focus, except for supply control programs in the United States, has been to extend price support on an unlimited quantity with little effort to control production.

Export Subsidy and Disposal Programs

A wide range of indirect actions can be taken to ease the way for exporting price support commodities on world markets. These include tax concessions, transportation subsidies, and the use of support programs which differentiate price between domestic use and export. Market discrimination programs are based on the assumption that demand elasticities are different in domestic and international markets and that farmers benefit from a greater return if prices are maintained high in the more inelastic domestic market and reduced in the more elastic foreign market. The primary purpose of this kind of market discrimination is to expand exports yet maintain a level of protection for agriculture.

Two major direct export subsidy programs have affected world markets: those operated by the United States and those used by the EEC. Subsidies are flexible and tailored to the levels needed for consummation of sales. Prior to the 1960 change in U.S. programs, most major export commodities received substantial per unit subsidies. The general level of subsidies has declined, but even after the shift in programs, important payments remained.[5]

EEC subsidies are paid under an export restitution system which is an integral part of the price support mechanism. For any commodity, subsidies are available for export equal to the difference between domestic support levels and world prices and are equal to the import levies set for the commodity.

The effect of these direct subsidy programs on world markets is profound. In theory, subsidies are used to cover the difference between domestic support and world market prices. However, when substantial amounts of a commodity are placed on world markets at a subsidized level, the domestic support price less the subsidy tends to determine world market price, not vice versa. In a sense, world market prices become administered prices, with the level determined by or at least strongly influenced by price support and export subsidy programs in major countries.

Export subsidies have an important effect on the creation of income transfers among nations, depending upon whether such countries are buyers or sellers. Buyers receive a cheaper product; sellers receive a lower price and, in some cases, are faced with greatly restricted markets. The international effect of domestic support programs is thus a twofold problem. First, imports are restricted and markets tend to be reduced in supporting countries; second, where surpluses arise, exports are subsidized and create a major price and quantity effect on world markets.

Food Aid

The second major dimension of agricultural export programs has been food aid, primarily in the United States. This system originated in 1945 when Commodity Credit Corporation exports of surplus agricultural commodities were made exempt from the rule limiting sales to parity prices or above. Early post–World War II disposal programs were imbedded in a series of interim measures, special grants, and credits designed to help lower income countries overcome food shortages. The most important of these was an emergency aid act to India in 1951, which provided a $190 million loan for the purchase of U.S. food grains. Major food exports also were provided under the 1948 Marshall Plan. The initiation of continuing programs of export surplus disposal began in 1953 under the Mutual Security Act. Provisions were made for the sale of surplus commodities to friendly governments for local currencies. In 1954 the more comprehensive Agricultural Trade Development and Assistance Act (P.L. 480) was passed. Since that time, P.L. 480 has been the foundation of massive food exports by the United States. The initial objectives of this act were surplus disposal and humanitarian assistance. More recently, greater emphasis has been placed on the use of government-programmed exports for economic development. Over time, food has represented a substantial portion of total U.S. foreign aid and resulted in total shipments through 1970 of approximately $21 billion in commodities for all programs.[6]

P.L. 480 exports are made in a number of ways. Through 1970, sales for local currency represented the largest portion. The United States also donates food for emergency and disaster relief under this program and until 1969 traded on a barter basis for strategic commodities. P.L. 480 local currency sales are being replaced by sales on long-term credit, which means that recipient countries must repay in dollars. The terms are very liberal; no interest or principal payments are required for the first two years, and long-term repayment is at very low interest rates. Despite liberal terms, the change from local currency to long-term credit sales means that the aid component in the P.L. 480 program has been reduced, and P.L. 480 shipments will begin to cost foreign exchange in recipient countries.

This particular program reached a peak of $1.6 billion in 1965 and since has declined to approximately $1 billion in 1971. Shipments have been made to over 50 countries in virtually all parts of the world, concentrating in Asia, particularly India and Pakistan. Part of the decline can be attributed to improved production and the Green Revolution in these areas.

Although P.L. 480 has served economic and welfare objectives, the program has been subject to considerable criticism and evaluation. Its effects can be viewed from three perspectives: implications for (1) U.S. agriculture, (2) other export countries, and (3) recipient countries.

Other exporting nations have been critical of P.L. 480, asserting it has infringed on their markets and effectively lowered prices for certain commodities. Probably with some justification, much criticism was aimed at the barter program; it permitted the exchange of specific commodities for food and removed recipients from the international hard currency market for food imports to the extent that their requirements were met through commodity bartering.

The most complex issue is the effect P.L. 480 has on recipients. Evidence suggests that P.L. 480 imports increase the total assets available to a nation and, thereby, foster increased savings and investment.[7] These assets are acquired without any expenditure of foreign exchange, and net capital formation can be increased. P.L. 480 commodities also can be used as wages to enhance a country's ability to employ labor on development projects. Very important is the fact that increased consumption levels can be achieved, and, in the case of disaster relief, a humanitarian end can be served.

These positive effects, however, have not been adequately weighed against the negative ones in order to arrive at a generalized idea of the net results of the program. Food aid may depress agricultural prices and lower incentives to increase production. More important, flexibility to postpone hard policy decisions and implementation of programs needed for domestic agricultural development may result. P.L. 480 shipments also may distort economic development, creating the need for massive investment in docking, handling facilities, and the infrastructure required for food imports. P.L. 480 shipments tend to be available in large port cities, and facilities for redistribution to internal areas are inadequate. As wages for labor they complement capital expenditures in port cities, and investments in these areas may receive a higher priority than desirable in a balanced development program. Because food shipments are obtained through ports, the infrastructure required for commercialization of agriculture, the movement of food from internal areas to cities, and the market mechanism needed to develop domestic agriculture may be neglected.

Finally, a question arises as to the rationality of the food aid program from the viewpoint of U.S. agriculture. Clearly it has provided a basis for disposal of a substantial amount of farm products. In this sense, it reduced the need for supply control programs and changed the emphasis between demand expansion and supply control as vehicles for overcoming the imbalance created by agricultural protection.

Beyond questions of economic cost and domestic program balance, P.L. 480 has complemented commercial export programs and has furthered U.S. political interests. It has increased rates of economic development in some countries that subsequently have become important commercial markets for U.S. agricultural products. Outstanding examples are Japan, Taiwan, and, at an earlier date, Western European countries. A secondary commercial impact thus may stem from P.L. 480 and other forms of aid. Political interests also have been enhanced in that P.L. 480 shipments have represented an initial interaction with some socialist countries which, over time, have become more closely oriented toward Western commercial interests.

Negotiations and Multilateral Action

Recent efforts toward liberalization of agricultural trade have been by-products of the general U.S. program of trade liberalization under the Reciprocal Trade Agreements Act and the Trade Expansion Act of 1962. Some efforts were made to negotiate a reduction in trade barriers prior to World War II, but these achieved only limited success. For numerous reasons, actual agreements were concluded only on a limited basis between the United States and the United Kingdom and Canada. First, three major countries, Germany, Italy, and Japan, were under dictatorial government and were not amenable to trade negotiation on any basis. Second, all negotiations were bilateral and undertaken on a commodity-by-commodity basis and therefore could not move rapidly. Third, the climate of international relationships within the worldwide depression of the 1930s and the building political tensions were not conducive to widespread commercial negotiations. The second era of negotiations got underway in about 1945 when Congress extended the Trade Agreements Act and provided authority for a 50 percent reduction in tariffs based on 1945 levels.

Formation and Early Role of GATT

Recognizing the limitations inherent in bilateral negotiations, in 1945 the United States initiated the creation of a multilateral international organization that would establish rules of procedure for handling international commercial policy and provide a forum for negotiations. A conference was convened in Havana, Cuba, and major trading countries agreed to set up the International Trade Organization (ITO). The ITO, however, was never established because the U.S. Congress failed to ratify the charter. Congressional approval was required prior to U.S. membership in an international organization, but it was not required for procedural agreements. As a result, the United States and other major trading nations entered into the General Agreement on Tariffs and Trade in 1947. Since then GATT has become a pseudo-international organization, although it has no legal standing and the secretariat continues to operate without formal recognition of its existence.

The General Agreement on Tariffs and Trade incorporated most of the major principles included in the charter of the International Trade Organization and has represented the framework within which all trade negotiations have taken place since 1947. The most important of these principles are noted below.[8]

(1) Reduction in trade barriers should be on a nondiscriminatory basis (that is, there should be no most favored nation), and any agreement to reduce tariff barriers would apply to all interested trading nations.

(2) The only acceptable means of protecting industry should be through tariffs, and negotiations should occur among contracting parties to reduce the level of tariff protection.

(3) No indirect subsidies, including income or price supports, should be undertaken that will prejudice international trade relationships.

(4) Consultations should be held between countries to avoid injury through unilateral action by individual countries.

(5) If unilateral action is undertaken that creates injury to another country, compensation should be paid to cover the damages.

An aspect of the general agreement that is more important than any of the individual rules is the underlying philosophy. GATT is built around the concept that the free market works and that the objective of international commercial policy should be to reduce trade barriers. Organized or arranged international marketing policies (such as commodity agreements) are justified only to overcome special difficulties.

A number of exceptions were included in the original agreement, and flexibility was retained to add others,[9] thus improving the acceptability of the general principles. An important early exception permitted various kinds of import restrictions for balance-of-payments reasons; another partially abolished the most-favored-nation idea. While this principle was retained in the sense that specific bilateral arrangements were not condoned, preexisting arrangements such as British Commonwealth preferences were permitted, and in the late 1950s exceptions were provided for the establishment of customs unions to allow formation of the European Common Market. This principle also was later extended to provide exceptions for free trade areas.

The most troublesome exceptions, however, were those developed specifically for agriculture. These cover both import restrictions and export programs. Early in the operation of GATT, exceptions on import restrictions were provided for countries that wanted to establish border protection with a view toward stimulating output to relieve food shortages. These soon were supplemented by restrictions to maintain grades and standards on products, as well as special exceptions for restrictions on animal products to regulate disease control. Exceptions granted to countries to implement domestic marketing and price support programs represented a major breakdown in GATT principles. This development was followed by GATT recognition of the need for export subsidies where domestic prices were maintained above world market levels and, in turn, resulted in surplus production. This latter exception was accompanied by special antidumping procedures to redress injury by nations excessively subsidizing exports to the detriment of other countries.

This formidable list of exceptions was not compiled all at once, but in one respect or another, virtually all important Western trading nations were involved. Initial exceptions to overcome food shortages were stimulated by conditions in Western Europe during the postwar period, but it probably is correct to say that the real breakdown in GATT's effectiveness in agriculture was due to U.S. actions in the early 1950s. In 1951 the United States stipulated that the Section 22 import restrictions be extended to make it mandatory for the President of the

United States to impose a quota or fees to restrict imports on price support commodities, irrespective of preexisting international agreements. In that year the United States also insisted that an escape clause be inserted into the general agreement, and if injury was proven to domestic interest as a result of actions taken in GATT, U.S. GATT obligations automatically would be suspended. Furthermore, in 1951 the United States passed specific legislation requiring quotas or even embargoes on certain dairy products.

Despite the numerous exceptions related to agriculture, it cannot be concluded that the role of GATT has been entirely ineffective insofar as agriculture is concerned. During the 1947–1962 period, major concern developed with problems in international trade in agricultural products, and two efforts resulted.[10] The first was an attempt to arrive at a special agreement on commodity arrangements which would serve as a guideline for world trading arrangements. A draft version of this special agreement included 21 separate articles and was a relatively comprehensive attempt to define and evaluate past experience with commodity arrangements in agriculture and establish new procedures for normalizing agricultural commodity trade. Article I stated that problems of production, consumption, and trade in primary markets could not be left to ordinary market forces. It stated that, through joint action, countries would try where possible to: (1) achieve a reasonable degree of stability on the basis of prices that are fair to consumers and provide a reasonable return to producers; (2) prevent shortages in world supplies or burdensome accumulation of stocks; (3) accomplish the equitable distribution of a commodity in short supply; (4) alleviate economic hardships in cases where a commodity has been produced in excess of long-term demand; (5) expand consumption and production with advantage to consumers and producers; and (6) direct production to places where world market requirements can be satisfied in the most effective and economic manner.

The formulation and discussion of this agreement was boycotted by the United States. This action, along with the general reluctance on the part of exporting countries to forego the notion of equal treatment for agricultural and industrial products envisaged in GATT, led to the breakdown of the attempt, and no formal resolution of the agreement was developed.

The second major agricultural effort during this period was essentially intellectual in that it involved a major study published in October 1958 by a panel of experts.[11] This important document attempted to analyze the cause of agricultural trade problems and make policy recommendations. Its final impact, of course, is difficult to assess. It did call to the attention of the international community the essential nature of the conflict between domestic agricultural and international trade policies. It also analyzed preexisting commodity agreements and developed rather specific evaluations of their role and potential in international agricultural markets.

GATT in the 1960s

An important influence changing the character of international negotiations during the 1960s was the formation of the European Economic Community. Formation of a customs union, by definition, changes international relationships through the elimination of trade barriers among member countries and by establishing a common external policy. Because of the major importance of the industrial and agricultural trading relationships among European Common Market countries, outside nations wanted a liberal common external policy, not one that was inward and protectionist. Under U.S. leadership, efforts were made to assure this outcome through negotiations in GATT. These attempts occurred initially in the Dillon Round of negotiations in 1961 and 1962 and were continued in the Kennedy Round from 1963 to mid-1967. Both rounds were promulgated by the United States, primarily with a view toward confrontation with the EEC, but also with a view toward general improvement in trading relationships in world markets. Following the Dillon Round experience, which indicated the ineffectiveness of item-by-item negotiation, the United States approached the Kennedy Round with the proposal that across-the-board cuts of 50 percent be instituted for all commodities and that negotiations be on exceptions rather than on tariff cuts as such. Furthermore, it was hoped that broad classes of commodities could be dealt with in total rather than item by item.

The Kennedy Round actually became two sets of negotiations: one for industrial products and one for agriculture. The industrial negotiators accepted the rule of a 50 percent across-the-board cut and proceeded from there to discuss exceptions. Two major issues were raised, both by the EEC: tariff disparities and U.S. customs procedures. In the former case, the EEC argued that because it recently had been through the process of equalizing its own tariff levels, the commodity-by-commodity dispersion around its average tariff level was much narrower than in the United States. The United States, on the other hand, was negotiating with tariffs that ranged from very low to very high, and its argument was that negotiating a 50 percent reduction on this basis would represent a smaller total reduction in tariffs than would negotiating a 50 percent reduction where the dispersion of individual commodities around that average was very small. The customs procedure question centered around the American selling price (ASP), where tariff rates applied to domestic prices rather than prices at which exporters were willing to sell. These two issues were resolved, and the final outcome on industrial negotiations was to achieve an approximately 35 percent across-the-board reduction in tariff, by any measure a highly successful result. The industrial countries were left with the most favorable tariff position on industrial products in recent history.

The negotiations on agriculture were completely different. Conflict was imminent from the outset, and although the negotiations continued for almost four years, the results were only nominal. Exporters entered the discussion hoping to achieve a reduction in EEC support levels for agricultural products and to achieve some form of guaranteed access arrangement into EEC and other importer markets. This desire was, in part, an outgrowth of the British grains agreement, wherein exporters felt that a negotiated access had been achieved.

While discussions in agriculture involved a broad range of commodities, the main focus of attention throughout was on grain. Grain exporters sought to bring the question of domestic agricultural policies into the negotiations and initially established three objectives. These have been stated as follows by one of the participants:[12]

> First the trade objective of obtaining acceptable conditions of access to world markets. Exporters set as their goal as acceptable conditions of access the opportunity to supply their present share of importers markets. . . . In practice the negotiations on access were directed primarily at the markets in the United Kingdom and the European Economic Community. Japan, the other major commercial grain market, has little potential for increasing domestic production and consumption is expanding rapidly. Conditions of access to the Japanese market were, therefore, generally regarded as satisfactory. Since World War II the United States and other grain exporters have seen their markets in the United Kingdom shrink as domestic grain production in the United Kingdom expanded under the stimulus of high returns the U.K. government guaranteed its farmers. With regard to the EEC, exporters were confronted with the prospect that the EEC common grain regulation would reduce access to the market — an apprehension which was aggravated by failure to negotiate concessions on grains in the Dillon Round to a place those previously held.

Second, an increase in the minimum floor price for wheat over those prevailing under the international wheat agreement. There was broad agreement also that the minimum floor price must be more specifically defined than under the present IWA. Under the IWA only the minimum price of Manitoba No. 1 wheat is specified. Exporters generally agreed that in a new arrangement minimum prices must be defined for all exporters in sufficient detail to indicate when the floor is reached.

Third, an equitable sharing among major grain producers of the task of adjusting supplies to available outlets including both commercial demand and food aid . . . . Price stabilization and higher prices, the United States argued, could only be achieved within the framework of an arrangement that assured acceptable conditions of access to importers markets and effective supply-management practices on the part of all exporters. This view met with sympathetic response from other exporters. The exporters, meeting in Washington in 1963, agreed that ways and means of controlling uneconomic production should be explored, and depending upon other elements in the overall arrangement, it might be necessary for all concerned to adopt appropriate supply-management measures.

This initial position by exporting countries was developed early in the Kennedy Round, but real negotiations had to await a response by the EEC and the United Kingdom. The latter, in general, can be characterized as unresponsive in the sense that it presented no real negotiating plan of its own but took a very tough position insofar as access arrangements were concerned. The EEC responded with its proposal for maintaining existing price support levels, including those recently established in the common agricultural policy in its proposal for "montant de soutien."

Evolution in the discussion on grains was slow and laborious. Its final outcome focused on an International Grains Agreement which was finally reduced to a modest one applying only to wheat. No agreement was reached on measures for supply control or on access arrangements. The principal stumbling block on the latter was the difference between the access sought by exporters and the access importing countries were willing to grant. In the case of the EEC, for example, exporters wanted a guarantee of approximately 14 percent of the market, whereas the EEC would not agree to more than approximately 5 percent. Other importing countries, particularly the United Kingdom, were no more generous.

When negotiations ended in 1967, the international grains arrangement was viewed as an important accomplishment in multicountry cooperation. International trading prices for wheat were specified by classes, and trading prices were raised substantially from those prevailing under the existing international wheat agreement. The management of surplus stocks received at least symbolic attention since the agreement included a provision for food aid of 4.5 million metric tons annually to be contributed by advanced countries. Deficit as well as surplus countries were included as donors. Although the agreement did not increase total food aid significantly because of the relatively small amount provided, it had the effect of shifting part of the burden of food aid from exporting to importing countries.[13]

Success in reducing the tariff levels on agricultural products was nominal. Figures compiled by the U.S. Department of Agriculture indicate that the United States received tariff commitments on a total of approximately $850 million of exports (based on 1964–1965 trade) and granted tariff concessions on a total of approximately $856 million of imports, of which $612 million were competitive imports.[14] By commodity, it appears that the most important concessions were received on livestock products and on fruits and vegetables.

The overall results of the negotiations, however, are difficult to assess. The figures on concessions include not only some very nominal tariff reductions, but also agreements to bind tariffs at preexisting levels. While some progress occurred, the principal objectives sought by exporters were not achieved. No progress was made in changing the basic price structure or support system of the European Economic Community. On the other hand, a major shortcoming of negotiations from the viewpoint of the EEC was that no legal recognition was obtained in GATT for the variable levy system, nor did the EEC achieve its goal of fixing preexisting support levels for agriculture in importing and exporting countries.

Problems and Conditions for the Future

The dominant fact about postwar agricultural negotiations in GATT is that those countries which have sought exceptions for agriculture from the general rules of GATT have, for the most part, been successful. However, in the Kennedy Round, where reduced trade restrictions on agricultural products were sought, success was only nominal. With the exception of tariff negotiations in the Kennedy Round, GATT activities in agriculture largely have been restricted to defining the problem and specifying and discussing various kinds of international market organization which would stabilize trading relationships in the light of the accepted commitment of governments to protect their domestic agriculture. Early discussions on agriculture were aimed at this purpose, and major efforts were made in the Kennedy Round to establish a framework for market organization for dairy products, meat, and grain. The problem that has not been overcome in any of these discussions is the unwillingness of governments to come to grips with the interrelationship between domestic protection programs and international policy. Possibly even more fundamentally, they have not grappled with the question of the economic differences in agriculture among major trading countries. Both these factors must be taken into account to achieve real success in harmonizing trading relationships among nations.

Direct market conflict can be overcome if methods of income support which do not interfere with prices as such are used. But, while income payments eliminate price differentials in the market, they do not necessarily eliminate or deal with the effects of protection on supply. Furthermore, many governments use extensive programs of input subsidy and subsidies for expanding production capacities as support measures for their agriculture. The direct supply effect of these programs can vary greatly depending upon the nature of the subsidy and its purpose. All forms of protection increase returns to agriculture and will have an effect on supply. The impact cannot be measured simply through the nominal price effect on commodities.

Conflict in international policy is related to differentials in the cost structure of agriculture and the relative need for protectionism in individual countries. The ultimate focus of international trade policy must go beyond the question of short-term supply and interference with market prices. At issue is what can be done to restructure agriculture so that a degree of specialization occurs among countries relative to available resources. Until recently, active restructuring programs have been nominal, although several efforts by governments are underway. The most important of these is the structural reorganization program of the EEC. Although its goals have changed since initially articulated, what is important is that sole emphasis no longer is being placed on price supports as a solution to the income problems of agriculture. The program calls for actions to (1) reduce the number of farmers through incentives for retirement, (2) expand the resource base for those who continue to farm, and (3) increase the productivity of resources remaining in agriculture.

Programs of this kind are expensive and can proceed only at a pace that is economically, socially, and politically feasible. The solution to problems of international conflict in agricultural markets cannot be accomplished quickly. Broadly based negotiations are required. Not only price support policies, but also the extent and direction of structural adjustments in agriculture, particularly in high cost countries, must be recognized in developing trade policies. As indicated in chapter 2, structural differences among countries are an important element in determining not only the nature of production, but also cost levels. The major need is for a basic restructuring of agriculture in high cost, import countries so that flexibility is achieved to adjust commodity outputs and so that cost levels can be reduced to a point below which severe protection is required.

Summary

It is apparent that future success in relieving the international conflict in agricultural markets requires that the scope of negotiation change considerably. As yet, no country has been willing to accept an indiscriminate reduction in tariffs that could have a major disrupting effect on its agricultural industry.

As long as various forms of domestic support and government intervention influence output and market access, trading prices will depend more on the willingness of governments to protect producers than on production costs and demand conditions. Given that varying degrees of domestic protection will continue, efforts should be made to move toward sound and interrelated policies that encourage an appropriate overall level of output and movement of production to low cost areas. The ultimate course is one that attempts to deal simultaneously with trade and domestic policy. This, of course, is not simply a matter of arriving at pricing and output agreements among exporting nations. The broad goal to be sought is some arrangement that places responsibility on importing as well as exporting countries. This will require a much broadened format of international discussion to deal with issues of price support level, import protection, export subsidization, the orientation of domestic farm policy, and agreement by individual countries to cooperate in programs of supply adjustments and structural reorganization.

The aspirations of exporters will have to be defined in terms of political reality and the potential for change in importing countries.

Furthermore, importing countries must realize that support for high cost agriculture is expensive in economic terms and that, in the long run, satisfactory incomes in agriculture can be achieved only through basic structural reorganization. In this context it must be recognized that change can come about only relatively slowly. Lower tariff barriers benefit importing countries if accompanied by changes that reduce the cost of agricultural production and result in a more rational balance between employment of resources in agriculture and in other pursuits.

The post–World War II need for agricultural adjustment has focused on problems of surpluses, production cost differentials, and conflict in trading relations. These problems recently have been partially overshadowed by shortfalls in food production, reduced levels of food reserves, and higher commodity prices. This new dimension clearly emphasizes, rather than diminishes, the need to restructure agriculture to achieve both flexibility and the capacity for agriculture in industrial countries to reduce wide fluctuations in world food supplies and prices and permit growth commensurate with market demand and humanitarian needs. These conditions add to, but do not displace, the problem of achieving adjustment among industrial countries to improve resource allocation and reduce policy conflict.

7

Trade Problems and Issues:
Less Developed Countries

In previous chapters the principal focus has been on trade problems and policies in the advanced free world. In these countries two issues loom largest in creating policy conflict: the reduction of trade restrictions to achieve greater international economic efficiency and the role that these restrictions play in support of domestic programs aimed at shifting income toward farmers. Major price differentials among countries are associated with varying levels of farm costs due to differences in technology, farm structure, and relative resource deployment in agriculture and other pursuits. While policy conflict is centered on domestic income protection for farmers, other factors such as national security, balance of payments, and rural fundamentalism complicate the search for solutions. Because shifts in resource use and structural change require time, market imbalances must be corrected gradually. Trade policy should be aimed at seeking improved adjustment to comparative advantage and lower cost agricultural production. Determining the rate and the cost relative to costs of perpetuating existing imbalances remains an important consideration.

Trade and Development: Issues and Arguments

In the case of less developed nations, trade problems and policies are somewhat less clear and are considerably different from those facing advanced countries. The largest economic issue concerned with questions of trade and resource use is their relationship to economic growth and development. *Economic development* is the process of moving from low income and traditional methods of economic activity to higher levels of income. Various kinds of economic transformation are involved, including the accumulation of capital, improvement of human skills, and diversification and expansion of output to achieve improved economic well-being. There is another and more subtle element: the achievement of institutional changes that will provide the basis for continued growth and development. Economic development must include innovations that provide a foundation for perpetuating improvement and expansion of industry and agriculture, specialization and division of labor, the use of technology and innovation, improvement in skills of the labor force, incentives for improved entrepreneurship, and the mechanisms required to upgrade resource use and create economic expansion.

While the process of economic development is primarily a matter of internal transformation and change, no country advances rapidly without integrating its economy into a regional and world framework of commodity trade and resource transfers, including both capital and technology. Gain can occur in a number of ways. Contact with the outside world through trade can provide the commodities and resources needed for consumption and development. More important, as some authors argue, such contact will provide a competitive stimulus for improving the institutions needed to sustain dynamic change and, in the case of economically small countries, expand the market and permit specialization to achieve scale economies in production.

Despite general agreement on the overall importance of trade in development, neither the precise role it plays under modern conditions nor the policies needed to optimize its contribution are easy to define. The major issues at stake in assessing trade problems of less developed countries concern the economic and policy conditions in world markets and within the countries themselves that reduce the rate of trade expansion or inhibit achieving the desired effect on economic development where trade does occur. In examining these issues, we need to study the logic developed by economists, as well as the historical perspective that sheds light on the role trade may have in economic growth.

Trade as a Leading, Balancing, or Lagging Sector

Viewed empirically, three classifications for the relation between trade and growth have been proposed: export-led growth, trade as a balancing sector, and trade as a lagging sector. Each of these models can be cited historically as applying to different economies at different periods of time.

Export-led growth implies a general increase in commercialization and expansion of output where the export sector is the leading one. Growth will occur in the first instance because of expanded production in the export sector, but by implication the process will not stop there. Expansion in exports will create secondary effects arising from increased income through the employment generated to produce exports. This, in turn, will create new demands within the exporting country that can result in expanded opportunities for resource employment in domestic industries and can lead ultimately to pressures for technological advance, improvement in infrastructure, and increased investment opportunities. General economic growth is stimulated as a result of initial expansion in the export sector.

Export-led growth appears to have had considerable relevance during the nineteenth century.[1] Following the Industrial Revolution, the United Kingdom became the major industrial power of the world and required major imports of raw materials. The development of sources of supply on the periphery was stimulated, aided by British investment capital, technical assistance, and the development of communications, trading methods, and institutions. The less advanced areas, in turn, provided a market for British manufactured products, and a complementary interaction occurred which provided export-led growth for British industrialism and raw material production in outlying areas.

The concept of trade as a balancing sector also can be verified intuitively. The reasoning is that as economic growth progresses, output expansion is not maintained in line with consumption and resource needs; imports or exports are required to fill the gap. An internal imbalance can arise between production and demand for final products, intermediate products, or raw materials. Increases in income create the basis for a broad expansion of consumption, and consumption imports in lagging sectors may be required. Input imports also may be required for the expanding sector. The basis for acquiring imports is to sell part of the product of the expanding sector in foreign markets and use the proceeds to import the goods needed to correct internal imbalances. Trade in this case is assigned a balancing role in the process of development. It is neither a positive force in stimulating growth nor a negative force inhibiting it; rather, it results from growth determined by other forces.

Trade results from development, not vice versa. Viewed ex post facto, trade is always the balancing sector, and no specific verification is needed to accept this concept. Viewed in the light of the classical model, this process of correcting imbalances moves toward conformity with comparative advantage. Individual countries fill the gap between their requirements and production by importing commodities for which they have a disadvantage and exporting commodities where a comparative advantage exists. But unless extended beyond the concept that trade simply fills a gap between production and consumption, this form of trade plays a neutral role in development.

Trade is a lagging sector when it becomes an inhibiting factor in economic growth. This occurs when emphasis is placed on generating internally balanced production in line with established goals. Trade becomes a lagging sector when countries place undue emphasis on development of import substitution industries. Conceptually, this situation exists whenever domestic industry requires protection to maintain itself and grow in the face of external competition, except where the infant industry argument is clearly applicable.

Individual countries can carry a policy of import protection to the extreme and develop high cost industries (sometimes for prestige purposes) that inhibit economic development. On the other hand, there are limitations on the amounts developing countries can import because of their low potential for export. This potential, in turn, may be limited for a number of reasons. External markets may stagnate because demand grows slowly or because substitutes are found for the type of product available for export. A worldwide pattern of import substitution policies may arise through individual country actions, and thus no markets exist. Finally, high populations within developing countries may leave little available for export even if a competitive advantage exists. This has happened in certain heavily populated, traditionally food exporting countries such as India and China.

Descriptions of the role trade plays as a leading, balancing, or lagging sector are useful as a starting point in raising questions about trade and development policy issues. Description, however, is inadequate for specifying cause and effect relationships, or for arriving at policy prescriptions. To do this we need to look at some of the conceptual frameworks that have been applied to analysis of the role trade plays in development.

Free Trade and Development

The guidance that economic theory provides for trade sector

analysis is both limited and controversial. As indicated in chapter 3, comparative advantage is determined by numerous variables. These include the land, labor, and capital base; the technology and skill available to producers; the organization and scale of agriculture and industry; the adequacy of infrastructure and facilities for coordination in the economy; and prices that apply to inputs.

The traditional theory of comparative advantage provides relevant guidelines for assessing trade position, but leaves important issues unresolved. It says nothing about the dynamic questions concerning interaction and change that may arise from commerce between nations. This is different from the statements on trade by Adam Smith, who essentially dwelt on what Hla Myint has termed the productivity doctrine.

> The productivity doctrine differs from the comparative-costs doctrine in the interpretation of specialization for international trade. In the comparative cost theory specialization merely means a movement along a static production possibilities curve constructed on the given resources and the given techniques of the trading country. In contrast, the productivity doctrine looks upon international trade as a dynamic force which by widening the extent of the market and the scope of the division of labor raises the skills and dexterity of the workmen, encourages technical innovation, overcomes technical indivisibilities, and generally enables the trading country to enjoy increasing returns and economic development.[2]

This statement suggests the basic issue to be considered when assessing the role trade policy plays in economic development. A question posed by Gerald Meier asks: If a country specializes or attempts to specialize according to comparative advantage, does this also lead to economic growth; or, alternately, is there a conflict between this kind of single period efficiency and some multiple period efficiency or expansion?[3]

In general, the comparative cost doctrine assumes that adjustment in production is a completely reversible process in response to demand and price changes. The dynamic productivity analysis involves restructuring a country's economy and economic process so that it is not reversible, but is a continuing process of growth. The elements of this growth process have been set forth as follows:[4]

1) Trade leads to increased division of labor and raises the skills of workmen, encourages technical innovation, creates economies of scale, overcomes technical indivisibilities, and generally encourages improved productivity.

2) International trade has a demonstration effect on consumption and serves to stimulate industrialization and growth.

3) Trade permits and encourages the introduction of foreign know-how and capital.

4) Trade can affect domestic factor supply through wider markets and the stimulation of increased savings.

5) Trade, by virtue of the contact among individuals from different countries, has a general educative effect, and this leads to economic development.

The mechanics of trade and economic growth have been built into essentially two kinds of theoretical structures. One is the vent-for-surplus argument which assumes that, given the opportunities, trade will lead to further development of unemployed resources — labor and capital — and to expansion of markets. Another builds on the classical productivity doctrine and recently has been described in terms of the cumulative circle of causation.

Vent-for-Surplus

The vent-for-surplus doctrine is based upon two assumptions: A vent (market) is available and open for the exports of developing countries, and unused capacity exists to produce an export surplus. As a policy guide this theory would argue that less developed countries should export commodities produced with surplus resources where world demand exists. Where surplus resources are available, exports can be expanded without reducing output for domestic use; hence, economic expansion occurs.

This theory differs fundamentally from the comparative cost doctrine, wherein the assumption of full employment requires that export expansion can be achieved only at the cost of reducing output of domestic goods. The net gain from trade is determined by the difference in the resource cost of imports that can be obtained with the resources diverted from domestic to export production. On the other hand, if surplus resources are used for export production, the domestic opportunity cost of acquiring imports is very low or, in the extreme case, zero.

The most important question to be answered is under what circumstances developing countries will have surplus productive capacity. Traditional analysis relates this issue to conditions that existed in many parts of the world during the early nineteenth century and phrases the question in terms of why an isolated economy opened up to international trade should have excess productive capacity. Myint concludes: "The answer which suggests itself is that given its random combination of natural resources, techniques of production, tastes and population, such an isolated economy is bound to suffer from a certain imbalance or disproportion between its productive and consumption capacities."[5]

The implication is that effective commodity and resource markets do not exist. In addition, the developing countries of the nineteenth century were not heavily populated and in some cases had vast, unoccupied land areas. This was true of North and South America, Russia, and to a lesser extent certain other areas. Vast untapped natural resources for agricultural and raw materials production were available and provided a base for expanded output. This resource base and available labor were supplemented with substantial capital investment in the form of transportation, communication, marketing, and production facilities.[6] To expand output, labor and natural resources were recombined and supplemented with capital and technology from external sources.

Viewed in a historical perspective, the source of surplus productive capacity does not appear to be a great mystery. But do conditions exist for similar developments today? A number of sparsely populated and resource rich developing countries can be cited. In Brazil, the Congo, and Nigeria additional output could be achieved with the application of appropriate capital and technology to the existing resource base and labor supply. The issue at stake is much less whether a vent-for-surplus theory can be defined than whether, in some general way, a process can be defined whereby the interaction between developed and developing countries results in trade as a positive force in economic development. The basic argument among policy makers is to what extent this process can be left to market forces and to what extent interference and direct policy manipulation are required.

Cumulative Circle of Causation

The argument for free trade is strong among economists. The question of trade and growth recently has been stated most forcefully by Harry Johnson in what he terms the cumulative circle of causation that generates economic pressures for peripheral development.[7] Of special importance in this argument is the growing pressure of demand for natural resources in advanced economies. The result is rising prices and a search for cheaper sources of supply on the periphery, which in turn results in an outflow of capital and technology to develop them. The periphery becomes linked to the industrialized countries and also creates specialization among countries. Incomes in the periphery rise, creating a demand for industrial development on the periphery, which results in a natural transfer of income through the market. The second aspect of the cumulative circle of causation as an automatic diffusion process relates to the international immobility of labor. Technology and progress cause rising wage rates at the center, which makes it increasingly profitable to establish production facilities on the periphery. In particular, there is pressure to develop labor-intensive industries in peripheral countries; hence, a resulting push toward factor price equalization occurs.

Johnson argues that, given normal market processes, there will be natural pressures through demand, wage rates, and prices to allocate resources efficiently and encourage economic development. He asserts this system worked well in the nineteenth century; if it does not work now, the reason should be sought within individual countries, not in international markets or the price mechanism. The effect may be offset by such things as a too rapid population growth, which prevents growth in income per capita. In some countries capital-intensive industries may dominate, and additional employment for export may be too small to provide growth in income. Furthermore, traditional societies might not provide an appropriate form of training and the conditions necessary to take advantage of opportunities. Finally, there may be resistance to becoming economically interlocked and dependent upon advanced countries when business cycles in those nations have a direct impact on the economy of a developing country. Thus, there is a political reason for pursuing planning and balanced growth rather than relying on the free market and the development of comparative advantage.

Is There a Conflict between Trade and Growth?

The traditional arguments for free trade and the role of trade in economic growth are countered by other arguments that maintain there is a conflict between free trade and growth. Economists in this camp use both a theoretical approach and empirical arguments. Theoretically, they state that trade theory in its static cross-sectional sense provides no basis for asserting a diffusion or growth process. Given its *ceteris paribus* conditions, one cannot infer a dynamic growth effect from adjustment to comparative advantage. Furthermore, they take into account the question of differences in asset distribution and assert that, with any given starting point of unequal incomes, greater factor price spreads and a disadvantage to developing countries will result from uncontrolled international trade and factor movement.[8]

Empirically, they argue that for a number of reasons market forces tend toward a cumulative process of greater inequality. First, development is retarded by the unfavorable effects of international factor movements. The inflow of foreign capital to developed export sectors leads to a tendency to neglect domestic sectors. The result is capital-intensive export sectors which provide a minimum level of employment; hence, economic enclaves or technological dualism arises, creating an advanced export sector and a traditional domestic sector. There is little impact on overall economic development. To support this argument many countries cite agricultural plantations and large-scale, highly mechanized extractive industries isolated from the basic economy. These industries also drain capital from the countries through removed earnings. At the same time, capital items associated with the investment have all been imported, so the amount of generated income left in the country is very small.

The full implication of this effect can be seen only if one looks at its structural impact on the developing economy. A growing society changes from a largely rural to an increasingly urbanized population. Urbanization is based on the development of secondary and tertiary urban industries. Urban centers represent the dynamic poles of technological, educational, and cultural advance. In balanced economic development this process is accompanied by commensurate technological change in agriculture and mining and the building of an infrastructure to provide an information and market linkage between economic activity at the primary, secondary, and tertiary levels. Commodities and factors flow between sectors, including labor migration and the distribution of capital and technology.

Where capital and technology are injected from external sources into agricultural plantations and the extraction of minerals, commodities flow primarily to foreign countries and complement urban development there. Technology flows only to specific kinds of primary production in the producing country, and if capital-intensive production and improved technology follow, it is isolated within these specialized subsectors. The employment and development effects are limited. Only specialized infrastructure required for export is built, which may do little to further general economic development. In this circumstance, complementarity is developed between primary production in developing countries and manufacturing in investing countries. Because the gains from technological progress and economies of scale largely are usurped by the investing country, the development effect is limited to that directly measurable as increased output in plantation agriculture and extractive industry. The dynamic internal interaction between primary, secondary, and tertiary industries and between rural and urban society is stimulated little, if at all. The mechanism through which industrial development based on domestic raw materials leads to direct effects on other industries and secondary effects on education, technology, demand creation, and so forth, is not stimulated by investment in enclaves designed to produce raw materials for external use.

A second major element of this argument is the international transfer of income from poor to rich countries through a secular deterioration in the terms of trade for commodities exported by poor countries. The general case has been argued by Hans Singer based on the structural differences in the economies of industrial and developing countries and the implication for distribution of the gains of technological progress. As summarized by Singer:[9] "The fruits of technological progress may be distributed either to producers (in the form of rising incomes) or to consumers (in the form of lower prices). In the case of manufactured commodities produced in more developed countries, the former method, i.e., distribution to producers through higher incomes, was much more important relative to the second method, while the second method prevailed more in the case of food and raw material produced in the underdeveloped countries."

As pointed out in chapter 9, there is no clear evidence to verify the thesis that the terms of trade turn against developing countries. Increasingly, however, the conceptual foundation for this outcome has been developed. Market factors are important. Low income elasticity of demand for food and increasing inroads by substitutes for raw materials mean that demand expansion is relatively slow. More fundamentally, export industries in developing countries, especially in agriculture, may compare with agriculture in industrial countries in terms of a seeming incapacity to adjust to market conditions. Conditions that have led to the development of price support and protection programs were listed in chapter 6. Theoretical explanations argue that where agriculture is faced with these conditions, that is, slow growth in demand and continuing change in technology and organization, imperfectly informed farmers will continue to make mistakes in committing resources to production.[10] The result will be:

(1) the production of more output than can be sold at prices (to the firm) which will cover acquisition costs (to the firm) of the resources used to produce that output.

(2) MVPs for resources which will not cover their acquisition cost but exceed their salvage value if the firm disposes of them which is to say, of course, that such fixed resources are priced internally according to the opportunity cost principle.

(3) ex post capital losses relative to acquisition costs.

(4) the determination of firm size by past mistakes in organization which fix important resources in firms, thereby activating the law of diminishing returns as successive quantities of the remaining variable resources are used in conjunction with the fixed resources.[11]

The implications of this process for the terms of trade are straightforward. Once production of a commodity has been established, adjustment to lower price conditions may be slow. In a static sense, the lag between a price change and adjustment will depend upon how rapidly the existing stock of fixed assets is used. On the other hand, if the dynamics of international markets are such that declining prices are interspersed with high price periods, increased investment can occur quickly. Disinvestment, on the other hand, depends upon the use rate of assets, and the combination of these two can lead to continuous overinvestment and chronic excess production. This conceptual foundation that has sought to explain excess capacity and low resource returns in the agriculture of industrial countries may be equally relevant to the often modernized, agricultural export sector in developing countries. Furthermore, the characteristics of the market and imperfections in knowledge that lead to overinvestment and overproduction may be greater in developing nations than in the agriculture of industrial countries.

A third, although somewhat less emphasized, argument against free trade is the adverse effect that occurs through the international demonstration effect. The propensity to consume through emulation, especially in the urban component of the society, encourages importation of consumption goods, thus reducing savings for investment and development. This argument can be looked at in a number of ways. If domestic gains from international operation are distributed broadly, the consumption "demonstration effect" easily can become an incentive effect. Small producers have markets that otherwise would not exist, and production for export can lead to increased income and demand for a variety of producers and consumer goods.

On the other hand, if domestic gains from trade are highly concentrated, "luxury" consumption standards in industrial countries might be emulated. Beyond personal consumption, demand will increase for government expenditures to provide the public facilities and services that complement high personal consumption. Distorted infrastructure investment may result; for example, construction of roads to recreation facilities may take precedence over roads needed for commercialization of agriculture. The issue is not that there is a demonstration effect and that international investment leads to increased consumption; the real issue is what form it takes. A broadly based demonstration effect that increases consumption of commodities produced or producible domestically can represent a powerful incentive to development and should be encouraged. Concentrated increases in luxury consumption can be deleterious to development; the most deleterious is the search for security through export of funds that otherwise might be used for domestic investment.

The general problem is the development consequence of permitting highly concentrated incomes and asset ownership, which can occur in domestic as well as export industries. The solution rests in domestic tax and income policy and only peripherally in policy related to external investment. External investment can have a number of additional benefits, such as the transfer of technology and managerial know-how, that often can outweigh any negative consumption effects that do occur. Here again, the problem is to channel these gains into broader use and not permit them to be isolated in enclaves or expatriate interests. Domestic participation in enterprise with a view toward transfer of technical and managerial competence to indigent personnel could be a requirement attached to much foreign investment. This would create a highly useful demonstration effect.

Import Needs of Developing Countries

Viewed in a more applied sense, an important question concerns defining the import needs of developing countries and determining how they can be paid for. A useful model defining such needs has been developed by S. B. Linder.[12] As illustrated in Figure 11, the model allows for inputs of consumption goods as well as raw materials required for operations and imports required for investment. Investment imports are broken down into replacement and new investment for expansion.[13]

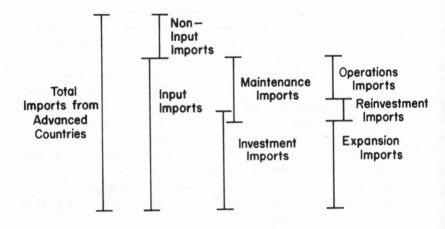

Figure 11: Structure of Imports for Less Developed Countries

The import minimum for any planned rate of growth is a composite of imports needed for investment, reinvestment, and operations. These are the input imports required to avoid underutilization of existing resources and frustration of the growth process. "The input-import problem constitutes a factor proportions problem, which if not solved, would lead to underemployment of existing resources and frustrate the accumulation of further resources."[14] Factor requirements are of two kinds: (1) those derived needs necessary to maintain existing capacity in production, both reinvestment and operational inputs, and (2) new capital that can be combined with domestic capital and labor for growth and expansion.

A key issue in planning development thus is the relation of economic expansion to this factor proportions problem. Much import substitution investment in less developed countries has served to increase the need for imported raw material and maintenance investment to the point that no real import substitution measured in foreign exchange requirements has occurred. In assessing this phenomenon based on a comparative analysis of seven countries, a recent study for the OECD concludes that import substitution investment tends to create a demand for new and different types of imports. Also,

> it tends, paradoxically enough, to increase the economy's dependence on imports. . . . Not only does the policy of import substitution create demand for imported inputs and equipment; but the rise in per capita income is likely to raise the developing countries' propensity to import, all the more so, because, as we have seen, import restriction tends to shift the distribution of income in favour of the urban sector and the higher income groups, whose expenditure pattern typically has the highest component of imports. All this needs stressing, because the chronic foreign-exchange shortage of many developing countries is partly due to an underestimation of the tendency of import substitution to generate demand for imports and consequent overoptimism about its ability to reduce the economy's dependence on imports.[15]

The question of self-induced import requirements for operations and maintenance is not, of course, strictly related to efforts at import substitution. It becomes an important variable in general development planning. Economic growth and employment, for example, can be expanded by importing a plant and parts for automobile assembly. Domestic resource use is limited to expanded employment of labor, and fixed proportions exist between labor and imported parts. Growth based on indigenous raw materials and labor both will have a secondary effect on employment through expanded raw material production and will not call for continuous foreign exchange expenditures to maintain output. The flow can go both ways. There are numerous examples of export industries based on imported raw materials and plants that have contributed to the balance of payments where exports of a product more than compensated for total imports needed to establish and maintain production.

Most developing countries are faced with technical limitations in producing certain types of capital equipment and, hence, require capital imports for growth. The question, both at the aggregate planning and the micro level, is what form investment should take. In general, except in the case of raw material needs and imports for maintenance of existing production capacity, factor substitution probably exists. Planning that emphasizes industrial expansion creates a greater import requirement than agricultural expansion. Planning for import substitution probably creates a greater foreign exchange burden than planning for export expansion.

Factor substitution and factor requirements as they relate to imports versus domestic factors must be included as ingredients in the general planning process. In assessing these questions there are few general rules that apply to developing countries. Each case will vary depending upon domestic resource base, level of development, and opportunities for profitable investment in relation to potential domestic and international market opportunities.

Export Potential and the Trade Gap

As is the case with import requirements, aggregate export potential of less developed countries is difficult to estimate, and very great differences exist among countries. A study by Barend DeVries noted that recent growth of exports among 29 developing nations varied considerably depending upon the size of the domestic market, degree of inflation, and the commodity composition of exports.[16] An assessment by Willard Cochrane concludes that the potential outlet for agricultural commodities produced by developing countries on world markets is relatively limited, but much could be gained if appropriate policy adjustments were made by developed nations.[17] A recent analysis of the export experience of seven countries indicates varying patterns related to policies followed by developing nations and the extent of their export orientation.[18]

A number of estimates of the aggregate import requirements of less developed countries and available export potential have been made. These efforts have sought to estimate and project trends in the aggregate trade gap facing these nations, and they have required the development of projections or reasonable assumptions about population and GNP growth in developing countries and assessment of world market conditions and export trends for them and their import propensities. Economic growth projections are related to historical trends, growth rates implied by development plans, and, in some cases, desired levels to achieve long-term development goals. When a projected rate of growth is estimated, the next question is how this relates to import needs. The empirical studies have computed or assumed an import elasticity relative to income growth. Of the several that have been completed,[19] two continue to have relevance in that they extend in one case to 1975 and in the other to 1980. The general results of these two studies are shown in Table 15.

Table 15. *Projected Trade Gap for Less Developed Countries, 1975 and 1980*

Study		Exports	Imports	Balance
Balassa 1975	A	38.5	42.4	−3.9
—		38.5	43.7	−5.2
—		38.5	45.1	−6.6
	B	41.9	47.0	−5.1
—		41.9	48.7	−6.8
—		41.9	50.0	−8.6
ECE 1980	A	71.7	79.4	−7.7
ECE 1980	B	50.3	60.0	−9.7

SOURCE: ECE (Economic Commission for Europe) data from John Pincus, *Economic Aid and International Cost Sharing* (Baltimore: Johns Hopkins Press, 1965), Table 2.1, p. 26. Data by Balassa from Bela Balassa, *Trade Prospects for Developing Countries* (Homewood: Richard D. Irwin, Inc., 1964), Table 4.5.2, p. 95.
NOTE: Values expressed in billions of dollars for both studies.

In estimating import requirements, the Economic Commission for Europe (ECE) study uses an import elasticity of 0.85. Both cases in this study assume an annual population growth of 2.2 percent. Version B differs from A in that it excludes petroleum exporting countries. The annual growth in exports implied for the study period is about 4.5 percent in each case, and the import elasticity value is low relative to
Bela Balassa's study is based on two rates of expected income growth and three alternative assumptions of import elasticities. Assumed growth rates in gross income vary from 4.1 to 4.3 percent for case A and from 4.8 to 5.2 percent for case B. Import elasticities (the percentage change in imports due to a one percent change in national income) vary from 0.7 to 0.8 in Latin America, 0.9 to 1.0 in Africa, 1.15 to 1.25 in the Middle East, and 1.0 to 1.1 in Asia. Exports are estimated to increase annually by 4.7 percent (case A) and 4.5 percent (case B) in the ECE study. Balassa uses annual export growth rates for all developing countries of 4.6 percent in case A and 5.6 percent in case B.
The most recent and comprehensive assessment of developing countries' trade position was made by UNCTAD in preparation for the Third Conference, held in Santiago, Chile, in April and May 1972. Alternative rates of growth were assumed for each country and aggregated for all countries, excluding major oil producers. The average growth rate in variant one is 6.6 percent and in variant two, 7.1 percent. These increase to an average annual growth of 6.8 and 7.3 percent if all producing countries are included. These projected rates are relatively high and compare with an achieved average for all countries of 5.3

percent per annum for the decade 1960–1970. Projections also were made for growth of developed market economies as a basis for estimating their potential imports from less developed nations. These rates were assumed to be 4.8 and 5.3 percent. For socialist countries a low growth rate of 6.6 percent and a high rate of 7.3 percent were assumed. The results of the UNCTAD projections are shown in Table 16, and the trade positions that arise from the analysis are summarized as follows:[21]

> Total exports of goods and services of all developing countries valued at 1960 prices are expected to rise from $54.4 billion in 1969 to $124.9 billion in 1980 for Variant 1 and to $132.5 billion for Variant 2. The implied average annual growth rates are 7.7 percent and 8.3 percent respectively, as against the historical growth rate of 6.5 percent during the 1960s. The projected rate of growth of commodity exports works out to 7.1 percent for Variant 1 and 7.6 percent for Variant 2, as compared to the rate of 6.7 percent recorded during 1960–1969.

> Exports of manufactured goods would grow at the highest rates (9.9 to 11.3 percent per annum), followed by petroleum (9.8 to 10.4 percent per annum). The remaining primary commodities as a group are projected to grow only at about 3 to 4 percent per annum during the 1970s.

> Import requirements were projected on the basis of import functions relating total imports to consumption and investment expenditures. The latter were projected as a function of GDP. For developing countries as a whole, the projections yield an acceleration of the rate of growth of imports from 5.7 percent per annum for the 1960–1970 period (and 7.3 percent during 1965–1970) to 7.9 percent (Variant 1) and 8.9 percent (Variant 2) during the 1970s. The income elasticity of imports, calculated as the ratio of the rate of growth of imports to the rate of growth of GDP, shows a slight increase.

The outcome these studies predict is dependent on several important assumptions. Assumed growth rates are essentially arbitrary and in the case of the latest UNCTAD study appear to represent a hoped for goal, influenced in part by developing countries' need substantially to increase their growth rates if they are to overcome chronic problems of under- and unemployment. One of the more crucial estimates in trade gap projections is establishing the import elasticity coefficient. As indicated above, imports depend upon consumption patterns, raw material needs, and both the level and composition of capital investment required to meet growth targets. Expansion of industrial capacity normally requires a larger component of imported capital than either

Table 16. Projections for Less Developed Countries, in Billions of 1960 U.S. Dollars

Variant	Africa[a] Actual 1969	Africa[a] Projection 1980	Asia[b] Actual 1969	Asia[b] Projection 1980	Latin America[c] Actual 1969	Latin America[c] Projection 1980	All developing countries Actual 1969 (d)	Actual 1969 (e)	Projection 1980 (d)	Projection 1980 (e)
Variant 1										
1 Gross domestic product	35.9	69.0	121.7	249.0	102.0	210.9	299.2	263.2	621.5	535.4
2 Imports of goods and services	9.4	19.9	23.3	57.1	12.4	26.4	55.6	47.4	130.5	107.9
3 Exports of goods and services	9.0	17.7	18.7	44.5	11.5	20.9	54.5	40.8	124.9	86.1
4 Import surplus (=5−6)	0.4	2.2	4.6	12.6	0.9	5.5	1.2	6.6	5.6	21.8
5 Factor income payments (net)	1.1	4.0	0.8	4.5	1.6	6.3	7.8	3.5	26.6	14.8
6 Trade gap (=7+8)	1.5	6.2	5.4	17.1	2.6	11.8	9.0	10.1	32.2	36.6
As percentage of gross domestic product:										
7 Imports of goods and services	26.2	28.8	19.1	22.9	12.1	12.5	18.6	18.0	21.0	20.1
8 Exports of goods and services	25.1	25.6	15.4	17.9	11.3	9.9	18.2	15.5	20.1	16.1
Variant 2										
1 Gross domestic product	35.9	74.1	121.7	260.3	102.0	222.5	299.2	263.2	654.7	564.3
2 Imports of goods and services	9.4	22.7	23.3	60.7	12.4	29.8	55.6	47.4	142.3	118.7
3 Exports of goods and services	9.0	19.2	18.7	46.5	11.5	22.5	54.5	40.8	132.5	91.4
4 Import surplus (=5−6)	0.4	3.5	4.6	14.2	0.9	7.3	1.2	6.6	9.8	27.3
5 Factor income payments (net)	1.1	4.4	0.8	5.0	1.6	6.6	7.8	3.5	28.2	16.0
6 Trade gap (=7+8)	1.5	7.9	5.4	19.2	2.6	13.9	9.0	10.1	38.0	43.3
As percentage of gross domestic product:										
7 Imports of goods and services	26.2	30.5	19.1	23.3	12.1	13.4	18.6	18.0	21.8	21.0
8 Exports of goods and services	25.1	25.8	15.4	18.0	11.3	10.1	18.2	15.5	20.3	16.2

SOURCE: UNCTAD, *Financial Resources for Development: Trade Prospects and Capital Needs of Developing Countries During the Second United Nations Development Decade.* TD/118/Supp. 3, 22 December 1971.

a Excluding Libya.
b Excluding Brunei, Iran, Iraq, Kuwait, Saudi Arabia, and other major oil exporters in the Middle East.
c Excluding Trinidad and Tabago and Venezuela.
d Including developing countries not elsewhere specified.
e Excluding major oil exporters.

agriculture or service industries. Great variation also would exist among countries given the resource base, structure of the existing economy, and level of development already achieved.[22]

Despite the uncertainties involved, these and other studies lead in one direction: If developing nations are to achieve economic growth at the relatively rapid rates sought in most countries, import requirements will rise faster than export growth. This raises the questions of how increased imports and improved trading relationships can be achieved and what relevance the policy proposals put forth by UNCTAD have.

The UNCTAD Proposals

The role of trade in development among the less developed countries has been the focal point of considerable analysis and policy discussion in UNCTAD. In documents prepared for each of three UNCTAD sessions,[23] evaluation of developing country trade problems has covered a broad perspective from basic changes in total trade structure to the specific problems associated with commodity trade, manufactures and semimanufactures, aid, and monetary and financial questions.

At the first conference, participants argued that, due to a basic structural shift in the world economy, the less developed countries have become disadvantaged and have moved to a position of inherent trade imbalance. This is in part because the center of world industrial activity has shifted to North America, where many of the commodities exported by less developed countries are produced domestically, and in part because the advanced countries in total have, as a result of the depression of the 1930s, adopted policies for domestic self-sufficiency and import substitutions of many of the agricultural commodities available at a lower cost in less developed countries. The inability of developing nations to export those commodities in which they have an advantage limits their ability to import manufactured products which are produced at lower cost in advanced countries. Consequently, it has been necessary to adopt import substitution policies and develop high cost manufacturing. Export of manufactured goods has been hindered by discriminatory tariffs against processed or semiprocessed raw materials, and the demand for raw materials has been seriously eroded by the proliferation of synthetic substitutes. The end result is a major problem in export expansion which cannot be overcome without concerted international action involving both industrial and developing countries.[24]

In seeking a solution, the less developed nations reject the philosophy of a multilateral reduction in trade barriers that has been the foundation of GATT negotiations. Rather, UNCTAD has promulgated a set of policy recommendations that focus on three major approaches: (1) improvement of world commodity markets and expansion of commodity exports from less developed countries; (2) improvement of the competitive position of the less developed in processed, semiprocessed, and manufactured products; and (3) increased transfer of resources to the less developed outside trade channels through aid and financial assistance.[25]

Commodity policy recommendations are broad, although among these, three are of primary importance. One deals with provisions relating to market access. Developed countries are asked to declare a moratorium on tariff and nontariff barriers against imports of primary products of particular interest to developing nations. They also are asked to initiate action for removal or reduction of tariff and internal fiscal charges and elimination of quantitative restrictions on products of particular interest to developing countries. With respect to trade policies, it is suggested that, as a transitional measure, existing preferences between developed and developing countries (such as EEC and United Kingdom preferences for former colonies) should be abolished. Advanced nations are asked to avoid subsidizing the exports of primary products and, when this is not possible, consult with developing countries with a view toward eliminating their adverse effects on the foreign exchange earnings of the less advanced. Furthermore, disposal of surplus agricultural products should be undertaken in accordance with internationally determined criteria.

A second major recommendation calls for the implementation of commodity arrangements with a view toward stimulating a steady and dynamic growth of developing nations' exports and to ensure reasonable predictability in real export earnings. It is suggested that agreements should be negotiated on a commodity-by-commodity basis and that procedures ranging from formal agreements, including possible compensation arrangements, to less formal methods, such as intergovernmental consultations within commodity study groups, should be developed.

A third major recommendation deals with competition from synthetics and substitutes. It is suggested that actions of a national and international character should be taken to do the following: raise the technical efficiency of the production of natural products; improve quality and grade; intensify technical and market research in the use of natural products; give consideration to the interchangeability of certain products in the determination of agricultural and industrial policies; exchange information on investment, planning, and consumption trends in the natural and synthetic sectors; give special attention to all these matters in study groups; and, through the negotiation of commodity agreements, mitigate fluctuations in the price of natural products facing competition from synthetic substitutes. The recommendation further suggests that coordination of investment planning and policies should be developed, and, where appropriate, financial measures should be introduced to reduce the impact of synthetic substitutes on the export earnings of developing countries.

In addition to these three major recommendations, others call for research in improved marketing techniques and promotion of consumption of primary products of interest to developed nations. Developing countries also are encouraged to liberalize their trading relationships with each other, strengthen their monetary relations, and integrate external trade into their development plans.

As a final point it is suggested that measures taken by the less developed be supported and aided by the UN as an international agency and independently by the developed countries and that measures taken by the advanced nations should not require reciprocity from the less developed.

A second set of recommendations, although somewhat less broadly oriented, has been made with respect to manufactured and semimanufactured products. Two are of major importance. One suggests that action be taken by developed countries to expand access in their markets to the less developed by reducing and, where feasible, eliminating all tariff and quantitative barriers on imports of manufactures of interest to less developed countries. The other recommendation is that tariff preferences be established by developed nations for imports of manufactures from the less developed nations without reciprocity and that, where feasible, reciprocal preference systems among developing countries (free trade areas or customs unions) be established to improve trade and development.

A number of subsidiary recommendations also are made by UNCTAD. Possibly the most important is the suggestion that, through the appropriate international bodies, advanced countries should participate in analyzing the development plans and policies of individual developing nations and examine trade and aid relationships with a view toward devising concrete means to promote exports. Another proposal is that governments and competent international organizations collaborate in the field of financial assistance for economic development through systematic studies of trade and aid relationships. Principles for international financial cooperation are suggested, including fairly specific statements advocating improved terms of aid and action to lighten the burden of existing debts. UNCTAD also advocates a substantial extension of international financial assistance for countries which have suffered short-term declines in their export proceeds and the study and development by the International Bank for Reconstruction and Development of schemes for longer term income transfers.

Whether or not UNCTAD has had a significant impact on international policy is difficult to assess. The first session in 1964 was devoted to defining the broad range of international actions needed to improve the trade prospects of less developed countries. The central issue was to devise means through trade or aid whereby these nations could acquire larger quantities of foreign resources needed for accelerated economic growth. The second and third conferences pursued the broad program defined in 1964 and placed specific emphasis on commitments by industrial nations to provide general preferences for developing countries' imports. A positive response was obtained from most industrial nations, and subsequent action to provide trade preferences has been taken by a number of them.[26]

On the other hand, the trend in industrial countries has been toward increased protection for agriculture, and there is little evidence that greater weight is being given to the problems of the less advanced in certain other basic matters. Ad hoc measures to patch up the international monetary system during the 1960s were consistently the exclusive products of a limited number of advanced nations. Recent major changes and current negotiations to establish a new system are based on unilateral action by individual industrialized countries or involve consultation among a limited group. There is also the prospect that discussions of monetary issues will be followed by another round of trade negotiations among industrial countries without major participation by the less developed. In all, while the impact of UNCTAD has been felt in international policy deliberations, it does not appear to have had a major effect on the subsequent course of events.

Summary

The central concern of developing countries is to establish the basis for an international trading system and a system for international transfer of capital that will permit them to finance their import needs.

These needs include consumption goods and raw materials, but the less developed elaborate policy issues largely in terms of their investment capital needs. Imports can be paid for through exports, aid, or inflows of private capital.

Trade projections indicate that, in order to achieve acceptable rates of economic growth, import needs substantially will exceed potential exports. Furthermore, even with the relatively optimistic assumption that capital transfers from industrial countries will reach one percent of their GNP (a target proposed by UNCTAD), a more modest but significant trade gap will continue to exist.

The thrust of trade recommendations proposed by UNCTAD is to reduce existing international policy obstacles and implement new policies that will close this gap. The UNCTAD proposals rest on a macro analysis of the role of trade in development, focusing on the relation between GNP growth rates and the investment and savings and export-import aspects of development. The assumption is that if resources are made available from domestic savings and external sources, development will occur. Presumably the generating mechanism will be economic planning and public guidance. In its international perspective, closing the gap — between imports and payment or, in the case of aid, reducing the need for payment — has become the policy game. Developing countries, in general, reflect the notion that multilateral reduction in trade barriers and movement toward international trade based on comparative advantage will not achieve this result. Thus a range of preferential policies designed to benefit developing nations is proposed to overcome inherent disadvantages faced by them in international markets. Some of these will be discussed in the two succeeding chapters.

8

Commodity Agreements and Compensatory Financing Schemes

Bargaining among countries for the reduction of trade barriers on the initiative of exporters is the time-honored approach to trade policy. Collective restructuring of trade systems through preference arrangements and customs unions among groups of countries is largely a post–World War II development. Programs to organize trade and intercountry flows of income through negotiated commodity arrangements also have been a relatively recent development. Commodity policy has taken two forms: international commodity agreements and international compensatory financing. Both these devices are aimed at stabilizing and increasing the flow of income to exporting countries.

Price Variations and Terms of Trade

As indicated in Tables 17 and 18, there is a great deal of variation among commodities and among countries, but the general pattern is one of substantial instability in export prices and quantities. This condition results from a combination of changes in demand, fluctuations in output due to weather, and cyclical production patterns that result from overreaction to market price signals by agricultural producers.

Table 17. *Total Exports of Individual Commodities from Less Developed Countries: Fluctuation Indexes and Trends for Prices, Quantities, and Earnings, 1953–1965, in Percentages*

Commodity	Indexes of fluctuation			Annual trend rates of growth		
	Prices	Quantities	Earnings	Prices	Quantities	Earnings
Minerals						
Petroleum	3.0	1.3	3.3	−1.2*	7.9*	6.7*
Copper	11.0	4.8	10.7	−1.0	5.3*	4.3*
Iron Ore	5.1	8.4	10.6	−0.7	12.6*	11.8*
Tin	8.1	8.7	15.9	3.2*	−1.9	1.3
Bauxite	10.6	5.2	15.6	7.6*	6.9*	14.9*
Phosphate	2.4	3.7	4.4	−0.1	5.6*	5.6*
Lead	11.4	3.8	13.9	−2.5*	−1.2*	−3.7*
Manganese ore	13.5	13.1	15.1	−2.4	2.9*	0.4
Zinc	18.9	4.2	23.0	3.0	0.9*	3.9
Agricultural raw materials						
Rubber	13.1	3.9	15.5	−0.8	1.6*	0.8
Cotton	4.3	7.1	9.1	−2.8*	2.5*	−0.4
Timber	8.8	4.7	10.3	−1.1	11.3*	10.1*
Jute textiles	7.2	4.5	6.7	2.5*	3.3*	5.9*
Jute	7.7	6.6	5.2	2.3*	−2.1*	0.2
Hides and skins	6.0	5.2	6.6	0.5	1.3*	1.8*
Sisal	16.0	5.4	11.8	3.2	3.5*	6.8*
Abaca	12.1	9.2	14.4	0.6	−1.9	−1.3
Tropical products						
Coffee	12.4	6.6	8.0	−5.2*	4.0*	−1.4
Tea	4.4	3.3	4.3	−0.9	1.9*	1.0
Cocoa	15.4	6.3	10.1	−5.5*	5.1*	−0.7
Bananas	5.9	3.3	5.1	−2.5*	4.7*	2.1*
Other food and feed						
Sugar	10.5	6.1	8.8	1.6	2.3*	4.0*
Rice	11.4	5.8	9.5	−2.3*	3.4*	1.0
Wheat	5.2	30.4	31.0	−1.2*	0.9	−0.3
Maize	7.7	18.6	20.9	−2.2*	12.8*	10.4*
Fishmeal	10.0	16.7	12.7	−2.3	35.4*	32.4*
Mutton and lamb	13.9	17.3	25.6	0.0	−6.7*	−6.7*
Oils and oilseeds						
Copra	10.9	6.6	6.5	0.5	−0.1	0.3
Groundnut	5.3	8.8	6.8	−1.3*	4.3*	2.9*
Palm oil	5.5	3.7	6.6	0.6	−0.2	0.4
Groundnut oil	5.9	12.4	8.4	−2.1*	5.6*	3.4*
Coconut oil	11.7	14.4	14.5	0.0	3.5*	3.5*
Linseed oil	12.0	16.5	11.0	−0.9	2.4	1.5
Linseed	5.5	46.6	45.4	0.3	1.7	2.0

SOURCE: IMF and IBRD, *The Problem of Stabilization of Prices of Primary Products,* A Joint Staff Study (Part I) (Washington, D.C.: 1969).

NOTE: The trends for a given commodity's prices, its quantities, or its earnings are estimated by fitting a linear relation between time and the logarithms of their annual observations. The fluctuation index is the average over the period of annual percentage differences between observations and the calculated trend value, disregarding the signs of the differences and expressing them as percentages of the trend value. An asterisk (*) indicates that the probability of obtaining the trend value in question by chance, when no such relation exists among the observations, is 5 percent or less. Commodity groups and the commodities within them are listed in order of their importance in the total export value of less developed countries over the period (1963-1965) of Table 9.

Table 18. *Total Exports of Individual Less Developed Countries: Fluctuation Indexes and Trends for Prices, Quantities, and Earnings, 1953–1965, in Percentages*

Country	Indexes of fluctuation			Annual trend rates of growth		
	Prices	Quantities	Earnings	Prices	Quantities	Earnings
Argentina	7.4	4.8	9.1	−0.8	4.0*	3.2*
Bolivia	11.1	10.9	30.4	2.3*	−1.8	0.5
Brazil	8.7	6.0	6.8	−3.4*	2.7*	−0.5
Burma	11.7	11.0	6.8	−1.9	2.1	0.2
Ceylon	3.4	2.8	4.1	−1.2*	2.0*	0.7
Chile	7.1	2.6	7.2	−0.8	4.3*	3.5*
China, Republic of	7.9	11.1	15.6	−1.9*	14.8*	12.6*
Colombia	10.7	5.9	9.3	−3.9*	2.0*	−2.0*
Costa Rica	8.0	7.7	8.2	−3.6*	6.5*	2.6*
Cyprus	6.0	3.8	7.2	−0.6	3.1*	2.5*
Dominican Republic	9.0	10.9	10.5	0.3	2.8*	3.1*
Ecuador	4.9	4.1	6.2	−3.4*	6.8*	3.2*
Ethiopia	10.8	9.5	9.4	−2.4*	6.6*	4.1*
Ghana	12.4	8.1	6.4	−4.0*	6.8*	1.9*
Guatemala	11.0	7.6	9.6	−4.0*	8.3*	4.0*
Haiti	10.2	11.0	12.7	−3.0*	3.0*	−0.9
Honduras	8.4	11.2	10.7	0.3	4.7*	5.0*
India	2.2	5.6	5.0	0.3*	2.4*	3.2*
Iran	4.6	27.6	31.3	0.3	19.7*	20.1*
Iraq	4.3	8.5	6.5	−0.6	7.3*	6.6*
Israel	4.8	6.6	5.3	0.3	16.8*	17.2*
Jamaica	4.6	5.4	6.0	1.3*	8.0*	9.4*
Kenya	3.1	4.9	4.3	−1.6	9.2*	7.5*
Malaysia	9.4	2.9	8.0	0.2	4.0*	4.2*
Mauritius	4.9	8.1	10.6	0.9	1.2	2.2
Morocco	4.7	4.4	4.5	−0.4	3.6*	3.2*
Nicaragua	6.7	12.3	13.4	−2.7*	10.3*	7.3*
Nigeria	3.7	5.5	7.6	−0.7	6.0*	5.3*
Pakistan	5.3	9.7	10.8	1.2	1.2	2.3
Peru	6.6	7.3	6.7	0.2	10.0*	10.1*
Philippines	4.6	5.2	5.7	0.1	5.8*	5.9*
Sudan	6.1	14.0	10.9	−0.2	4.8*	4.6*
Tanzania	6.7	5.9	6.4	−0.2	6.0*	5.7*
Thailand	2.5	9.1	8.6	−0.1	6.0*	5.8*
Uganda	8.0	5.6	9.8	−2.8*	6.9*	3.9*
United Arab Republic	7.5	7.0	5.8	0.4	2.2*	2.6*
Uruguay	8.7	15.0	20.6	−1.0	−1.5	−2.4
Venezuela	2.0	4.7	6.0	−0.2	4.8*	4.6*

SOURCE: IMF and IBRD, *The Problem of Stabilization of Prices of Primary Products,* A Joint Staff Study (Part I) (Washington, D.C.: 1969).

NOTE: The trends for a given country's export prices, its quantities, or its earnings are estimated by fitting a linear relation between time and the logarithms of their annual observations. The fluctuation index is the average over the period of annual percentage differences between observations and the calculated trend value, disregarding the signs of the differences and expressing them as percentages of the trend value. An asterisk (*) indicates that the probability of obtaining the trend value in question by chance, when no such relation exists among the observations, is 5 percent or less.

A recent study by A. I. MacBean concludes there has been no correlation between economic growth in developing countries and short-term export fluctuations.[1] This does not mean that no problem exists. Short-term balance-of-payments fluctuations can arise and require international borrowing. Furthermore, the impact on specific industries through lower profits and reduced employment can be severe. In countries highly specialized in one or two commodities, the effects can create a general impact on the economy, and where export taxes are important they seriously can affect government revenue. It is safe to conclude that the export instability issue is important for less developed nations and cannot be overlooked in determining international policy.

A second major issue concerning international commodity arrangements is whether effective actions can be taken to transfer income from rich to poor nations. This emphasis stems from the search by many underdeveloped countries for accelerated rates of economic growth. Major capital imports are required to fulfill growth targets, and these must be paid for. The overwhelmingly important source of foreign exchange earnings for the underdeveloped has been the export of agricultural commodities and raw materials. In the short run, the most apparent basis for expansion of foreign exchange earnings is through increases in the value of commodity exports.

The case for setting up commodity arrangements in which poor nations receive income transfers is based on the argument that, over time, there is a tendency for the terms of trade to turn against countries that produce primary commodities. Conceptually, the argument centers around the fact that the demand for primary products grows slowly relative to income; at the same time, there is a tendency for the long-run supply to increase even at low prices because of a lack of alternative opportunities for primary product producers. This tendency is aggravated by import substitution and price support policies in industrial countries that stimulate output and aggravate market price conditions.

A structural argument also is made that advanced countries are characterized by rigid pricing patterns brought about by large-scale labor organizations and large-scale business. Both have power to maintain prices and retain gains in productivity that arise from technological or institutional developments. This pattern, along with greater technological sophistication in developed countries and protection of producer incomes through support policies, results in the development of low cost substitutes and, in extreme cases, the stimulation of production that is dumped on world markets at subsidized price levels. In this way, the developed countries alleviate their domestic problems at the expense of the less developed.

Only limited empirical evidence is available to assess the terms of trade questions. Figures 12 and 13 are based on a study completed by Theodore Morgan for different time periods and for somewhat different groups of countries.[2] In each case, some major nations are not included, and the results must be accepted with reservations. From these studies, however, Morgan concludes there is no long-run tendency for terms of trade to turn against the less developed. C. P. Kindleberger,[3] on the other hand, concludes the evidence is clear that commodity terms of trade have tended to move in favor of the developed and against the less developed, but he argues it is not true they have moved against primary production in favor of manufacture.

The evidence either way is inconclusive. Much depends upon the base period used, as shown by Morgan. Also, the convention of using commodity terms of trade to estimate secular trends can be seriously contested since it contains neither a productivity nor a quality adjustment factor. Shifts in commodity terms of trade are not accurate indicators of changes in real income, particularly over a long period.

Commodity Programs for Stabilization

International commodity arrangements have much in common with domestic programs in industrial countries. The mechanics involved in marketing agreements are closely related to those in direct price maintenance programs, while the mechanics of compensatory financing are similar to deficiency payment systems where prices are allowed to reach market levels and additional payments are made to maintain a given price equivalent. The income transfers involved are among countries rather than from consumers or taxpayers to producers within a country.

The issue of international commodity arrangements recently has taken on new impetus from two sources. First, long discussions in the Kennedy Round were aimed at establishing trading arrangements for commodities of primary interest to advanced countries. Second, UNCTAD has stressed the special role commodity arrangements should play in economic development. The 1964 UNCTAD conference stated that "a basic objective of international commodity arrangements is in general to stimulate a dynamic and steady growth and insure reasonable predictability in the real export earnings of developing countries,

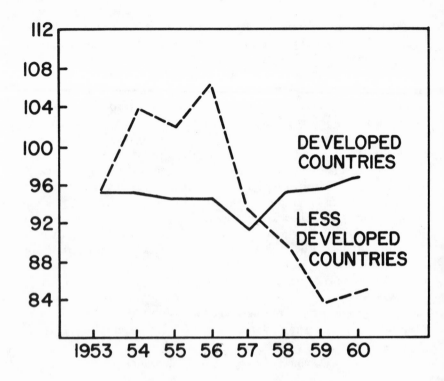

Developed Countries		Less Developed Countries		
Australia	Japan	Angola	Ecuador	Nicaragua
Austria	New Zealand	Argentina	El Salvador	Nigeria
Belgium	Norway	Bolivia	Ghana	Pakistan
Canada	Portugal	Brazil	Greece	Philippines
Denmark	Spain	Burma	Guatemala	Sudan
France	Sweden	Ceylon	Honduras	Turkey
Germany	Switzerland	Chile	India	Uruguay
Ireland	United Kingdom	Colombia	Indonesia	Venezuela
Italy	United States	Costa Rica	Malaya	Viet Nam
		Dominican	Morocco	
		Republic		

SOURCE: Theodore Morgan, "Trends in Terms of Trade and Their Repercussions on Primary Producers," in *International Trade Theory in a Developing World,* R. F. Harrod and D. C. Hague, eds. (New York: St. Martins Press, Inc., 1963).

Figure 12. Trends in Terms of Trade (1953=100)

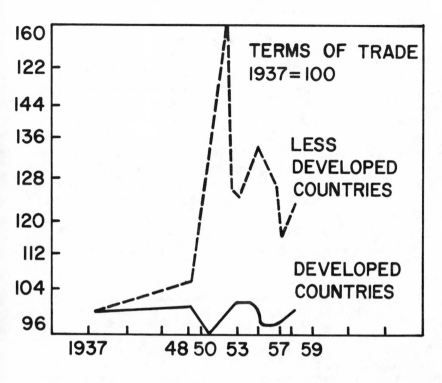

TERMS OF TRADE
1937=100

LESS
DEVELOPED
COUNTRIES

DEVELOPED
COUNTRIES

Developed Countries		Less Developed Countries	
Australia	Japan	Bolivia	Honduras
Belgium	New Zealand	Burma	India
Canada	Norway	Ceylon	Malaya
Denmark	Sweden	Colombia	Philippines
France	Switzerland	Costa Rica	Sudan
Germany	United Kingdom	Dominican	Turkey
Ireland	United States	Republic	Uruguay
Italy		El Salvador	Venezuela

SOURCE: Theodore Morgan, "Trends in Terms of Trade and Their Repercussions on Primary Producers," in *International Trade Theory in a Developing World*, R. F. Harrod and D. C. Hague, eds. (New York: St. Martins Press, Inc., 1963).

Figure 13. Terms of Trade (1937=100)

so as to provide them with expanding resources for their economic and social development, while taking into account the interests of consumers in importing countries."[4] To achieve this objective, UNCTAD also established a number of conditions required in international commodity arrangements. These were stated in the Final Act of the Geneva Conference as: (1) secure remunerative, equitable, and stable prices for primary commodities, especially those exported by developing countries, having due regard for the import purchasing power of the commodities exported; (2) aim to increase, particularly in developed countries, the consumption of primary commodities, including those in semiprocessed and processed forms, from developing countries; and (3) assure satisfactory access to the markets of the developed countries for the primary products of developing countries as appropriate in the context of the commodity arrangements.

In commenting on the UNCTAD position E. M. Ojala makes the following observation:

> This seems a far cry from the Havana Charter. The interest has moved from "stable" prices to "remunerative" prices; from the treatment of "special difficulties" to the promotion of dynamic and steady growth; from the interests of both producers and consumers to the problems of developing countries "taking into account" the interests of consumers. The indicators are that under UNCTAD the developing countries will seek to obtain through commodity agreements, not a balance of concessions and obligations as between exporters and importers, but a tilting of world commodity markets in favor of the developing country exporters — in other words, aid through trade.[5]

But policy positions are not reality until implemented, and this has been a slow process. Despite attempts since the 1920s, agreements have been signed for only five commodities (wheat, sugar, tin, coffee, and olive oil), and only those for wheat, tin, and coffee have operated with any degree of continuity. The use of compensatory financing has been equally limited.

International Commodity Agreements

The economic literature does not present an optimistic view of the future role of international commodity agreements. Most writers point out that agreements are both difficult to negotiate and to administer. Furthermore, even if these problems are overcome, such arrangements lead to a malallocation of resources by stimulating too much production and can prevent movement of production to the lowest cost locations. Critics thus question whether agreements can or should be implemented.

Difficulties in arranging and administering agreements stem, in part, from technical problems surrounding the production and trading of products. Among other things, commodities must be identifiable by grade, in some cases storable, and they must not be subject to competition by close substitutes. But even when these problems are not severe, conflicts of interest between importers and exporters must be overcome. On competitive imports, importers want low quantities and high prices. On noncompetitive imports they want lower prices with quantities determined by demand. Exporters would like both higher prices and greater quantities. While these limitations are real, the premise for discussion here is that there are a number of commodities or combinations of commodities for which technical limitations are not prohibitive, and that compromise of short-term, special economic interests to seek broader goals is at least worth discussing. In some cases, they may even be amenable to effective negotiation.

The second part of the argument — that commodity agreements have limited usefulness because they lead to malallocation of resources — should not be accepted without reservation. The implication is that economic efficiency, in the utopian sense defined by the perfectly competitive model, is the sole criterion for judging the effect of a policy action. This kind of argument overlooks three issues. First, a central contention in welfare economics is that, in today's world of oligopolistic industrial structures and government guidance of economic activity, there is no basis for assuming the best outcome is achieved by making any given market conform more closely to the perfectly competitive model.[6] Second, no government acts strictly on an efficiency criterion, either in its domestic agricultural policy or its international commercial policy. Achieving other ends may be worthwhile even at the expense of some economic efficiency. Third, given current conditions in agricultural markets, it is possible that commodity agreements, if properly designed, can serve to improve resource use.

In advanced countries the price and terms of trade issues have been handled by price support programs, border protection, and, where there were differences in domestic and world price levels for exporters, export subsidies. Developing countries, on the other hand, have not had sufficient resources or in many cases the internal political foundation to differentiate internal and external prices. Their approach more often has been to accept world prices on commodity exports and to tax domestic producers through export marketing boards. They have argued that their export earnings and development have suffered seriously from variability and long-term deterioration in the prices of export commodities. Given these conditions, the question arises whether formalized agreements that have as their central purpose orderly and gradual international adjustment of production have a potential role in the future.

If we accept that the case against commodity agreements on efficiency grounds is at least ambiguous, this question should be placed in context with other effects in assessing their consequences and potential role in international markets.

There are at least two other issues. One is to what extent commodity agreements can achieve greater stability and whether or not such stability is desirable. Market stability is important to most trading nations and has been a central issue in all commodity agreements developed during the postwar period. Their stated direct aim has been to moderate price fluctuations, but since the principal source of such fluctuations is variation in supply, the methods used also involve some form of stabilization of quantities exported, or specification of the proportion of the product traded under the agreed pricing relations.

Second, and particularly as a result of the UNCTAD discussions, major attention recently has been given to the role of commodity agreements in transferring income from rich to poor nations. For commodities produced largely in poor countries and consumed largely in rich countries, the possibility of achieving longer term income transfers exists through agreements that maintain price above market levels if price-demand is inelastic. For commodities produced in both rich and poor countries, even greater income transfers are possible if agreements include provisions to regulate production or quantities traded so that poor nations increase their proportion of the supply consumed in advanced countries.

Regardless of the central purpose of an agreement, a number of interrelated effects are likely to result. The act of stabilizing prices may affect resource use by influencing producer expectations, even if average price levels remain at normal market levels. In agreements that seek price stabilization, the determination of an appropriate price or range of prices is at best a matter of judgment and may be weighted heavily by the negotiating power of the countries concerned. This means that the difference between price stabilization and price adjustment involving income transfers becomes obscured. Furthermore, it is obvious that any agreement designed to transfer income from rich to poor countries will stabilize prices and may affect resource use.

Given this range of effects, one of the problems encountered is to establish agreements that will maximize beneficial effects and yet not lead to uncontrolled surpluses or extensive resource malallocation. As suggested by Irving Kravis,[7] "the key requirement of a commodity agreement that will satisfy the aid and efficiency objectives is a means of separating the price or revenue received by the exporting country from that received by individual producers. A closely related requirement is that the producer price be uniform for producers in different countries." The first of these conditions will permit international pricing at a level that includes an income transfer component without creating an excessive price incentive to producers. Maintaining the same producer price for all countries should encourage movement of production toward areas of comparative advantage.

Objectives and Techniques of Control

The central objective of commodity agreements established to date has been the control or limitation of short-term fluctuations in world prices. In some cases this objective has been supplemented by secondary ones designed to adjust production toward a long-run equilibrium and to guarantee markets for producing countries.

Agreements have relied upon one or more types of control: (1) supply control through export regulation and efforts to adjust production; (2) storage (buffer stock) programs designed to iron out short-term fluctuations; and (3) contracts that specify maximum and minimum trading prices for a proportion of the internationally traded quantity. Each of these techniques requires different conditions and faces a variety of problems for effective operation.

Export Regulation

In theory, export regulation schemes can be devised to accomplish the short-term objective of regulating world exports to maintain prices within certain limits and to adjust production to longer run trends in export requirements at a given price level. There are, however, problems involved in managing export regulation schemes. One of these is the initial process of assigning production quotas. A major disadvantage in establishing quotas is that they tend to perpetuate the initial pattern of world trade, and adjustments designed to gain exports based on changing production potential and comparative advantage are difficult to achieve. Flexibility, in theory, can be obtained by periodic reviews of quota and production conditions in individual exporting countries, but even with good intentions, shifts in member quota proportions are politically difficult to achieve. One method of partially overcoming this problem is to establish quotas to cover only a part of the market and permit a competitive fringe that individual countries can compete for on a cost basis. This step must be accompanied by a rule that no government subsidies be used to capture this segment of exports. Even then, a two-price system is established whereby producer returns are dependent upon a pooling relationship, and price levels in the uncontrolled segment of a market are likely to be driven to an excessively low level.

Determining the desired price level or price range is a second main problem in international quota control arrangements. For most agricultural commodities, aggregate price elasticities of demand are low; hence, total returns can be increased by maintaining relatively high prices. On the other hand, depending upon the proportion of the commodity traded in world markets and upon the degree of competition from substitutes, price elasticities may be high for exports, and total earnings can be increased by reducing price levels.

Another complicating factor is the extent of variation in production costs among countries. If these costs are relatively similar, the guideline for establishing equilibrium level prices is more easily defined than if a wide range of costs exists. In the case of grain, for example, low cost producing countries have substantial capacity for expanding output, and setting a price near the median or higher cost range may create major problems of supply control.

Beyond these basic economic conditions related to supply and demand and establishment of workable price and quota guidelines, a number of technical problems can arise. These might vary substantially among commodities. Devising a workable scheme for quota regulation is essential, and questions related to price variation based on quality and varietal differences also may be important.

International Buffer Stocks

By definition, international buffer stocks must be limited in objective to reducing short-term price variations. Commodities are purchased during periods of excess supply and sold during periods of short supply to reduce price variations. If prices are maintained above an equilibrium level over an extended period of time, a buffer stock will continue to grow and require continued expansion of financial resources and storage capacity — as has occurred in some domestic price support operations. The first and main requirement for a successful buffer stock program is the ability to project realistic price levels and establish prices within a range the market will clear over a defined period of time. Thus the underlying conditions of world supply and demand must be estimated as a base point.

Establishing the financial basis for operating a buffer stock can be a difficult task. A buffer stock program implies the existence of a pool of money and commodities which shift proportionately in response to market conditions. The total pool of assets must be large enough to mitigate market variation effectively. The size of the pool required will depend both upon the total value of the internationally traded commodity and the extent of variability in market supply or demand. In practice, the most frequently encountered problem is instability due to fluctuation in supply as a result either of a cyclical production pattern or variation in weather. Theoretically, if the stocking program operates effectively, the cyclical pattern of production based on producers' responses to price could be eliminated and leave only fluctuations due to natural and weather conditions and demand. Alternately, a buffer stock program can be complemented by an export regulation scheme, and part of the cost of assuring continuous supplies can be shifted to individual countries rather than maintained in the international pool.

There are a number of technical problems in establishing buffer stock programs. One is the composition of stocks to be kept on hand, especially where quality and varietal differences are important. Problems also can arise concerning handling of stocks: whether they should be concentrated or held by numerous member countries, and how commodities can be moved through the storage program without incurring excessive costs. An alternative to the concept of international stocks would be an agreement among countries to maintain adequate levels of national stocks that in turn are subject to international coordination.

Contractual Price Arrangements

The most important requirement for the effective operation of contractual price arrangements is that the range of prices maintained as maximum and minimum levels must bracket the long-run world equilibrium price. If that price falls outside the range of the stipulated upper or lower limit, a price agreement alone, without one on supply control or storage stocks, would not be effective. If price exceeds the maximum range, sellers would be unwilling, over an extended period, to reduce international trading prices below world market levels. If prices are below the minimum range, buyers will not agree continuously to higher prices; furthermore, competitive interaction between sellers is such that maintaining minimum prices is difficult. As with a buffer stock program, the major problem in implementing effective price agreements is to estimate world demand and supply conditions accurately and, from a technical point of view, to be in a position to adjust to trends and developments that create major shifts in equilibrium prices and quantities.

The most important case of contractual price arrangement has been for wheat. The first wheat agreement was established in 1949 and included five exporters and 37 importers. Through 1967 this agreement was revised twice, but in each case included a maximum and a minimum trading price among members and specified quantities or percentages of trade. These earlier agreements were replaced by the Wheat Trade Convention arrived at during the Kennedy Round. The trading provision of the new convention differs somewhat from previous wheat agreements, but the basic concept of establishing maximum and minimum prices within which specified quantities of trade will occur is not changed. The wheat agreements appear to have had some, but probably only a limited, effect in stabilizing wheat prices. From 1949 to 1953 the agreed price maximum was below world market prices, and a saving accrued to importers. Prior to about 1964, world trading prices were above the minimum largely because of the storage program operated in the United States. From 1965 to 1967, a general decline in world food grain stocks maintained prices at relatively high levels.

Two changes in the late 1960s and early 1970s led to a new test of whether the wheat convention would affect world trading prices. The United States moved to a two-price program on wheat, and world supplies of wheat increased substantially due, in part, to the Green Revolution. Consequently, world prices declined on commercially traded wheat, and the major increases in output of food grains in Asia meant smaller quantities were removed from commercial markets as food aid. Pricing arrangements under the wheat convention broke down, and it is unlikely they will be effectively reestablished in the near future.

Commodity Agreements and Development

Past experience is not very instructive about the potential of commodity agreements to create longer term income transfers. Only two agreements of major consequence to less developed countries have operated effectively for any length of time, and both emphasize price stabilization.[8] In 1956 a buffer stock agreement was implemented for tin which set a range within which prices were allowed to fluctuate. A stocking agency was established to implement support purchases if prices reached the lower limit and to sell if they reached an upper limit. This arrangement was intended to protect both exporters and importers from extreme price fluctuation with a minimum of direct market interference. Theoretically, if prices are set to bracket the long-term supply-demand equilibrium and if the range is not too wide, a stabilization effect through buffer stocks can be achieved without a heavy financial commitment. Short of this kind of foresight, inability to control upward price fluctuations or heavy accumulation of inventories and burdensome financial requirements may emerge. The latter occurred with tin in 1948, and the program thereafter relied more heavily on export quotas as a method of control.

The other relevant case is coffee. A coffee arrangement was initiated in 1962, and a new long-term agreement was signed in 1968 by 66 member countries to be effective until 1973. The agreement prescribed price limits within which world prices would be maintained, and these limits would be enforced through export quotas allocated to member exporting countries in proportion to a historical base period.

The coffee agreement during its period of operation appears to have had some effect in stabilizing world coffee prices, particularly after 1964, when adjustable quotas were adopted that changed even within a marketing year in relationship to price pressures. Higher export earnings also may have been achieved for coffee producing countries than would have existed without the agreement. Despite encouraging results, the coffee agreement did not succeed in coping with the basic problem of periodic overproduction. Prices received by producers encourage excess production, and no international arrangement to specify producer prices was reached. Kravis argues that this omission encourages resource malallocation, and "the main rationale for the support by the developed countries of coffee prices — encouragement of economic development — is weakened to the extent that the extra revenues of the export restriction scheme go to coffee producers and make coffee production attractive compared to other alternatives."[9]

In viewing the future use of commodity agreements as instruments for furthering economic development, John Pincus suggests that only a limited number of commodities can be traded effectively. These agreements can be effective instruments for international income transfers only if a number of conditions exist:[10] (1) There must be an inelastic long-run demand for the commodity; (2) effective provision for control over supply must be developed; (3) means must be created by governments to channel the increased earnings into economic development rather than allow higher profits for plantation owners; (4) there should be a marketing organization in which a few producing countries dominate world supply so that they are willing to practice restraint in the face of the inevitable supply control violations by smaller producers; (5) there must be a large number of producers within each country to assure a fairly wide distribution of gains from higher prices; and (6) agreement must be reached to limit domestic production in those importing countries that can or do produce the commodity.

Based on these criteria, Pincus concludes that only coffee, sugar, bananas, tea, and cocoa can be brought effectively under agreement. His conclusion, however, appears to be based solely on the extent to which agreements can be used to achieve gains from monopoly pricing of commodities through upward price stabilizing activity. Certain differences in aid and stabilization arrangements could become important. While stabilization agreements are looked upon as a tool for effecting returns to producers in exporting countries, aid agreements could be more directly incorporated into a development plan and would be concerned primarily with increasing national export earnings without the proceeds necessarily going to producers of the export commodity. This procedure would have a major implication for the problem of supply adjustment and would overcome, at least to a degree, the supply control problem and thus potentially expand the range of commodities which could be handled under agreement.

A second important difference is that the premise for participation by advanced countries would change. They would be forced to consider aid-giving responsibilities along with the question of import prices in deciding the extent and nature of their participation in commodity agreements. In the case of competitive imports such as sugar, domestic price support programs would be called directly into question in terms of their relationship to aid objectives. Furthermore, aid

granted through commodity agreements would be extracted directly
from consumers or raw material users in the form of higher prices on
imports and would not require government appropriations, which
could be a political advantage.

An important perspective on the role of commodity agreements has
been provided recently by Gerda Blau. She cites two conditions that
have developed in commodity markets. First, growth in demand has
slowed and even stagnated for a large number of traditional commodities. Second, other commodities for which demand prospects are
good (such as meat and timber) depend upon production methods that
are labor extensive; hence, shifting to these commodities presents a
problem of internal adjustment under conditions of underutilization
of rural labor. These problems, she argues, could be compensated for
if a larger share of commodities were exported in processed form.
Against this background she sums up the main agreement objectives
for developing countries as the following:

(1) The main functions of international agreements ought to be seen
    as those of instruments of economic development. In particular,
    they ought to contribute to the processes of economic diversifica-
    tion which in turn form intrinsic parts of the process of develop-
    ment, both of its causes and of its effects;

(2) In order to enable a developing exporting country to get out of its
    concentrated economic dependence on a poor market risk, the
    very first step required will usually have to be that of making the
    risk less poor. Once the risk has been made less poor it may also
    become easier to make it less concentrated. The other way round,
    the process tends to get stuck. This is because the country's diver-
    sifying capacity depends in large measure on its earning powers,
    exchange resources, revenue surplus, and cash linkage derived
    from its established export sector.

(3) Simultaneously, determined efforts need to be made for develop-
    ing new opportunities of adequate market size for alternative
    export products. This second requirement will call in particular
    for the liberalization of access for processed products.[11]

This approach is not aimed solely at the narrower objectives of improving prices, balance of payments, or stabilization. Her argument rests on
the proposition that the main policy task consists of finding a more
effective system of international economic adjustment assistance. In
this context the traditional goals of agreements become instrumental to
more basic development objectives.

In the final analysis, the use of marketing agreements as tools for aid and improving international adjustment must be looked at in terms of whether appropriate institutional arrangements can be established to implement them and in light of their efficiency relative to alternative methods of giving aid. In assessing alternatives, not only should traditional methods of granting aid be considered, but also an approach that relates aid to level of commodity exports must be taken into account, namely, compensatory financing.

Compensatory Financing

Several compensatory financing schemes have been put forth by various international organizations.[12] All seek to provide compensation to underdeveloped nations to offset shortfalls in their export earnings through a fund financed primarily by developed countries. The level of financing is determined "after the fact" of the shortfall and hence does not interfere with market operations. Beyond these common features, considerable variation among proposals exists, particularly in relation to the basis for computing shortfalls and for making repayments.

The Organization of American States (OAS) suggests that credits be granted which are equal to two-thirds of the amount by which official export receipts are below average export receipts for the preceding three years. Repayment should be made over a three-year period by applying two-thirds of any surplus of export receipts over the average for the preceding three years of repayment. Where necessary, the repayment could be extended for two years with half of the balance due each year. The OAS scheme is designed to offset cyclical or random fluctuations around a trend and contains no long-term aid. Repayment including interest would be required.

Two general types of schemes have been suggested by the UN. One involves payment of premiums and grants for shortfalls in exports. Funds would be provided by a contribution related to national income for rich countries and export proceeds for the less developed. These latter automatically could draw up to 50 percent of their shortfall — measured in relation to average exchange earnings over the past three years. Shortfalls of less than some minimum amount (5–10 percent) would not qualify for grants from the fund. Under this program, developing nations would have no obligation for repayment, and a continuous transfer from rich to poor countries could occur. A second UN proposal would provide contingent loans from a credit fund where repayment would be required only if exports in the next five years exceeded the average for the preceding three years by a sufficient amount to permit repayment. If not, payment would be forgiven, and a loan essentially would become a grant.

The International Monetary Fund Program

In 1963 the International Monetary Fund (IMF) introduced a compensatory finance scheme patterned after the OAS proposal, to be operated strictly as a program to offset short-term market instability.[13] The principal features are noted below.[14]

1) All member countries may participate, but the plan is designed in particular for primary producing countries.

2) The purpose is to compensate for temporary shortfalls in export receipts rather than in export prices, terms of trade, or the importing power of exports.

3) *Temporary shortfalls* are defined as deviations from a medium-term trend in export receipts. The existence and amount of an export shortfall for the purpose of any drawing is determined with respect to the latest twelve-month period preceding the drawing request.

4) Compensation is paid in the form of a drawing subject to the normal conditions of repayments for fund drawings, including an outside limit of three to five years.

5) Compensation is paid to the full extent of the calculated shortfall, subject to the proviso that the total of compensatory drawings outstanding normally should not exceed 25 percent of the quota.

6) The policies of members drawing under the facility do not have to meet the tests that the fund would apply in the case of noncompensatory drawings in the same tranche. However, members do have to satisfy the fund that they are encountering payments difficulties, that the shortfall is of a short-term character and is largely attributable to circumstances beyond the member's control, and that the member will cooperate with the fund in an effort to find solutions, where required, for its payments difficulties.

In order to identify more clearly what are regarded as export shortfalls of a short-term character, the fund, in conjunction with the member concerned, seeks to establish reasonable estimates regarding the medium-term trend of the member's exports, based partly on statistical calculation and partly on appraisal of export prospects.

Procedural Issues in Compensatory Financing

A number of procedural issues have arisen in the operation of the IMF scheme. One of these involves the method used in estimating the amount of shortfall in export earnings and, hence, the amount that can be drawn by a country. Both quantitative and qualitative techniques are used.

The estimated shortfall is based on a five-year moving average of the last three years of exports combined with a forecast of the two future years. Therefore, a country never can know with certainty the exact amount that can be drawn until application actually is made. This method is considered a disadvantage by borrowing countries, who would prefer estimating procedures that permit the amount that could be drawn to be known with certainty by all countries at all times. However, the fund defends the five-year moving average approach by noting that the policy of estimating future exports along with weighted averages of past exports gives better estimates of trends than does consideration of past exports only. By estimating future exports, it is possible to more quickly differentiate a temporary shortfall from the beginning of a general downward trend.

Another area of concern involves the limitations on compensatory borrowing by individual countries. After its inception, the program increased the amount of funds allocated to compensatory financing from 25 to 50 percent of a member country's quota.[15] This increase was made with several qualifications. The first was that the 50 percent limit would apply in *all* cases, not just to "normal" ones, as did the original 25 percent limit. Furthermore, except in major emergencies or disasters, a country could not withdraw more than 25 percent of its quota in any twelve-month period. Last, any country drawing more than 25 percent of its quota must cooperate with the fund in an effort to find, where required, appropriate solutions for its balance-of-payments problems. The most difficult procedural questions are those concerning repayment. To achieve the objective of reducing fluctuations in available foreign exchange, repayment should be made in years when exports exceed estimated trend values and not on a fixed time schedule. On the other hand, this method can create problems in obtaining repayment and may result in loans that remain outstanding for a longer period than is compatible with the short-term character of a compensatory financing scheme designed to smooth cyclical variations in export earnings.

With this purpose in mind, the IMF defined a desirable system of repayment as one that contained at least three major provisions.[16]

(a) Because of the short-term character of the use of Fund resources by individual members, it is necessary to observe an outside limit of five years for repurchase.

(b) Repurchases should be made within the five-year period on the compensatory principle. It has been shown that compensatory repurchases amounting to one-half of the export excesses are likely to result in greater reduction of the fluctuations of export availabilities around the trend than would full compensatory repurchases.

(c) Enough flexibility must be maintained so that members may use less than one-half of an export excess in repayment or even to omit the indicated compensatory repurchase entirely.

In accordance with this philosophy, compensatory financing has retained a short-term focus as a result of being built into the procedures for computing shortfalls and for making repayments. The position that long-term income transfers to offset declines in export earnings fall outside the scope of compensatory financing has been maintained by the IMF.

Compensatory finance schemes have some general advantages compared to commodity agreements. They involve less interference with normal trading procedures. Problems of administration are greatly reduced since no supply control or stock management programs are involved. This simplicity of administration plus the automatic nature of the credits and the fact that there are no strings attached to compensatory loans are an attraction to developing countries. The only obligation is repayment.[17] Needless to say, any measure that automatically brings financial assistance when exports decline, while leaving national governments free to follow their own policies, is very welcome.

Despite these advantages, there are reservations concerning the validity of compensatory financing as a tool for stabilizing export earnings. Such financing is justified on the basis that export instability is caused by circumstances outside the control of governments, which assumption is not entirely valid. Internal policy also may cause shortfalls in export receipts, and in this case the solution should be sought internally. Also, the assumption that fluctuation in export earnings is a major determinant of changes in the domestic economy and of the foreign exchange position of a country is crucial.

There is the possibility that a compensatory scheme with automatic credits and repayments may not stabilize foreign exchange earnings and, in fact, may cause greater instability. The importance of this development is illustrated by the results of empirical tests of various automatic schemes for compensatory financing of short-term fluctuations of export earnings performed by members of the IMF staff.[18] They tested 137 different schemes by varying the provisions of the OAS proposal related to the weighting system employed to establish the export norm, the aggregate debt limit imposed on the borrowing country, and the repayment of the debt. Their conclusion was that several variants of the OAS plan would achieve only very partial success in approximating the targets or trends. Some of the variants examined had deviation ratios in excess of unity, showing that availabilities under these programs deviate from the target more than do actual exports.[19] The deviation ratio of the OAS scheme as originally drafted is 0.92, and the lowest deviation ratio for any scheme tested was no lower than 0.77. These results suggest that compensation plans of this kind would make only a limited contribution to stabilization of export earnings. Whether that contribution would be worth its cost depends upon the value assigned to the stabilization that could be achieved.

Compensatory financing schemes might be designed to transfer resources from richer to poor countries simply by financing shortfalls at too high a level and by foregoing repayment unless major surpluses above trend are generated. Continuous contributions by the industrial nations would be required for this kind of program to remain solvent. Under any such plan, long-term aid would tend to be transferred in accordance with the value and time pattern of a country's exports and the extent of shortfalls and surpluses in relation to average export receipts. Within the whole group of developing nations, this type of aid would not necessarily flow either to those in need of it or to those best able to make use of it. Furthermore, these expenditures would be completely free of supervision; donor countries would have no guarantee against misuse.

Summary

Whether viewed as a short-term device for achieving stability or as a method of income transfers, compensatory financing schemes have some advantages over commodity agreements. They remove uncertainty from the market and avoid many of the technical and administrative problems associated with commodity agreements. They are attractive to less developed countries inasmuch as a system or formula is established whereby the drawing of funds is automatic without specific policy commitments other than the promise to repay at some time. It is, of course, only a short step from low interest loans with repayment required only if certain price conditions arise, to proposals for commodity related income payments to meet a specific price (as is much the case with domestic U.S. farm policy based on deficiency payments).

Commodity agreements would achieve income transfers through manipulations of prices or quantities sold, while with compensatory financing commodity prices seek their own level, and supplementary or deficiency loans are made. In either case, a major disadvantage is that tying aid to commodity sales means that the greatest amount of aid or income supplements go to those who sell the most. This is not necessarily the best way to redistribute income, either domestically or internationally. For this reason, and because of the costs associated with their operation, commodity arrangements and compensatory financing schemes can be considered inferior methods of providing aid. From the viewpoint of less developed countries, however, they have great political appeal and may have some political advantage in advanced nations. And in any policy question, but particularly in international policy, the political element cannot be ignored.

9

Reducing and Changing Trade Barriers to Assist Developing Countries

A second major policy concern of developing countries is whether trade restrictions can be reduced or restructured to increase exports substantially. This aspect of trade policy encompasses three major issues: (1) the significance of developed countries' import restrictions on primary commodities and whether a reduction in trade barriers can improve the trade position of less developed nations; (2) whether preferences by developed countries have affected exports of the less developed or whether action can be taken to improve the latters' position; and (3) whether free trade areas or customs unions among less developed nations offer any hope for improving development by expanding market size and providing dynamic stimulus to investment and growth.

Trade Restrictions on Agricultural Commodities

The extent to which the trading position of the less developed can be improved through reduction of import barriers by advanced countries can be measured only partially. As implied in chapter 4, such measurement is complicated by variations in international specifications of products, quality differences, and the variety of techniques and methods used for protection.[1] While tariffs are an element of agricultural protection, nontariff barriers are also important. The scope of these restraints as they apply to agricultural products in the four major industrial trading areas is indicated in Table 19.

Table 19. *Primary Commodities: Nontariff Barriers to Imports into Major Industrial Countries, 1971*

Commodities	European Economic Community		Japan		United Kingdom		United States	
	A	B	A	B	A	B	A	B
Food, beverages, and tobacco								
Wheat	CMA	Se	QM	S	—	Sd	Q	Se
Rice	CMA	Se	QM	S	—	—	—	Se
Barley	CMA	Se	QM	S	—	Sd	—	Se
Maize	CMA	Se	—	—	—	—	—	Se
Sugar	CMA	Se	—	S	Q	S	Q	S
Beef and veal	CMA	Se	Q	—	—	Sd	Q ^{a}	—
Pig meat	CMA	Se	M	S	q	Sd	—	—
Mutton and lamb	q ^{b} m ^{b}	—	—	—	—	Sd	Q ^{a}	—
Poultry	CMA	Se	—	—	—	—	—	—
Eggs	CMA	Se	—	O	—	Sd	—	—
Butter and milk	CMA	Se	QM	Sd	Q	S	Q	Se
Fish	CMA	—	q	—	—	S	—	—
Citrus fruit	CMA	Se	q	—	q	—	—	—
Bananas	Q ^{b}	—	—	—	Q	—	—	—
Wine	CMA	S	—	—	—	—	—	—
Tobacco	CMA m ^{b}	Se	M	S	—	—	—	Se
Oilseeds, oils, and fats								
Soya beans and oils	—	—	—	Sd	—	—	—	Se
Groundnuts and oil	—	—	—	—	—	—	q	Se
Cottonseed oil	—	—	—	—	—	—	—	S
Rapeseed and oil	CMA	S	—	Sd	—	—	—	—
Linseed and oil	CMA	S	—	—	—	—	—	S
Sunflower seed and oil	CMA	S	—	—	—	—	—	—
Olive oil	CMA	Sd	—	—	—	—	—	—
Agricultural raw materials								
Cotton	—	—	—	—	—	—	Q	Se
Wool	—	—	—	—	—	S	—	Sd
Jute and bagging	q ^{b}	—	—	—	q	—	—	—

Source: UNCTAD, *Commodity Problems and Policies: Access to Markets*, TD/115, 27 January 1972. Calculated from: EEC Commission, *Fourth General Report on the Activities of the Communities, 1970* (Brussels: February 1971); Great Britain, Ministry of Agriculture, Fisheries and Food, *Annual Review and Determination of Guarantees, 1971* (Cmnd. 4623) (London: H.M.S.O., March 1971); United States, Office of the President, Commission on International Trade and Investment Policy, *United States International Economic Policy in an Interdependent World: Report to the President* (Washington, D.C.: U.S. Government Printing Office, July 1971); and GATT, documents prepared in connection with the work of the Agriculture Committee and the Committee on Trade and Development.

Note: Column A shows the general nature of the restraint at the frontier, a small letter indicating that the measure is applicable to only part of the item in question: M,m indicates state trading or trading by an authorized monopoly; Q, q indicates quota restrictions; and CMA indicates commodity falling under Common Market arrangements.

Column B indicates the general nature of explicit official intervention on domestic markets, not including direct or indirect subsidies of inputs of the primary sector or fiscal privileges accorded to that sector: O indicates organization of the domestic market without official price fixation; S indicates price supported or production subsidy paid; Sd indicates price guaranteed by deficiency payment; and Se indicates support accompanied by provision for export subsidy.

[a] Contingency quotas on beef and veal and mutton, authorized by legislation (not so far applied), accompanied by restraints by supplying countries.

[b] Certain member states only.

A recent study by L. J. Wifp analyzes the protection pattern for U.S. agriculture (Table 20).[2] Wipf reveals a number of things about these programs. First, despite recent changes in U.S. agricultural policy, rather substantial protection continues, but with considerable variation among commodities. Second, there is substantial variation in the relationship between nominal and effective protection levels. Third, a change in the nominal tariff level does not necessarily cause a corresponding change in effective protection. For example, nominal tariff levels for grains in 1968 were substantially lower than 1958 and 1963 levels, but effective protection did not decline measurably. In the case of cotton, nominal tariff levels declined to near zero in 1968, but effective protection increased substantially. The fourth important relationship demonstrated by Wipf is that nontariff barriers dominate for commodities subject to direct price support, while in the case of nonprice support commodities, tariffs continue to be the major form of protection.

As Wipf suggests, these protection levels are likely to be equalled or exceeded by rates of protection in the agricultural sectors of other industrially developed countries. Some indication of this state of affairs is included in Table 21, which shows the ad valorem tariff equivalent of variable levies in the EEC. EEC equivalent tariffs not only are very high, but also have increased substantially in recent years. This contrasts with a substantial decline in nominal protective levels in the United States and a maintenance of the level of effective protection.

In addition to measuring the level of restrictions, other questions must be dealt with in assessing the impact of protection on exports by developing countries. First, the effect of removing protection on a commodity with a high elasticity of demand in advanced countries, where consumption responds substantially to change in price, will be

Table 20. Nominal and Effective Protection in U.S. Agriculture: 1958, 1963, and 1968, in Percentages

Input-output sector	1958 protection rates				1963 protection rates				1968 protection rates			
	TOT NOM (1)	TOT EFF (2)	EFF TRF (3)	EFF NT (4)	TOT NOM (5)	TOT EFF (6)	EFF TRF (7)	EFF NT (8)	TOT NOM (9)	TOT EFF (10)	EFF TRF (11)	EFF NT (12)
Farm level sectors												
Meat animals	8.6	10.8	14.5	3.7	9.2	14.6	14.7	0.1	7.5	13.8	13.2	0.6
Poultry and eggs	0.5	−28.0	−5.2	−22.8	0.3	−11.7	−6.4	−5.3	0.8	−19.6	−16.6	−3.0
Farm dairy products	17.6	41.3	−5.8	47.1	13.6	31.9	−9.8	41.7	16.8	48.2	−3.4	51.6
Other livestock products	0.7	−4.8	−1.9	−2.9	0.2	−5.4	−5.2	−0.2	2.5	3.3	3.5	−0.2
Food grains	40.3	144.4	−2.7	147.1	41.3	158.5	−2.8	161.3	8.4	143.5	−2.7	146.2
Feed crops	13.2	22.6	3.4	19.2	3.7	8.8	7.4	1.4	0.4	8.1	0.0	8.1
Cotton	19.8	57.1	−1.2	58.3	32.2	95.0	−1.3	96.3	0.3	100.8	−1.3	102.1
Tobacco	11.7	19.0	20.5	−1.5	15.0	24.4	15.2	9.2	17.0	28.2	24.5	3.7
Oil-bearing crops	7.2	9.2	13.6	−4.4	10.3	13.6	−0.5	14.1	11.3	16.4	−0.8	17.2
Vegetables	16.6	25.5	26.6	−1.1	16.4	24.8	27.7	−2.9	12.4	17.9	20.8	−2.9
Fruits	15.2	19.8	21.8	−2.0	14.1	17.5	20.2	−2.7	8.4	9.1	11.8	−2.7
Tree nuts	23.0	32.9	40.1	−7.2	13.2	12.4	22.1	−9.7	20.1	25.5	35.2	−9.7
Legume and grass seeds	4.5	5.1	7.1	−2.0	4.7	4.9	7.5	−2.5	6.9	8.7	11.3	−2.6
Sugar and syrup crops	57.4	227.7	34.1	193.6	−6.3	72.6	17.5	55.1	195.8	662.2	72.2	500.0
Miscellaneous	5.2	12.1	13.5	−1.4	8.3	19.7	21.9	−2.2	5.8	13.0	15.2	2.2
Forest products	0.0	−0.7	−0.1	−0.6	0.0	−0.9	−0.1	−0.8	0.0	−0.9	−0.1	−0.8
Greenhouse products	5.2	5.1	6.0	−0.9	4.8	4.5	5.7	−1.2	3.7	3.2	4.4	−1.2
Aggregated sectors												
Livestock and livestock products	9.2	14.6	8.4	6.2	8.7	16.1	7.5	8.6	8.5	18.9	7.5	11.4
Other agricultural products	17.5	33.0	9.5	23.5	14.2	29.5	9.6	19.9	7.6	32.3	6.0	26.3

SOURCE: L. J. Wipf, "Tariffs, Non-Tariff Distortions and Effective Protection in U.S. Agriculture," *American Journal of Agricultural Economics* 53 (August 1971): 423–30.

NOTE: The following abbreviations are used: total nominal rate (TOT NOM); total effective rate (TOT EFF); effective tariff rate (EFF TRF); and effective nontariff rate (EFF NT).

Table 21. *Ad Valorem Tariff Equivalents of Variable Levies in the EEC, 1967–1971, in Percentages*

Commodities	1967–1968	1970–1971
Soft wheat	90.7	89.3
Durum wheat	62.6	82.0
Rye	68.9	72.4
Barley	62.5	46.0
Oats	54.4	42.4
Maize	65.5	40.8
Sorghum	61.0	49.2
Rice, husked or polished, excluding broken	18.0	110.2
Rice, broken	0.0	60.4
Sugar, raw	—	110.0
Sugar, white	—	155.3
Olive oil	24.1	4.5[b]
Pig meat	43.7	53.3
Eggs in the shell	34.2	37.2
Chicken, eviscerated	22.9	23.5
Turkeys, eviscerated	23.8	26.0
Butter	—	214.2
Fat cattle (excluding calves)[a]	—	20.7
Calves[a]	—	1.1

SOURCE: UNCTAD, *Commodity Problems and Policies: Access to Markets*, TC/115, 27 January 1972. Calculated from EEC, *Marchés agricoles, Prix*, various issues.

NOTE: As a rule figures shown represent yearly averages of levies imposed expressed as percentages of average c.i.f. prices of imports to which levies applied during the year. The yearly averages relate to the period 1 August – 31 July, except for rice (1 September – 31 August), sugar (1 July – 30 June), and olive oil (1 November – 31 October).

[a] Excluding *ad valorem* tariff of 16 percent for live animals. (As regards beef and veal, an *ad valorem* tariff of 20 percent — to which variable levies are added — is applied).

[b] Average for first 10 months of year.

quite different from the effect on a commodity with low price elasticity. Second, there is the issue of the competitive relationship in production both between advanced and less developed countries and among the less developed. Little is gained by less developed countries if one or more advanced nation is the low cost producer. It would be hard to visualize any gain to the less developed from a reduction in trade restrictions on dairy products, for example. Third, there is the matter of competitive relationships in processing and the implications of locational economics in terms of transport costs on unprocessed versus processed products. If transport and processing costs are minimized by shipping raw materials and when processing plants are located near consuming centers, no gain necessarily arises from reducing protection on processed products. If, on the other hand, both production and processing costs are lower in outlying areas, potential for gain is possible by reducing the restrictions that protect producers and processors. Finally, in assessing the potential effect of reducing trade restrictions, attention must be given to the nature of competition and potential flow of gain and losses resulting from expanded trade. Competition can exist on commodities produced generally by advanced countries and generally by the less advanced, or generally by the less advanced and by a few advanced countries. Or the reverse may occur, and competition can exist between one or two advanced nations and among many or few less advanced countries. Some commodities are produced by large numbers of less developed countries, and trading relationships are general. Other commodities are produced by only a few nations, and the flow of gains, if any, are concentrated. Within individual countries, gains may accrue to many or a few domestic producers or, in some cases, largely to foreign investors. These variations suggest that broad generalizations concerning the effects of reducing trade restraints and market intervention by advanced countries always must be qualified and that changes will have differential impacts among underdeveloped nations. Very few changes would be Pareto better in the sense that no country would be made worse off.

While a full analysis of the effect of barriers on developing nations' exports is infeasible, useful insight can be gained by looking at differences among major commodities groups. Those that should be considered include temperate zone products, temperate-tropical food commodities, tropical food commodities, and raw materials. Competitive conditions, policy problems, and the potential gains from reducing trade barriers vary substantially among these.

Temperate Zone Products

The major commodities included in the temperate zone agricultural category are wheat, feed grains, and livestock products, both meat and dairy. Historically, these items have been traded almost exclusively among advanced countries with the major exception of exports by Argentina and of exports of grains — largely wheat — to less developed areas. It could be argued that the major restrictions and support programs in advanced countries result in a net benefit to the less developed. Surpluses, particularly of wheat, have been generated, and export subsidy programs have led to lower cost commercial imports. In addition, major food aid shipments have been created as a result of surplus production in industrial nations. Controversy exists over the effect of food aid on receiving countries, and no doubt its impact has varied greatly among recipients, but empirical evidence indicates that food aid has been a positive element in overall economic development by increasing the total assets available for investment and consumption.[3]

With the exception of limited amounts of rice, developing countries generally are not competitive on world grain markets. Livestock commodities have both a high income and price elasticity of demand. If support levels and prices were allowed to drop substantially, particularly in Western Europe and Japan, consumption would increase measurably. Price reductions also would increase consumption in North America, although probably less so than in these other areas. If this drop were to occur, there is some question whether the advanced exporting nations plus Argentina could supply the market, or whether room would be left for major exports from potential livestock producing areas in the less developed countries. Exports of livestock products could be of importance, for example, to Brazil, which has massive resources to produce livestock and feed grains, and to a lesser degree to several other Latin American countries and to parts of Africa. In the case of livestock products, historical trade patterns do not provide a foundation for estimating the potential effect of reduced trade barriers. Both the questions of the competitive relationship between historical export areas, primarily Australia, New Zealand, and Argentina, as well as the ability of new producing areas to enter these fields would become important.

Temperate zone commodities dominate in total agricultural production and are at the center of programs for income improvements in agriculture in industrial countries. Reductions in protection levels become closely related to conditions within individual countries, and changes in trade policy will be contingent upon major shifts in domestic policy. Major domestic policy decisions thus are prerequisite to changes in trade policy.

Temperate-Tropical Products

The temperate-tropical category includes commodities produced and traded both by less developed and by advanced countries. Sugar provides a classic example of disruption of world markets by the action of advanced nations. The most extreme situation exists in Western Europe, where most countries protect and promote the production of sugar at very high prices. Less developed nations could satisfy demand at much lower prices — probably at no more than one-third of the level consumers presently pay for domestic production. The six-member European Economic Community recently has become fully self-sufficient and has spent major sums of money for domestic support of sugar in surplus production. Subsidized diversion to livestock feed has been used to reduce periodic surplus.[4] Furthermore, EEC import policy is based upon a levy system that excludes the possibility of income transfers over and above market price to less developed countries.

The U.S. sugar program has been based on a complicated policy that calls for a domestic quota; in recent years it has increased from about 45 percent to approximately 60 percent of total U.S. consumption. It differs from the EEC program in that U.S. imports are paid for at domestic price support levels, creating competition among foreign countries for the U.S. sugar quota.

Although sugar is the most highly politicized of commodities in this group, there are major protection programs for others. Extensive protection against imports of fruits and vegetables exists in the EEC. The United States maintains prohibitive quotas on protected oils and oilseed such as peanuts and flaxseed. It would appear that considerable gain could accrue to developing countries by reducing protection and permitting forces of comparative advantage to operate for these commodities. Not only would lower prices have a demand effect that would result in increased consumption, but also supply displacement — the movement of production from industrial to less developed countries — could be important for some items. As with temperate zone commodities, lowering protection will require changes in domestic policy, but would involve only limited numbers of producers. These groups, however, tend to be well organized and have substantial political power. Liberalization will be difficult to achieve.

Tropical Food Commodities

Since tropical products are produced exclusively in less developed and imported largely by developed countries, the question of trade expansion centers around potential increases in demand in the advanced countries and the price-consumption response that would occur if existing trade barriers were reduced. These barriers are primarily consumption taxes levied on several commodities in European countries (Table 22).

While the tax is significant, demand is relatively inelastic for most of the items, and its abolition would not result in massive new revenues to developing countries. UNCTAD has suggested other actions to im-

Table 22. *Revenue Proceeds from Internal Fiscal Charges and Tariffs on Specified Commodities in Major Industrial Countries, 1969, in Millions of U.S. Dollars*

	Coffee	Cocoa	Tea	Bananas
EEC				
Internal charges	459	10	10	44
Tariffs	55	19	4	10
Belgium				
Internal charges	5	—	—	—
Federal Republic of Germany				
Internal charges	283	—	10	—
France				
Internal charges	51 [a]	—	— [b]	—
Italy				
Internal charges	120	10	—	44
Netherlands				
Internal charges	—	—	—	—
Japan				
Internal charges	5	—	—	—
Tariffs	—	1	4	59
United Kingdom				
Internal charges	—	—	—	—
Tariffs	2	—	—	—
United States				
Internal charges	—	—	—	—
Tariffs	—	—	—	—

SOURCE: UNCTAD, *Commodity Problems and Policies: Access to Markets*, TD/115, 27 January 1972.

NOTE: Fiscal charges exclude general turnover or sales taxes and taxes on value added in the EEC. Tariff proceeds generally were estimated by applying ad valorem tariff rates extant in 1969 to the value of dutiable imports in 1969.

[a] This figure relates to the year 1967, since when the "taxe unique sur les cafes et les thes" has been replaced by taxes on value added. It includes revenue from indirect taxes on tea.

[b] Included in figure for coffee.

[c] The profits (or excess of revenue over expenditure) of the state trading monopoly in tobacco are regarded as "internal charges" in the context of this table.

prove revenues from these commodities.[5] Because demand is inelastic, action by exporting countries could include imposition of uniform export taxes or minimum levels of export prices through collective agreement. Possible action by advanced nations could include payment to exporting countries of all or a portion of the revenue duties collected on imported tropical products, or compensatory arrangements under which all or part of the difference between actual prices and an agreed reference price would be paid. These payments could be financed from direct budgetary appropriations or by levies against consumers, which would influence prices. As indicated in Table 23, the amounts involved in programs of this kind, especially for coffee, could be

Table 23. *Estimated Effect of Alternative Fiscal Policies on the Export Earnings of Main Producing Countries, in Millions of U.S. Dollars*

	Coffee	Cocoa	Tea	Oranges[a]	Bananas	Total
Imports						
EEC and EFTA countries	707	243	333	283	159	1,725
Total revenue collected	591	70	20	77	27	785
Revenue as a percentage						
of imports	83.0	29.0	6.0	27.0	17.0	45.0
Effect of:						
(a) Abolition of all						
fiscal charges:						
Assumption A[b]	41	9	—	17	8	75
Assumption B	51	12	—	26	16	105
(b) Transfer of revenue						
20 percent	101	14	4	15	5	139
50 percent	253	31	10	37	13	344
Exports						
Values of countries						
included (to all markets)	1,460	450	550	270	270	3,000
Percentage increase under:						
(a) Assumption B	3.5	3.0	—	10.0	6.0	3.5
(b) Transfer of 50						
percent of revenue	17.0	7.0	2.0	14.0	5.0	11.0

SOURCE: Data from UNCTAD, *Commodity Problems and Policies,* vol. 2, Second Session, New Delhi, 1968, p. 49.
NOTE: Prepared on the basis of 1961 data.
[a] Including tangerines.
[b] Assumptions A and B refer to the behavior of retail margins in case of elimination of charges. Under A the (gross) retail margin per unit, and under B the total margin, would remain constant. In the second case, the decline of the retail price (and hence the increase in demand) would be greater.

considerable, and the gains to developing countries far exceed those which would accrue from eliminating the charges. While reducing trade barriers on exports may be easier than for products produced domestically, the gain to developing countries appears limited. Recognizing this, UNCTAD has proposed direct action to increase returns beyond those that would accrue from a freer market.

Nonfood Primary Products

The economic framework surrounding the nonfood primary products is complex and diverse. Import demand is not based upon direct human consumption, but is related to industrial raw material requirements. These in turn are closely related to rates of economic growth, both in manufacturing and service industries, and are complicated by technological gains that utilize substitutes. Major policy programs influence trade in these commodities, especially for cotton and, to a lesser degree, other fibers, minerals, and agricultural products.

The U.S. cotton price program has been a classic case of market interference having a direct impact on less developed countries and without a clear perspective of the consequences. These latter have not always been detrimental to less developed countries. During the period of high price supports, U.S. storage and stockage programs substantially reduced U.S. exports, and the slack was taken up by expanded production in developing areas, primarily North Africa. But after stimulating this kind of structural shift, the U.S. program changed and currently is aimed at recapturing markets for U.S. producers. If this is accomplished, export sales by less developed countries will be reduced sharply.

Restrictions on imports of nonfood primary commodities are diverse and often severe. Tobacco is heavily taxed by most countries and is often subject to almost total monopoly control by states. U.S. price support policy and quota arrangements place severe limitations on imports of both cotton and wool. Major importing areas maintain protection on most mineral imports, and in the case of petroleum, heavy taxation for revenue purposes tends to depress consumption.

The problems facing exporters of nonfood primary products include direct restrictions on primary product trade, competition from synthetic substitutes, and restrictions on processed products derived from their raw materials. A broad program of trade negotiation along with technical advance and improvements in production of raw materials and products that are competitive with synthetics is needed to improve developing nations' export earnings.

Consequences and Policies

Protection of the kind used in industrial countries can have two principal effects on markets. First, consumption in protected markets declines. Second, domestic production is stimulated, often resulting in a surplus of high cost products. Trade is affected both because this process tends to close off or reduce levels of imports and surpluses are placed on world markets at subsidized prices. World market prices are depressed and outlets are reduced in competing nonsupported import markets. Developing country exporters absorb these losses.

The 1964 UNCTAD conference envisaged the improvement of access to primary commodity markets in developed countries as involving a series of measures which can be summarized as follows:[6] (1) removal or reduction of direct obstacles, such as quantitative restrictions, tariffs, and internal fiscal charges; (2) modification of domestic policies which stimulate uneconomic production and adversely affect trade; (3) guarantees to developing countries which ensure fair and reasonable shares of markets and market growth; (4) avoidance of subsidization of primary commodities exports in a manner injurious to the exports of developing countries; and (5) exercise of special care in the disposal of agricultural surpluses.

Reduction of barriers to agricultural commodities in industrial countries will prove difficult. If it can be achieved only with major structural reform in agriculture, as argued in chapter 6, the process will be very slow. In the case of temperate zone products, conflict among advanced countries has generated extensive discussion in international forums. For commodities protected primarily by industrial countries against exports from the less developed, bargaining has not been extensive. Little or no progress was made or even attempted on most temperate-tropical or tropical products during the Kennedy Round.

The number of commodities of export interest to developing nations is increasing due partially to the Green Revolution and the resulting expansion in output of grain and partially to developments such as the expanded output of maize in Thailand and the discovery of oil in Nigeria. These events have occurred during a time when little has been achieved toward reducing the trade barriers on primary products of export interest to the less developed.

In the future, increased efforts should be made to expand developing nations' earnings from primary product exports. To achieve this, the industrial countries will have to take the initiative and generate concrete terms for improved market opportunities for these countries. A standstill on protection by the more advanced will not achieve this objective. Gradual reduction in both the level of protection for primary commodities and the proportion of protected output should be sought.

Another approach would be to change the form of protection. The use of deficiency payments often has been suggested as being less in conflict with trade than direct price support. To the extent that these payments do not influence consumption, this is true. Yet, movement is clearly in the other direction, and with the entry of the United Kingdom, Ireland, and Denmark into the EEC there has been a move not only toward higher support levels but also away from the use of deficiency payments to that of direct price support. Even without deficiency payments, one step that could be taken to reduce the demand effect of protection would be to provide income or subsidy payments on agricultural commodities that, in turn, are inputs for other agricultural producers (subsidizing grain, for example, which is used in production of livestock products). Removal of the demand effects of price supports would have the greatest implication for livestock products, and a major reduction could be achieved with lower grain prices.

A second approach to traditional agricultural programs would be to eliminate their stimulus to output, including adopting more programs that control and reduce production of certain commodities (such as sugar) in industrial countries. If appropriately guided, this policy could be translated into a market-sharing approach that would stabilize domestic production and potentially provide the basis for expansion of exports by developing countries. A counterpart recommendation is that consideration be given to expanding the number of commodities subject to agreed price levels, such as existed in the U.S. sugar program and in the British sugar agreement.

Another approach advocated by less developed countries is that industrial nations which do not wish to change their import programs or reduce restrictions should compensate the less developed for resulting losses. In theory, there are two approaches: Exporting countries could levy a tax and raise prices to some preagreed level, or industrial countries could compensate developing ones for losses due to import restrictions. In either case, compensation could equal or exceed the gains to developing countries from the elimination of trade barriers if demand is price inelastic.

In theory, price compensation schemes could be implemented on a comprehensive basis. J. E. Meade has suggested such a scheme be based on the principle of a compensation agreement between any two countries covering both a standard or reference price for commodity and a standard quantity, with compensation by one party to the other if deviations from the norm occur.[7] The chief problems would be establishing prices and quotas and estimating deviation from normal prices and quotas for compensation purposes. Long-term adjustments in the norm to account for general market trends would be required for continued workability.

Less developed countries could gain from a commodity policy in several ways. As indicated in the previous chapter, improvement for a limited number of items could be achieved through international commodity agreements and financial measures in support of export earnings by developing countries. Although there are major technical problems in operating these kinds of arrangements, recent experience with the coffee agreement and with the IMF compensatory financing program indicates they are not insuperable. The most crucial issue involved in shifting commodity policy is the extent to which industrial countries will be willing to reduce the level and coverage of protection for their agriculture. Until and unless this is achieved, developing nations will have limited opportunity for expansion of exports, even in those commodities where they have competitive advantage. A corollary question — short of major trade liberalization — concerns the extent to which industrial countries will permit imports to share in expansion of their domestic markets as economic growth occurs. As indicated above, the reverse has occurred for some commodities, such as sugar. If extended to primary products of export interest to developing countries, market sharing programs could help expand foreign exchange earnings for these nations and at the same time minimize domestic political problems that might arise if protection were withdrawn.

The gains from such actions, of course, are not limited to increased foreign exchange earnings by developing countries. Immediate gains accrue to importing nations through lower cost raw materials and food supplies. Even modest initial actions, if designed to fulfill the objective of reducing or eliminating protection for high cost production or of increasing market shares for low cost producers, could open the way for consideration of national policies through international trade negotiation. Such actions also could result in more comprehensive arrangements that would increase export opportunities for low cost producers in both industrial and developing countries.

Protection for Processing and Manufactures

Another major area of concern for the less developed is industrialization and trade in processed products and manufactures. Primary commodities still represent the bulk of exports for these nations, but increasing emphasis is being placed on the need to develop manufactures as a source of expanded exports. Faced with the difficulties of export market development and problems associated with generally lower levels of skills and technology, less developed countries, with a few notable exceptions such as South Korea, have emphasized industrialization for domestic use. But continued progress in development increasingly will require competitive exports of processed and manufactured products.

Problems encountered in developing industrial exports will vary among countries, and it is unlikely that any single model or format of industrialization will be generally applicable. Variations in level of development, natural resource base, size and skill of the labor force, nature of institutional and technical infrastructure, and a variety of other considerations will condition the individual situation. In addition, all will face high rates of technological development in advanced countries that will lead to increasingly difficult competition in international markets. Unknown factors are the impact multinational corporations will have on industrial growth in less developed countries and the kind of policy format that will be required to provide a positive rather than an exploitative relationship between these corporations and their hosts. Multinational corporations can represent an important means of transferring capital and technology to less developed nations, yet the issues of controlling and guiding their operations to complement development plans will have to be met if maximum benefit is to be achieved.

In looking at data on exports of manufactures from less developed countries, two facts become clear. One is illustrated in Table 24, which shows that a large proportion of manufactured exports are based on agricultural raw materials; thus, we do not leave the realm of agriculture in dealing with policy issues related to manufactures. In 1965, 74 percent, in terms of value, of the developed market economy countries' imports of manufactures and semimanufactures from the developing countries consisted of 20 products or product groups. The second fact is that during the decade of the 1960s manufactures were the most rapidly growing category of less developed country exports. In fact, during the latter part of the decade they accelerated more rapidly than did total world trade in manufactures. Exports of manufactures grew at an annual average rate of nearly 11 percent for the period 1960–1969, and increased from approximately 10 to 18 percent of total developing nation exports.[8] While these aggregate results are encouraging, they conceal a number of factors which make the overall results far less so. One is the distribution of exports. In 1969, six developing nations and territories accounted for almost 60 percent of the exports of manufactures from developing countries to developed market economies, while approximately 80 percent of the exports to socialist countries originated in three developing nations, only two of which were among the six major exporters to developed market economies.[9]

For the future a paramount issue facing the less developed is whether an expanded basis can be established for trade in industrial

Table 24. *Imports by Developed Countries of Manufactures and Semimanufactures from Less Developed Countries, 1965, in Millions of U.S. Dollars*

Product	Value of imports, 1965
1. Clothing	432
2. Fabric (other than cotton)	252
3. Shaped wood	216
4. Alcoholic beverages	200
5. Cotton fabrics	194
6. Fruit, preserved, and fruit preparations	154
7. Meat, preserved, and meat preparations	143
8. Floor coverings	138
9. Plywood and veneers	118
10. Leather products	97
11. Textile products n.e.s.[a]	91
12. Manufactured articles n.e.s.[b]	91
13. Inorganic chemicals	86
14. Vegetables, preserved or prepared	78
15. Pig-iron, and so forth	65
16. Perambulators and toys	65
17. Silver, platinum, and so forth	63
18. Fish, preserved, and fish preparations	62
19. Textile yarn and thread	56
20. Essential oils and perfumes	53

SOURCE: UNCTAD, *Problems and Policies of Trade in Manufactures and Semi-manufactures* (Report of 2nd Session), New Delhi, 1968.

[a] SITC group 656: Bags and sacks, tents, blankets, and so forth.
[b] SITC group 899: Handicrafts, toilet articles, artificial flowers, articles of human hair, and so forth.

products both among the less developed and between the less developed and the advanced industrial countries. As indicated in Table 25, tariff levels facing processed and manufactured exports by less developed countries are still significant and rise as the degree of processing increases. These data represent nominal tariffs and do not indicate the extent of protection as would be measured in effective tariff rates, nor do they include any measure of nontariff barriers, which in some cases are extensive.

Some indication of the relationship between these nominal and effective rates can be obtained from Table 26. These computations are based on estimates of the relationship between nominal and effective rates for groups of manufactured products of interest to less developed countries using 1963–1964 tariff levels. There are variations in commodities due to differences in input mix and the degree to which inputs are imported, but a general consistency is apparent. The difference between nominal and effective tariffs on imported construction material is relatively small, but for other categories the range is from a low of 1.5 to a high of 2.4. On the average, for all commodities the effective rate was 1.6 to 1.8 times the level of the nominal rate in the individual country or groups of countries in 1962 (see Table 26). This relationship is probably not greatly different today; hence, some indication of effective tariffs in 1969 can be inferred from data in Table 25.

Viewed in this context there is substantial room for improving the trade position of less developed countries by lowering tariffs, despite the reductions made during the Kennedy Round. The extent of the gain will depend upon existing input-output relationships and the leverage effect that reductions in nominal tariffs have on the effective rates. Where a high effective rate is created by a small nominal one, even a minor shift in the nominal rate can create a substantial shift in competitive relationships.

The issue of nontariff barriers also is important, but there are no data to quantify their effect on developing nations' exports. The following catalog of the kinds of nontariff barriers in existence has been made by UNCTAD:

    I. Foreign Trade Policies
        License requirements, quota restrictions, negotiated export limitations, foreign exchange restrictions, state trading, procurement policies favoring domestic products, antidumping and similar regulations, subsidies to exports.
    II. Administrative Practices
        Classification of goods for custom purposes, documentary mark-

Table 25. *Average Tariff Protection in Developed Market Economy Countries for Four Groups of Products Arranged According to Different Stages of Processing*

Products, dutiable imports from developing countries	Six member Common Market	United States	Japan	United Kingdom
Raw rubber	3.3	8.2	7.2	5.0
$3.0 million	0-5	3-16	0-8	0-8
Rubber, semimanufactured products	6.3	11.0	7.5	8.7
$0.8 million	3-10	3.38	3-10	5-18
Rubber, manufactured articles	8.3	8.7	10.8	11.1
$62.7 million	8-10	2-35	8-15	8-18
Wool	2.3	14.9	5.0	7.0
$39.0 million	0-3	0-43	0-5	0-10
Wool yarns	6.8	16.8	5.5	10.3
$0.9 million	4-11	5-30	5-8	8-13
Wool fabrics	11.8	35.2	10.3	17.5
$5.4 million	8-18	9-100	8-16	17-5
Cotton	1.5	5.9	0.0	5.0
$43. 1 million	0-2	0-9	0	0-5
Cotton yarns	7.4	11.6	7.8	10.3
$29.2 million	4-12	4-20	6-11	8-13
Cotton fabrics	13.0	18.4	11.2	20.0
$104.9 million	9-15	7-35	7-14	18-25
Jute	0.0	6.3	0.0	5.0
$0.001 million	0	5-8	0	5
Jute yarns	8.0	10.4	10.0	13.3
$0.6 million	8	7-13	10	10-15
Jute fabrics	19.0	8.5	20.0	20.0
$12.8 million	15-22	3-23	20	20
Clothing and clothing accessories	11.6	22.6	17.3	19.4
$417.8 million	5-20	3-65	10-30	5-25
Raw hides and skins	0.0	25.7	10.0	0.0
$1.4 million	0	2-41	5-20	0
Semimanufactured products of leather	5.0	6.4	15.1	10.3
$61.5 million	3-8	0-19	8-25	5-20
Manufactured articles of leather	8.7	17.5	15.0	15.3
$13.4 million	5-13	3-87	8-25	8-25
Wood and cork in the rough	3.9	7.0	3.8	4.3
$4.2 million	0-7	0-12	0-10	0-5
Wood based panels	12.7	12.6	18.0	10.8
$70.5 million	12-13	6-20	15-20	5-18
Wood and cork, semimanufactured products	5.3	6.6	9.0	6.2
$30.7 million	3-10	0-14	0-20	4-15
Wood and cork manufactured articles	7.9	10.4	11.4	8.0
$21.8 million	4-16	3-26	5-40	3-15

Table 25 — *Continued*

Products, dutiable imports from developing countries	Six member Common Market	United States	Japan	United Kingdom
Paper pulp and paper waste	2.8	0.0	5.0	7.5
$6.8 million	2-3	0	0-5	5-10
Paper and paperboard	10.6	6.2	9.2	14.5
$5.2 million	3-14	1-34	3-20	10-18
Printed matter	8.4	4.8	7.5	9.8
$0.8 million	0-13	0-10	0-8	0-12
Pulp and paper, manufactured articles	12.4	6.7	7.9	13.5
$1.5 million	8-15	1-14	5-15	10-18
Copper, unwrought	0.0	3.9	7.4	7.5
$496.1 million	0	2-11	3-15	5-10
Copper, semi-manufactures	7.4	8.0	16.5	11.3
$14.6 million	2-10	2-16	10-20	8-15
Nickel, unwrought	0.0	4.9	18.7	5.0
$0.2 million	0	2-9	11-23	5
Nickel, semi-manufactures	5.1	8.9	14.5	8.5
$0.3 million	1-9	2-16	0-23	8-10
Aluminum, unwrought	6.0	4.5	6.8	5.0
$10.4 million	4-9	4-5	3-9	5
Aluminum, semi-manufactures	10.9	7.7	14.9	8.7
$7.7 million	8-12	2-20	10-18	8-10
Lead, unwrought	5.4	9.0	8.4	5.0
$58.0 million	5	8-10	5-12	5
Lead, semi-manufactures	9.2	7.8	15.6	9.0
$0.5 million	3-11	5-15	10-20	8-10
Zinc, unwrought	4.6	11.2	4.4	3.3
$22.4 million	5	5-19	3-8	2-5
Zinc, semi-manufactures	9.2	7.9	10.4	9.0
$4.7 million	6-10	2-12	8-15	8-10
Gas	1.5	0.0	15.3	5.0
$31.3 million	2	0	11-20	5
Crude petroleum	0.0	3.6	12.2	0.0
$2,262.2 million	0	3-5	12	0
Products derived from coal, petroleum or gas	4.5	9.1	11.5	5.0
$1,206.8 million	0-7	0-27	0-62	3-10

SOURCE: UNCTAD, *The Generalized System of Preferences*, TD/124, November, 1971.

Table 26. *Average Nominal and Effective Tariff Rates on Manufactures of Export Interest to Less Developed Countries, 1962, in Percentages*

	United States	United Kingdom	Common Market	Sweden	Japan
Group I[a]					
Nominal	8.8	11.1	7.6	3.0	11.4
Effective	17.6	23.1	12.0	5.3	23.8
Ratio	2.0	2.1	1.6	1.8	2.1
Group II[b]					
Nominal	15.2	17.2	13.3	8.5	16.6
Effective	28.6	34.3	28.3	20.8	34.5
Ratio	1.9	2.0	2.1	2.4	2.1
Group III[c]					
Nominal	17.5	23.8	17.8	12.4	27.5
Effective	25.9	40.4	30.9	23.9	50.1
Ratio	1.5	1.7	1.7	1.9	1.8
Group IV[d]					
Nominal	10.3	17.0	11.7	8.5	17.1
Effective	13.9	23.0	15.0	12.1	22.0
Ratio	1.3	1.3	1.3	1.4	1.3
All Groups					
Nominal	11.6	15.5	11.9	6.8	16.2
Effective	20.0	27.8	18.6	12.5	29.5
Ratio	1.7	1.8	1.6	1.8	1.8

SOURCE: Based on data in Harry G. Johnson, *Trade Policies Toward Less Developed Countries* (Washington, D.C.: The Brookings Institute, 1967), pp. 174-75.

[a] Average of 9 manufactures that make up intermediate products and whose main inputs are natural raw material.
[b] Average of 10 manufactures that make up intermediate products but at a higher level of fabrication than Group I.
[c] Average of 10 manufactures that make up consumer goods.
[d] Average of 5 manufactures that make up investment goods.

ing and packaging requirements, incomplete or delayed publication of customs information.

III. Internal Economic Policies Affecting Imports
Internal taxes for revenue purposes, taxes applied to imports to compensate for indirect taxes borne by comparable domestic goods, pricing policies and price control regulations, restrictions on advertising.

IV. Internal Health and Safety Regulations Affecting Imports
Sanitary regulations, technical specification requirements, regulations applied for national security reasons.[10]

In addition to these governmental procedures, informal arrangements both by governments and the branches of multinational corporations must be taken into account in assessing the range of controls on exports of manufactured products. Voluntary agreements among governments, such as those in cotton textiles and the U.S. beef import system, have become increasingly important.

Cotton, in particular, has been subject to formal international control and to voluntary restriction. An initiative on cotton undertaken by the United States in 1961 in GATT to establish a long-term cotton textile arrangement aimed at regulating imports into the United States of cotton textile products with a controlled rate of expansion. The arrangement was agreed to by European countries and represented the first international trade agreement that dealt with market access on a controlled basis. The 1961 agreement permitted any nation to establish a restriction for the following year on cotton textile product imports not below that which existed the previous year. As noted by John Evans,

> the stated objective of the arrangement was "orderly" expansion of international trade in cotton textiles, but its most important operative articles provided that:
>
> a. If imports from a participating country "should cause or threaten disruption" in the market or another participating country, the latter might ask the exporting country to restrict its shipments.
>
> b. If no agreement on the level of restraint were reached, the importing country might, regardless of the provisions of the GATT, impose quantitative restrictions on imports from the exporting country in those categories of textiles causing the market disruption.
>
> c. Any import quotas so imposed could be no lower than the level of imports in the year ending three months before request. Where such quotas were maintained for more than one year they were required to be increased by at least 6 percent each year.[11]

Recent U.S. actions to negotiate "voluntary" constraints on exports of cotton textiles to the United States by main suppliers is a step beyond the restrictions imposed through the preexisting formal international arrangements. Producers of other raw materials and derived manufactures also have been put on notice that success in market expansion at the expense of producers or industries existing in the United States will not be permitted.

An exhaustive study would be required to determine whether the expansion of multinational corporations has been a negative or a positive factor in the growth of manufactured exports from developing nations. These corporations' development within individual countries for import substitution purposes could well have the effect of expanding input import requirements, and they could have a negative effect on the balance of payments. On the other hand, if they are moving to less developed countries in order to be more competitive in world markets, the general effect can be to stimulate export development. The problem of measuring the extent to which tariffs and other forms of protection inhibit the development of export industries in less developed countries is a difficult one. Two major questions are involved. One is determining the actual level of protection and measuring the demand effect that would occur in industrial nations if tariffs were reduced. Initially the demand effect would depend upon price elasticity which, in turn, would be conditioned by consumer preferences, the closeness of substitute commodities, and the degree of price change. In a longer term perspective, the competitive reaction that occurs in developed countries due to substitute commodities and the stimulus to lower cost production that follows will have an important effect. A second major uncertainty is the extent to which the less developed could increase production if markets were available. The assumption by spokesmen for developing nations seems to be that the elasticity of supply for most commodities and derivative products is infinite. This is hardly likely. In some areas, the capital and technical know-how greatly to expand production of existing industries probably is not available. Over the long run, training and capital accumulation for expansion could occur, but probably not rapidly. Even more crucial is the question of whether new industries can be developed that will broaden the base for industrial development and restructure the economy in such a way that a foundation for continuing adjustment and innovation is developed. Aside from policy at the international level, these become crucial internal issues within developing countries, and policy should be formulated to complement international policy adjustments.

Trade policy for the less developed must be created in light of the role they can play in the world economy and the interaction between this role and economic development. Historically, the less advanced have traded primarily with the advanced, with only limited exchange among themselves. Their exports have been raw materials, their imports manufactures. A basic issue in international policy as viewed by developing countries is how this structure can be changed. The less advanced have sought to eliminate their dependence on external sources through import substitution. This policy has led to high cost industries in small markets and often to expanded import requirements for raw material and replacement capital that create severe balance-of-payments problems. Basically, import substitution has sought to isolate developing countries from international markets, although in many cases unsuccessfully or at great economic cost. The limitation of import substitution as a viable policy for individual nations is now generally recognized, and developing countries have accepted a new approach to trade policy that seeks to increase exports of manufactured goods to industrial countries and expand trade among themselves.

The GATT Model for Trade Liberalization

Whether or not GATT has or can be effective in negotiating policies that will materially improve the trade position of developing countries is not clear. The GATT model of trade negotiation is based upon the conviction that, if allowed to, international price systems will work and that movement toward universal competition is correct in trade policy negotiations. Within this philosophical framework, two major concepts are involved in guiding GATT's bargaining procedures. One is reciprocity, or the notion that all concessions by a given country must be offset by concessions obtained from a bargaining adversary. The other is the concept of nondiscrimination, or the belief that a concession granted to one country also must be granted to all others, hence, bilateral bargaining will result in the general reduction of tariff levels.

These two principles plus general political conditions surrounding GATT negotiations have ensured that limited benefit would accrue to developing countries. In point of fact it is clear that since its conception in 1947, GATT negotiations primarily have been bargaining sessions between and among industrial countries. Negotiations have focused on interrelationships between North America and Europe and have centered on industrial products. Gain to the less developed has been minimal. On the other hand, quotas and protection in industrial countries have tended to increase on some items of export interest to the less developed, especially those of agricultural origin, and a number of special arrangements, such as the Cotton Textile Agreement, have been developed under GATT auspices. These kinds of actions reflect internal conditions within individual countries, but also can be encouraged by the most-favored-nation principle. If concessions between two countries are passed on to all others, incentive is provided to maintain protection levels at or above production cost in the two bargaining countries. An implication of nondiscrimination is that bargaining parties will not create a situation where they are no longer adequately protected from third countries which have a cost advantage. Some nations in Europe, for example, have maintained protection against Japanese goods by failure to extend most-favored-nation treatment and, more recently, through quota arrangements. Another implication of the GATT program is that many of the sanctioned exceptions to GATT principles have impinged heavily on agriculture and raw materials; these have been the commodities of greatest interest to the less developed.

While no quantitative assessment has been made of the gains and losses to developing countries as a result of GATT negotiations, it would appear that both the principles upon which GATT was established and the context within which negotiations have occurred would confirm developing nations' contention that GATT has been of little direct benefit to them. Where negotiations have been fruitful for industrial commodities, less developed countries often have little basis for offering a quid pro quo. High cost import substitution industries do not provide a basis for seeking trade concessions that will increase exports. To seek these kinds of concessions on specific commodities, a planning decision would be required to channel industrialization toward exports of specific commodities where concessions can be obtained. This implies internal decisions on development that very few countries have been in a position to make. Scarce capital has been oriented toward industrialization for domestic markets, and only a few nations, of which Japan is the outstanding example, have succeeded in achieving broadly based industrialization to help fill the demand in the domestic market and expand exports.[12]

A major input into the analysis of GATT's role in trade policy was developed in a 1964 United Nations study, "The Developing Countries and the GATT."[13] This UNCTAD study points out GATT shortcomings in relation to the problem confronting developing countries and makes some final recommendations: "(a) A full recognition of the significance of the problem of economic development for world trade; (b) differentiation between countries of various levels of economic development and of different economic and social systems; and (c) positive and deliberate action to promote the exports of developing countries, overcome the obstacles of agricultural protection and industrial discrimination, and provide for preferential treatment and other special measures of aid and encouragement."

Discussions of trade policies in UNCTAD were followed by recognition in 1965 by industrial countries of the special nature of trade problems facing the less developed. A new chapter was added to the GATT agreement. The major principle enunciated by UNCTAD, namely, that positive efforts beyond multilateral and reciprocal reduction in tariffs are needed to improve trading positions of less developed countries, appears to have been accepted. The GATT chapter contains three important articles.

> Article 36 on principles and objectives, states the need for rapid and sustained expansion of export earnings by these countries and for positive efforts to insure them an appropriate share in the growth of world trade: the need to provide better conditions of access to world markets for primary products and wherever appropriate to devise measures designed to stabilize and improve conditions of world markets in these products including, in particular, measures designed to obtain stable, equitable and remunerative prices: the need for increased access to markets for processed and manufactured products of particular current or potential interest to less developed countries and the principle that developed countries do not expect reciprocity for commitments to reduce barriers to the trade of less developed countries. Article 27, on commitments, pledges the developed contracting parties to accord high priority to the production and elimination of barriers to products of particular export interest to the less developed contracting parties, including barriers that differentiate unreasonably between such products in their primary and processed form; to refrain from increasing barriers against such products; and to refrain from increasing, and give high priority to reducing, fiscal measures hindering the growth of consumption of primary products wholly or mainly produced in less developed contracting parties. Article 28, on joint action, provides for collaboration in implementing the objectives.[14]

While there appears to be rather broad agreement that some form of policy unique to the trade problems of the less developed is warranted, only limited progress has been made in specifying the detailed nature and content of policies. During discussions in the Kennedy Round and in UNCTAD sessions, major cleavages appeared between the United States and Europe and between developed and less developed countries. The European model of aid for the less developed and, in fact, in the case of agricultural trade policies, centered on the need to organize international markets. The EEC, under the guidance of French thought, accepted the concept of nonreciprocal concessions, but only on a special bilateral basis which would permit differentiation among countries and specific situations. The United States, on the other hand, retained its philosophy of multilateral, nondiscriminatory reduction of trade barriers and remained reluctant to accept the concept of preferences except insofar as these apply to customs unions. The developing countries, in addition to seeking reduction of trade barriers by developed nations, especially those that discriminate against processed products and manufactures, have pursued policies aimed at restructuring tariff systems to achieve preferences from advanced countries and to create preference systems among themselves. The first of these requires that developed countries reduce barriers to imports from developing ones on a nonreciprocal basis and at the same time maintain restrictions on trade among themselves. The second approach requires that groups of developing countries maintain restrictions against imports from other areas and reduce or eliminate barriers among themselves through the formation of free trade areas or customs unions.

The UNCTAD Model: Trade Preferences

The arguments for trade preferences by less advanced countries rest upon three interrelated concepts: (1) the infant industry argument; (2) the economy of scale question; and (3) the notion that industrial exports must become an important vehicle of development for many countries.

The need for increased industrial exports by the less developed has evolved over time and has been articulated most directly by Raul Prebisch.[15] He begins by asserting that, because of declining markets for agricultural products and raw materials, the ability of less developed countries to purchase industrial imports required for development is diminished. As a result, import substitution industries were created to produce domestically those commodities for which there was insufficient foreign exchange to purchase them internationally. But many countries have completed the easy phases of import substitution and some have reached the point where high cost domestic industries, particularly those that produce inputs for agriculture, have begun to have a detrimental effect on economic development. Further reduction of import requirements is no longer feasible. Developing countries, on the other hand, need to expand their capacity to pay for capital equipment and technical assistance, and a major portion of this will have to be accomplished by expanding exports. Because of the low demand elasticities for many primary products, the inroads synthetic substitutes have made, the effects of protection policies in industrial countries, and the effects of stimulated production which reduces the need for imports, rapid expansion in traditional commodity markets cannot be expected. The alternative is to expand industrial exports. In order to compete in advanced country industrial markets, efficient and low cost production must be stimulated. But because of major differences in technological sophistication between developed and developing nations, infant industry protection will be required to foster export industries.

Furthermore, as these industries develop they will have to achieve economies of scale to remain competitive. Because the markets available in many developed countries are small, economies cannot be achieved without expanding external market outlets; hence, exports are required.

The rationale for tariff preferences is built upon a philosophical as well as a practical economic analytical basis. Philosophically, it is argued that equal treatment of unequals becomes by definition inequality, thus, preferences are justified in the name of equity.[16] But even with an accepted rationale, a number of important problems exist in developing a workable preference system.

One of the practical issues is this very question of equity. The range of development is great among less developed countries, and the resource base and the kind of treatment needed to stimulate development also vary greatly. If equal treatment represents inequity between developed and less developed countries as a group, then equal treatment represents inequity between the more and least advantaged countries among the underdeveloped. The issue of how treatment should be differentiated in setting up a system of preferences is important. At one level, the equity question concerns determining which nations should be considered underdeveloped; at another level, it concerns determining which kinds of special needs and concessions should be granted, how they will complicate the problems of administering a system of preferences, and what special provisions will be required for operating the system.

The least advantaged of the developing countries need the most assistance if they are to break away from traditional export systems. This could be accomplished in a number of ways. Part of the gains available to the more advanced developing countries, as the result of preferences, could be distributed to the less advanced. This is not simply a matter of transferring income, but rather of providing technical and capital assistance that can influence development. Another approach would be to couple preferences with programs of active assistance and aid by industrial countries to the least developed. Or a system to establish differentiated preference rates could be used so that greater preferences are granted to the least developed. But all these approaches assume that sufficient analysis and knowledge is available to program and guide the kind of industrial export capacity that will be of long-run benefit to individual nations. That this can be achieved is a heroic assumption. At minimum, a very broadly based analysis of the economic development in each country would be required to make even preliminary judgments about internally and externally oriented industrial structures. In countries which rely largely on a single agricultural commodity, the first direction for industrialization might be toward processing that commodity. However, this is no guarantee that an individual country will achieve competitive status vis-à-vis other less developed countries exporting to industrial nations.

Another major question concerns the duration of the system and, in particular, the point at which competitive operation is reached by less advanced countries so that preferences no longer are needed. If preferences stimulate economic development, by definition they should be temporary. If they are viewed as perpetual, this might remove the stimulus for producers and policy makers to increase efficiency and improve production systems. The threat of change, if not actual preconceived plans for reduction or elimination, should be built into preference systems. Phased reduction could be based on a time pattern in which, following a specified period, preferences could be reduced on a scheduled basis with complete elimination at some stated time. Another measure to ensure that the system is temporary is the suggestion that preferences granted to the developing countries be extended on a most-favored-nation basis to all countries after a certain period. This plan would link preferences with a commitment by industrial countries to reduce general tariff levels and would have an overall trade liberalizing effect. Such an agreement, implemented in a future period, would be very difficult to achieve among industrial nations.

Special relationships between industrial countries, such as the EEC and former colonies, have to be taken into account in establishing preferences and devising administrative procedures. It would appear from progress to date that problems of this kind will not be handled systematically. Individual industrial nations will grant preferences in line with internal feasibility, and it is not likely that procedural coordination will be forthcoming.

A major issue concerns the procedures for establishing preferences, including questions such as the extent of reduction, exceptions to protection, the way nontariff barriers are to be handled, and how private trade practices can be encompassed within a preference system. Management of the escape clause presents special problems. Under GATT regulations, no countries will permit substantial injury to domestic industries as a result of tariff preferences. Both developing and less developed countries appear to accept the facts that various initial exceptions have to be stated and that industrial countries need to be flexible and retain internal political options concerning imports.[17] A problem arises in that great variation can exist among countries in implementing the escape clause. In situations where political pressures are great, it can become a method of raising trade barriers in the guise of accepted international procedure for trade policy.

Another approach is to eliminate escape clauses and require that individual importing countries commit a portion of their markets to foreign suppliers. Such a tariff quota approach has the advantage of automaticity and could be established so that industrial countries agree to a gradual expansion of the import quota as consumption rates increase. This would provide a high degree of predictability in import requirements and remove a great deal of uncertainty from production planning in exporting countries. The program would operate very similarly to that specified in the British grains agreement and thus is not without precedent.[18] That agreement, however, had no specifications concerning the participation by individual exporters in the market. An extension of this form of quota arrangement could assign quotas to individual exporting countries, as existed for U.S. sugar. Obviously, competition among less developed nations easily could be eliminated, and the political factor involved in administering preferences would be greatly increased. Not only would domestic policy be important in allocating the market between domestic and foreign producers, but also foreign policy would become important in allocation among individual exporters.

General or Selective Preference

Nations disagree about whether preferences should be a generalized system applicable to all developing countries and all commodities with only specific negotiated exemptions, or whether they should be granted only selectively. A number of industrial countries accept the position that preferences should be general; others do not. "France has suggested a concept of preferential tariffs which are *selective* — as regards the countries which grant them or benefit from them — and are *temporary* and *digressive* as regards the products they affect."[19] There are several aspects to the problems of establishing and implementing preferential treatment. Two major arguments are used in support of selective preferences: One need select only those products for which the infant industry argument seems reasonable and for which the prospect for future competitiveness exists, and by giving preferences selectively by countries, allocation can assure gain for countries at different levels of development and in relationship to their capacity to take advantage of export opportunities.

The central issue in these conclusions is that those nations giving preferences retain a great deal more control over which countries benefit and which industries within a country receive preferences. If used appropriately, preferences can be differentiated among developing countries to serve efficiency and equity criteria. Selectivity also allows for a great deal of autonomy in granting preferences. International agreements on objectives and procedures need not be obtained. No internationally agreed upon principles or criteria need be defined, and wide differences could evolve among donor countries. In this framework, preferences also can be used as a political tool and can be devised on a regional basis or to promote special relationships among developed and developing countries.

General preferences would be nondiscriminatory in the traditional sense, and gains would tend to flow among less developed countries to those endowed with a better resource base. The less developed among the developing nations may be even worse off under an open system of nonselective preferences.

Assessment of Preferences

Trade preferences for developing countries encompass two major economic concerns. One is the short-term trade creation/trade diversion effect and its implications for closing the export gap and providing the basis for a short-run increase in capital and other imports in less developed nations. The second relates to the dynamic implications of the infant industry argument such as increased market size which could result in the development of scale economies and a stimulus to international transfer of capital and technology.

The extent of short-run gains will depend upon the degree of preference granted the relative supply and demand elasticities in the countries involved and the relationship between production costs in countries that grant preferences and those that receive them. Where developing nations have a cost advantage and demand is elastic, even nominal reductions in restrictions could increase their exports measurably. Inelastic demand will inhibit short-run trade shifts. If supply displacement occurs, trade shifts will follow. An outstanding case in point is sugar. Preferences on sugar and sugar products or even free trade would cause massive displacement of sugar production from North America and Europe. A major benefit could accrue to developing countries through increased foreign exchange earnings, increased employment, and the beginnings of diversification through expansion of processing industries.[20]

The overall effect of trade preferences cannot be clearly judged without more quantitative research than is currently available. Depending upon previous production and trade arrangements, the principal effect may be for producers in the preference receiving countries to displace production in the preference granting country. If the latter has previously imported, the displacement may be largely against producers in other exporting countries or a combination of this effect and displacement of producers in the preference granting countries. The extent to which each occurs for individual products will depend upon relative cost levels and the degree to which the importing countries previously were protecting their own producers from foreign competition.

Another effect is that income will be transferred from the importing country or from the competing exporting country that does not receive preference to the one that receives preference. Also, because the preference receiving country will not in turn grant reciprocal reductions in restrictions, its balance-of-payments position should improve.

A final issue in developing preference systems is determining how they should be related to other aspects of international commercial policy and in what way this form of aid should be coordinated with direct aid, commodity agreements, compensatory financing, and other efforts to provide a consistent noncontradictory program that will contribute to economic development and yet retain a semblance of equity and generality in international relations. A danger lies in the temptation to develop spheres of influence and regional isolation among groups of countries as the extent and form of administered aid and trade programs increase. In the future even greater emphasis should be placed on achieving multilateral action through international organizations and on reducing unilateral, bilateral, and individual actions in relationships between industrial and less developed countries.

Free Trade Areas and Customs Unions

A final important element of the UNCTAD proposals is the development of preference systems among less developed countries. Economic integration may well be the most important method for expansion of their industrial development and improvement of economic efficiency. The proposal appears to be supported by virtually all industrial nations and is not in conflict with agreements reached in GATT. Developing countries have shown considerable enthusiasm for regional integration, and a number of arrangements have been made, including some of substantial duration. The Central American Common Market has been operating with some apparent success for approximately fifteen years, and the East African Federation has operated nearly twenty years. The largest of all, the Latin American Free Trade Association (LAFTA), has been operative since the mid-1960s, although it is less integrated than the other two units.[21] The belief that the less developed can benefit from integration seemingly emanates from the successful development of the EEC, coincident with rapid economic growth within the area. The assumption is that similar results can be achieved in less developed areas.

Broadly, the analysis of the gains or losses from economic integration can be viewed from three different welfare perspectives: that of the world as a whole, that of individual countries composing the union, or that of the nonmember country. Initial theorizing about customs unions was concerned largely with the first of these points and focused on trade diversion and trade creation and their impact on income distribution and resource use efficiency.[22] Our concern here is with the workability of preferences among developing countries and their effect on improving economic efficiency and growth rates. Improvement in production efficiency has to do with achieving higher output-input ratios, the gains from specialization, the gains from economies of size, and the reallocation of resource use within the area. The theory of customs unions has led to a number of rather specific criteria for evaluating this kind of potential gain. One is that the larger the economic size of the union, the greater are the possible gains from integration. Greater size leads to increased potential for the division of

labor and increased scope for specialization. The basis for the reallocation of resources within the area increases as the area becomes larger.

A second proposition is that the higher the initial height of tariffs or
trade restraints among the countries forming the union, the greater
will be the economic and welfare gain resulting from their elimination.
Balassa has observed that the smallness of GNP has been used as an
argument to stress the inherent limitations for the reallocation of
resources in a developing nations' union, especially considering the
considerable portion of the GNP which is produced in the subsistence
sector.[23] He rightly criticizes this position because it assumes as given
the economic and institutional structure of these countries and fails to
consider the causes of the low level of interregional trade as well as the
possibilities for change. It can be argued that the economic union is
precisely the tool that would allow increased trade and more efficient
allocation of resources among those involved. It consequently could be
argued that the larger the size of the union, but the smaller the degree
of economic intercourse, the higher the potential prospect for increased trade and more efficient division of labor. This development
would occur, however, only if the economic distance among countries
were sufficiently reduced and if tariffs or other policy restraints were
the principal reason for preexisting low economic intercourse. On the
other hand, if countries are geographically distant or if trade is hampered by transportation, communication, language, cultural, or even
political differences, the simple removal of trade restrictions may have
little impact.

Also of great importance for developing countries, at least in assessing the short-term effects of preferences, are the structural characteristics and the resource base of the economies involved. If all nations
produced the same basic mix of products based on similar resource
endowments with a similar quality of labor force and technical
capacities, the removal of trade barriers among them likely would have
little short-run impact on specialization or improvement of economic
efficiency. Such countries also are likely to be at similar levels of
economic development, and consumption patterns will contain the
same general mix of expenditures for food, clothing, consumer dura-
bles, transportation, and other industrial items. Demand is not likely to
be a differentiating factor that will stimulate trade among the parties.
However, if the participants differ basically, with some degree of initial
industrial specialization, particularly if based on varying resource endowments, specialization and development can be directly stimulated.
In this context the structure of internal demand and particularly price

elasticities of demand can have a significant impact. Specialization will occur more easily and most rapidly for those commodities which have a relatively high price elasticity of demand and if supply response is sufficient to fulfill the quantities needed. This situation will lead to expansion and capturing scale economies in those industries where they are relevant.

Economic integration among less developed countries also may provide a basis for coordinated regional development and investment planning. This concept should be viewed from two levels. One relates to regional planning, such as for transportation and communication infrastructures. In addition, coordination of educational facilities, particularly among small countries, can provide great savings and often is necessary for efficiency. The other aspect of integration is the question of economic polarization and the need to plan for the distribution of industry among countries. Regional integration is a technique for widening the basis for import substitution, but if this is implemented, the issue becomes one of where it will occur and who specifically will benefit. In general, industry tends to move toward areas where development is already well along and the needed infrastructure as well as labor resources and other facilities are available. Poor countries and poor areas within countries remain poor, while richer countries and richer areas gain. It is argued that this kind of distributional problem requires internal, coordinated planning for the location of newly developed industries. But this planning in itself presents a major problem. Some industries must locate close to sources of raw materials or to markets by virtue of the economics of transportation and transfer. Although other industries face no such constraints, the problem of effective investment planning has proven difficult to achieve. As stated by J. N. Behrman: "To avoid polarization, parts of complex industries or complete simple industries would have to go to the less as well as the more developed of the countries."[24]

But even if effective plans and coordination could be developed among governments, the problem of implementing these programs, vis-à-vis the private sector, is difficult. As indicated by S. S. Dell, "the basic difficulty lies in the tendency of new enterprises to gravitate to those areas where an industrial base and all the requisite facilities already exist. But the problem has been intensified by a system under which the poorer areas are compelled to buy high cost manufactures from the richer areas, thus in effect subsidizing their industries."[25]

Two major issues lie at the heart of the polarization problem. One relates to income distribution and the other to comparative advantage and efficiency. The distribution question has been dealt with by B. F. Massell,[26] and it is apparent that Dell's suggestions for Latin America hold true on a broader basis. The second issue was discussed in chapter 6. If there are trade-offs between efficiency and growth and equity, as by implication there will be in regional development planning, what are the criteria for decisions on plant location, infrastructure development, and so forth? The answer cannot be defined solely by economists and must enter the realm of political feasibility.

Administrative and political feasibility thus presents a major problem in generating successful integration among less developed countries. As noted by Dell,[27]

> proposals for economic fusion in Central America have been bedeviled for years by political animosities and upheavals, and similar friction has occurred in the south between Argentina and Chile and between Chile and Peru. In Africa and Asia there are pronounced rivalries between the neutralist countries and those following the political line of one or another of the Western powers. In Africa, moreover, it is inconceivable that any common market could be formed which would include the Union of South Africa, so long as the latter maintains its present policy of white supremacy. Similar policies followed in Southern Rhodesia have undermined the Federation of Rhodesia and Nyasaland despite the general need for greater unification in Africa.

A more comprehensive analysis of political problems in LAFTA confirms this observation and points out that, despite serious efforts at international negotiation, progress has been slow; "to override reliance on traditional means of problem solving and dependencies on speical interests, a crisis is needed."[28] If this is true, meaningful integration will not necessarily occur simply because economic gain can be demonstrated. It must depend upon a felt political need for cooperation among countries.

Summary

It has been said that preferential treatment for exports of developing nations "would help the industries of developing countries to overcome the difficulties that they encounter in export markets because of their high initial costs."[29] The foundation for preference thus is an extension of the infant industry argument. The issue at stake is whether preferences will lead to the kinds of change and adjustment that will result in efficient long-term industrialization and development of a viable economy. The starting point for the argument, both for preferences by industrial countries and preferences among developing countries, is the need for increasing the size of the market, permitting growth, specialization, and technological change that will reduce cost, stimulate dynamic growth, and permit more rational development planning. Whether this can occur is largely an empirical question, the answer to which can be arrived at only through experimentation or research.

Intuitively, however, a number of issues must be raised. Given the resource base available, with capital in relatively short supply and often with large supplies of labor, how broadly based is comparative advantage in less developed countries? Can they export to industrial countries even if no import restrictions exist? Which infant industries can grow up to become competitive in world markets? Economies of scale tend to be most important in such heavy industries as automobiles, machinery and equipment, and steel. In general, these are capital-using industries where plant economies are substantial. They require considerable research and development as well as large-scale coordinated distribution systems and follow-up service. It is not likely that less developed countries will compete actively with industrial nations in these areas. Another industrial category in which an inherent comparative advantage exists for developed countries is that subject to highly dynamic technological innovations such as aviation, computers, and the like. Here the scale question becomes one of the size of the national underpinning in education, management, and the ability to generate production systems from large numbers of firms and very often government.

The competitive position of developing countries is liable to be strongest in those areas where economies of scale are relatively less important, where technology is less sophisticated, and where the production system is not dependent upon broadly based and sophisticated education and management techniques. The toy industry, bicycles, small motors, sewing machines, and processing of domestic agricultural products are examples. If these are the only industries in which developing countries can compete even with preferences, preferences by industrial countries in themselves are not liable to carry many nations far on the path toward industrialization. Some growth potential would exist, but it would fall far short of that required for general industrialization and development.

But would preferences among developing countries be any different? In general, the pertinent questions are similar to those noted above. If one can assume that sufficient progress is made in any industry so that exports to industrial countries are competitive, it will represent low cost production, and displacement by exports from industrial nations is unlikely. If preferences are general, the competitive stimulus among the less advanced in seeking export outlets in industrial countries should result in production shifts on the basis of comparative advantage among countries, except insofar as special preference arrangements prevent this from happening. Furthermore, if forming a preferential area results in an influx of external capital, technology, and managerial capacity, as has been the case in the EEC, this could have major implications for improving production and reducing costs. On the other hand, a preference system may not create a situation in which exports from developing nations become broadly competitive in industrial market economies. While industry in a regional group of developing nations may be lower cost as a result of scale and other improvements than possibly could be achieved by the individual countries, they may continue to require protection from competition from industrial countries.

Industries that require very large-scale and sophisticated technology and substantial managerial know-how could be developed and protected ad infinitum from the pressures of international competition. Just as in the past there was a tendency for individual countries to overextend import substitution, the same could occur at a higher level in customs unions. The policy issue involved includes the potential positive effect of larger markets and the derivative consequences for production as well as the question of the level of protection, degree of self-sufficiency, and extent of import substitution sought by regional groupings of developing countries. The international policy questions facing integrated groups will not differ materially from those that face individual countries. Their magnitude and the decision-making process required in their resolution, however, will be very different.

10

Trade Sector Planning

The formation of UNCTAD in 1964 issued in an era of collective demands by less developed countries for changes in the rules concerning trade among nations.[1] Emphasis has been placed on the need to revise international policy so that export outlets can be expanded, terms of trade improved, and import capacities of developing nations increased, both through more exports and expanded aid. A vital and largely missing link in the UNCTAD program of trade and development analysis is assessment of the potential for economic change and policy response within developing countries to improve trade positions and to achieve greater development impact.

This perspective, which tends to "export" the policy problem, accepts trade as an important factor in development and emphasizes market limitations, structural differences among countries, and policy impediments as limitations on the rate at which countries can develop. By implication, if trade restrictions by importing nations were reduced, if income elasticities of demand for the products the less developed export were greater, and if market organization were such that the gains from improvement in productivity were distributed more equally to sellers and buyers, a major constraint on growth potentials for developing countries would be eliminated. Recommendations for policy change by UNCTAD are aimed at reducing these kinds of constraints.

Why so little emphasis has been placed on defining the policy adjustments and planning focuses needed to improve the linkage between trade patterns and development within individual countries is not easy to discern. As suggested by George Hicks and Geoffrey McNicol, "it is possible that modern study of the very different 19th century development experience and the anti-colonial reaction to the exploitive foreign-created export economies has succeeded not only in greatly advancing the knowledge of the various trading problems facing the developing countries (adverse terms of trade, instability of earnings, etc.) but also, on a less conscious level, in largely suppressing serious thought on the issue of the role of trade in economic development."[2] Whatever the reason, there tends to have been a "closed economy" approach to development in many countries at the working and planning level, with trade viewed largely as a constraint outside the control of individual governments. Even at the analytical level, emphasis has been on aggregate growth models which tend to treat trade as a constraint on planning flexibility rather than as an integral component of the planning and development mechanism.

A number of influential spokesmen and UNCTAD have accepted a limited and, in some cases negative, role for trade in development. This position is based on the argument that trade leads to a dualistic economic structure with a high productivity sector producing for export, coexisting with a low productivity sector producing for the domestic market. The linkage between these sectors is asserted to be limited if it exists at all; hence, the effect of exports on employment and development in the domestic sector is minimal. To the extent that this kind of dualism does exist, trade can become largely isolated from economic development, particularly if it is accompanied by increasing distortions in income distribution and if the isolation is supported by government policies on investment, imports, and taxation.

While the extent and nature of economic dualism has not been documented empirically, there is a distinction between the role of trade in development as visualized in classical economics and as it apparently materialized during the twentieth century. Recent gains in trade by developing nations do not appear to have created important development effects in many cases. The reason for this should be sought, in part, in the conditions and policies within these countries. As suggested by Gerald Meier, "instead of seeking an answer in the allegedly unfavorable effects of international trade, we may find a more convincing explanation in the differential effects of different exports and in the domestic market conditions of the poor countries."[3]

The essence of Meier's argument is that external phenomena are not the sole determinants of developing nations' trade position and that heterogeneity and variations exist among these countries with respect to export base and market conditions that influence the potential role of trade in development. While the less developed justifiably are concerned with external obstacles to exports and the effect of international trade policy on investment and development of their economies, a major policy concern is their ability to affect their own destinies and implement development policies that take account of the relationship between trade, both imports and exports, and the rate of development generated. This process requires explicit recognition of the interaction between trade and development and the formulation of policy and planning mechanisms that facilitate development of an open economy. The issues and policies involved in this kind of planning require a great deal of investigation before many conclusive generalizations can be stated. The need for exploration, even if tentative, of conceptual and applied guidelines, however, is apparent and is the focus of the remainder of this chapter.

Marginal Adjustment and Development

In classical theory, the development of trade is embedded in the principle of comparative advantage through which efficiency is promoted by specialization. Specialization and trade, in turn, will result in gain through such things as the transmission of knowledge and the accumulation of capital and will stimulate growth. The efficiency effect of comparative advantage arises from the assumption that production will adjust among regions or countries until the opportunity cost of producing a given commodity is equated with the import or export price as determined in perfectly competitive markets. Countries will export commodities in which they have a comparative advantage and import those for which a comparative disadvantage exists. Both the resource allocation effect and the growth effects are postulated on the assumption that freely operating markets will allocate resources to maximize total output at any point in time. By implication, if growth occurs as a result of the transfer of technology, capital, or know-how, adjustment to a new and efficient equilibrium follows. No conflict exists between achieving gains from specialization and trade and maximizing economic growth.

Much of the recent economic literature on trade and development explicitly or implicitly recognizes shortcomings in this classical approach and seeks to establish guidelines for planning under conditions where optimal adjustment does not occur automatically through the market. The movement from market economics to development planning creates the need for planning criteria. Contemporary economic theorists have taken two approaches. One seeks to build on traditional concepts of comparative advantage by providing decision rules for resource allocation and policy formulation that more clearly reflect current conditions and that seek to bridge the gap between allocative efficiency criteria and the dynamics of growth and development. The other essentially ignores the constraints of allocative efficiency and seeks to deal with development planning in the context of dynamic interactions among sectors and the need to generate structural change in the economy. This latter approach focuses on the question of balanced and unbalanced growth. The real distinction between the two is that one continues to reflect the concepts of marginal economics, while the other emphasizes nonmarginal or structural change.

The marginalist approach has sought to establish criteria for resource allocation under conditions where perfect markets do not exist or where optimum short-term resource allocation does not necessarily fulfill growth objectives.[4] The most widely advocated criterion is based on resource availability. This approach asserts that a country should seek to devise a development strategy that conserves its scarce factor and uses proportionately more of its abundant factor. This reasoning reflects the modern version of trade theory, which attributes comparative advantage largely to differences in factor endowment. One is led directly to the conclusion that less developed countries should produce and export commodities with limited use of capital and should import items that are capital intensive. The proposed criterion for selecting commodities to produce and sectors to develop is that planning should seek to minimize the ratio of capital to output or of capital to labor in determining production mix and growth objectives. This criterion will lead to defining comparative advantage in terms of capital availability since capital is the scarce factor in developing countries.

Exclusive reliance on capital-output ratios begs two very important questions. It in no way accounts for differences in the availability or productivity of other factors, either labor or natural resources, nor does it deal with problems of how to measure output. These shortcomings, in turn, have led to several efforts to measure more comprehensively the productivity of all resources by specifying input-output relations on a project basis and by introducing the concept of social marginal product (SMP). Whereas the capital-output approach focuses on assessing the increase in market value of output of alternative commodities from a marginal increase in investment, the SMP criterion seeks to define "the net contribution of a marginal unit (project) to the national product. The related decision rule is to rank investment projects by their SMP and go down the list until the funds to be allocated are exhausted."[5]

Another suggestion is that projects should be chosen to maximize income at some future date.[6] Planning should not be guided by increases in SMP, but should seek to create the highest rate of savings leading to potentially high future growth rates. Clearly this method can produce very different results. The SMP criterion seeks merely to redefine the measure of output within a static adjustment framework, whereas the reinvestment criterion could result in less than maximum short-term output in order to expand output at a future date. As indicated by H. B. Chenery, this method has been widely criticized for its extreme assumptions, "in particular for the use of a social welfare function in which the starvation of half the population in the near future would appear to be a matter of indifference and for the assumption that limitations on fiscal policy make a lower income preferable to a much higher one if the former has a higher savings component."[7]

Another contribution to marginal adjustment theory has been developed by Otto Eckstein. He argues that "achieving a maximum marginal growth contribution from any given investment should be defined to consist of two parts: (1) an efficiency term, consisting of the present value of the consumption stream, and (2) a growth term, consisting of the additional consumption to be achieved by reinvesting savings."[8] Both factors would be weighted in assessing project plans, and, in theory, trade-offs between efficiency and growth could be related to development objectives if adequate data and the measurement techniques were available.

The value of any of these criteria as policy guides is difficult to ascertain. First, each seeks a fixed rule for allocating investment, and each rule leads to a different outcome. Given the complexity of development processes and the diversity of conditions within most developing countries, establishing fixed rules hardly seems to be an enterprise that would enjoy much success. Second, the importance of specific criteria would change under different circumstances and levels of development. Both present and future consumption as well as goals related to employment, foreign exchange earnings, and other factors must be involved in choice. Rules based on a single or unchanging set of objectives probably do not fit many real world planning situations.

Balanced Growth

Another approach to establishing policy criteria for planning by
less developed countries is embedded in the balanced-unbalanced
growth controversy. This discussion has led toward minimizing the
role of trade in development and implies that the traditional concept of
trade-induced growth in the classical sense is no longer relevant. It is, in
fact, within the context of the uncertainty that developing nations will
be able to depend on growth induced from the outside, through
expansion of world demand for their primary products, that Ragnar
Nurske presents his argument for balanced growth.[9] He maintains that
development must be internally generated through expansion of production for domestic markets. However, since markets are limited,
private investment in any single industry considered by itself is dis-
couraged.
     The solution, he argues

> is a balanced pattern of investment in a number of different industries
> such that people working more productively, with more capital and
> improved techniques can become each others customers. . . . The case
> for balanced growth is concerned with establishing a pattern of mutu-
> ally supporting investments over a range of industries wide enough to
> overcome the frustration of isolated advance, in order precisely to
> create a forward momentum of growth. The particular factors that
> determine the optimum pattern of diversification have to do with
> technology, physical conditions and other circumstances that vary
> from country to country.[10]

Essentially, then, balanced growth is an investment strategy that
seeks simultaneous progress in a number of complementary lines or
sectors. In addition, as Nurske points out, the idea is closely related to
the classical law of markets, where supply creates its own demand
provided that supply expansion is along a path determined by the
income elasticity of demand for the product. With investments determined by income elasticities, the balanced growth concept is a free
market approach (behind the solid wall of protection which closes the
economy).
     Critics of the balanced growth argument point out that it is essen-
tially an exercise in comparative statics. The concept of balance is seen
as a successive set of equilibria, but with little insight into what happens
in moving from equilibrium to equilibrium. It is within this context that
A. O. Hirschman enters his "development as a chain of disequilibria"
argument from his theory of "unbalanced growth."[11]

Unbalanced Growth

Hirschman based his conclusions on Tibor Scitovsky's assertion that "profits are an indicator of disequilibrium and the magnitude of profits under a free market system can be regarded as an index of the degree of disequilibrium that exists."[12] Furthermore, it is argued, profits in an industry lead to investment in that industry, and investment tends to eliminate the profits which called it forth. Investment tends to bring equilibrium closer in a particular industry, but through external economies increases profits and creates disequilibrium in another industry.

Development occurs, says Hirschman, when this type of interaction takes place "up and down and across" the whole of an economy's input-output matrix over an extended period.[13] Development strategy or policy must concern itself with creating the kinds of sequences and repercussions described by Scitovsky. Balanced growth and the policies related to it by implication tend to suppress this kind of economic fluctuation.

Whereas Nurske argued for an investment policy within a closed economy where supply would create its own demand, Hirschman argues that the existence of imports provides the safest proof that a market is indeed there. Furthermore, he argues, imports "reconnoiter and map" the country's demand,[14] reduce uncertainty and selling costs, and bring the country closer to the point at which domestic production can be started.

Balanced versus Unbalanced Growth

A number of distinctions between balanced and unbalanced growth are pertinent. The balanced growth position, argues Myint, advocates horizontal industrialization in the area of light consumers' goods. On the other hand, unbalanced growth advocates suggest that more substantial economies can be obtained by a vertical group of industries at different stages of production, each of which is the other's supplier or customer.[15]

Myint points out distinctive differences between the two approaches in terms of protectionist policies. The "horizontal diversification" of balanced growth calls for a policy of protection "in breadth," whereas the "vertical diversification" of unbalanced growth calls for a policy of "in-depth" protection. Myint argues the Hirschman position explicitly favors manufacturing over agriculture because, through the vertical linkages possible, it is a more effective stimulus to economic development.[16]

Discussing the two approaches, Paul Streeten elaborates on the role of government planning implied (to him) by each.[17] Although Nurske argues that balanced growth is relevant to a private enterprise economy, Streeten states that the indivisibilities assumed by it imply the need for coordination. On the other hand, unbalanced growth, as propounded by Hirschman, states Streeten, does not require initial and continued planning. The role of the state can be limited to reducing and repairing disequilibria. Since in disequilibrium the potential exists for significant excess capacities which no private firm may be willing or able to carry, unbalanced growth may be significantly improved through the process of government planning. Both theories presuppose planning, albeit of different kinds.

As is the case with investment criteria, the extent to which either argument can be generalized is questionable. Analysis of intersectoral relationships and interaction among sectors is relevant to development planning. But to argue that balance or imbalance represents a generalized path to development, or even that they have sufficient general validity to justify protective trade policy by developing countries, is unwarranted. A firmer conclusion at this point is that no single theoretical structure exists that can provide a complete foundation for development planning. None can span the spectrum of differences in preexisting conditions that face individual countries with respect to level of per capita income, resource base, degree of infrastructure development, total economic size, and other diversities. Rather than concentrate on single comprehensive theoretical guidelines, the need in economic analysis would seem to be to draw upon various theories in analyzing specific situations. Differences among countries almost certainly assure that any single policy objective including free trade and market determined adjustment will have widely differing impacts on different nations. The potential for import substitution and balanced growth is greater in larger countries with a diversified resource base. But even when this is the case, some specialization for export normally will be required.

The relation between balance and imbalance would seem to shift as countries move up in income level. Ultimately, all seek to achieve a diversified economic structure with extensive vertical depth. All want to achieve industrialization with as broad a spectrum of support through production of agricultural products and raw materials as the natural resource base permits. The issue for developing nations, however, is how to start the process. For all countries, developing requires planning, and planning requires choice concerning which industries and activities to promote for domestic consumption, how to expand exports, and how much import substitution should be achieved and at what cost. While no general guidelines fit all circumstances, a set of conditions that should be weighted in most situations can be outlined. We now turn to these.

Demand Trends and Sector Planning

Whether formally programmed or not, effective reconciliation of development and comparative advantage criteria requires that specific attention be paid to a number of questions. One of these is the present state and potential development of demand for products that are being produced or potentially can be produced. International markets for agricultural raw materials have presented a particularly important dilemma for less developed countries. In 1972, UNCTAD identified a list of problem commodities:[18]

coffee	cotton	wool
sugar	rubber	hides and skins
tea	oil palm	sisal
rice	jute	essential oils
		vanilla

Growth trends for these items have been insufficient to maintain a favorable world market situation relative to supply growth. In some cases, where production is based on perennial crops, production is sustained for long periods beyond the point of severe price declines. On the other hand, at any time clear growth trends exist for some commodities. In general for agricultural products, world economic growth and the shift toward improved diets has been the underlying factor generating the growth trend. Livestock and feed products and fruits and vegetables tend to have been the most important groups involved. World import demand for minerals and petroleum and other raw materials is sustained by industrial growth in more highly industrialized countries, and relative predictability exists.

A second important demand component that should be encompassed in trade sector planning is that which is internal to individual countries and, in some cases, that which might develop in nearby less developed countries. Densely populated nations with rapid rates of population growth inevitably will have to gauge production toward necessities and subsistence needs. On the other hand, in countries where industrialization is occurring and where income levels, particularly in the urban sector, are increasing, the expansion in demand for higher quality foods, including livestock products, and a variety of durable consumer goods may be relatively rapid.

The overall mix of demand will be related to the structure of the economy and the nature of income distribution. A particularly favorable situation would appear to exist in countries where production planning can be organized to take advantage both of rapidly growing domestic demand and strong positive trends in international markets.[19] A case in point is the beef and livestock industry in Kenya.[20] Urban development in a number of cities, along with a major tourist industry, has resulted in a strong upward trend in domestic demand for meat and provides a foundation for development, particularly of the beef and poultry industries. This situation is strongly complemented by trends in international meat markets, where sales potential for beef in nearby oil-rich Mediterranean areas and other African countries provides a possible outlet beyond that which Kenya currently is able to provide. In addition, investment in disease-free production and slaughtering zones could mean that a potential in Western Europe can be tapped. This kind of demand complementarity for agricultural commodities may represent a special opportunity available to very few countries. It contrasts sharply with the more general situation where world market demand is expanding slowly and domestic demand is nonexistent or at a minimal level as a result of low and slowly increasing per capita incomes or because of the specialty nature of commodities. Although circumstances vary greatly, a key element in planning both for exports and for import substitution is attempting to project effectively domestic and foreign demand trends as a necessary foundation for project and sector planning.

The feedback effect of expanded production on new demand also should be taken into account. If production planning results in concentration of income and demand for consumption, imports may increase sharply. At a second level, demand for producer goods may be expanded greatly, and if this can be fulfilled only through imports, an adverse balance-of-payments effect may occur. On the other hand, any particular development effort, if income is widely distributed, may generate internal demand and provide a definite stimulus for further development. Both preexisting demand trends need to be taken into account with a view toward assessing their implications for generating future growth.

Supply Adjustment and Comparative Advantage

Differences in demand trends and in the demand effect of specific productive activities need to be complemented with concern for a wide range of production and marketing questions. The most thoroughly discussed of these is the extent to which economies of scale are relevant in production and their relationship to the size of the potential market. Internal markets in most developing countries are small, and export development is necessary for achieving substantial scale economies. A major factor in the efforts to create customs unions among the less developed thus has been the need to provide a market adequate for economic production organization.

There are other important questions concerning production organization. One of these is the nature of the production function, including differences among sectors and the extent to which change and improvement can be achieved. It appears generally valid to state that developing countries, particularly in considering export possibilities, should concentrate on those areas in which extensive use is made of resources in plentiful supply. In some countries this resource tends to be primarily labor; in others, natural factors such as land or mineral and petroleum reserves are important. Within the constraints of these generalities, normally there is need for programs of improvement in the effective use of these resources, usually with the requirement that capital be added. Improvements in production functions can be generated in various ways. Under most circumstances, if increased amounts of fertilizer are applied to crops, output will be increased, and costs will be reduced. Hence a short-run gain in comparative advantage will be achieved. Production functions, on the other hand, can be changed through investment in irrigation, improved roads, and various forms of capital investment that will, in general, have a long-term effect and can serve to induce secondary development that otherwise might not occur.

A third form of improvement can arise through internally generated research and development. This normally can be expected to have a permanent and cumulative, self-generating effect. One of the important questions concerning the balance between projects and sectors is the extent of the differences among sectors in their internal capacity to generate improvements in production function and the extent to which this capacity must be supplemented by external assistance. It is accepted that, in the case of agriculture, educational and research assistance must be provided from public sources. But even where this is the case, choices as to how aid should be applied among sectors and where the greatest pay-off can be achieved become an important planning factor. A new dimension, however, should be added for most agricultural commodities. Production can be organized on an integrated basis within the framework of a marketing-processing system where research development and training can be generated internally. In general, industries with large producing firms are more capable of research and of taking advantage of innovations that arise. But often this advantage can be emulated in less developed countries through vertical organization, such as marketing boards. This, in fact, is probably the soundest argument favoring the use of marketing boards.[21]

Another pertinent question concerning the direction of development is the extent to which sectors differ in their self-accumulation of capital. This factor is defined by Maurice Byé as "that part of capital formation directly imputable to productive activity as such and therefore includes the undistributed profits of companies and entrepreneurs."[22] On the one hand, this suggests a profitability criterion in deciding what pattern growth should take, and it could be used as an argument for a free market as opposed to planning. While profits are important, and capital accumulation results from savings, indigenous capital formation also is important, particularly in agricultural pursuits. Farm structures are built with family labor. Land drainage, tiling, and other permanent improvements often stem from indigenous activities which, in essence, reflect the conversion of labor into capital, usually with long-term implication for production and change in comparative advantage.

Market Interactions and Externalities

Another important consideration in relating short-term to long-term comparative advantage and in guiding policy is the nature of the complementarity among sectors and the extent to which gain in one industry or sector will induce change in others. Involved, for example, is the effect of development in a processing or fabricating industry on raw materials industries, or the effect of increased agricultural outputs on stimulating processing and fabricating industry. The complex of possible interactions is both horizontal and vertical and operates through the market system. As stated by Gottfried Haberler: "If industry A invests and expands, it is bound to have pecuniary repercussions on any or all of the following industries: (1) on industries which produce intermediate goods (machinery, materials, etc.) used by A; (2) through cheapening of A's own products, on industries which use A's products as intermediate goods; (3) on industries whose products factors used in A spend their additional income; and (4) on industries whose product is complementary in use to the product of A."[23] These interactions in composite create backward and forward as well as horizontal linkages through the market that, in theory (as argued by the proponents of balanced and unbalanced growth), should generate self-cumulating development. The economic conclusion reached is that, since individual proprietors are not aware of these external effects, the private gain from economic activity is less than the social gain. Market prices under these circumstances are not necessarily an adequate guide for production and investment. This theory can be used as a justification for subsidies or protection to further economic development.

A second form of externality arises because markets fail to operate and gains or losses occur that are external to the market or price system. The most important such externality is the general training and educative effect that arises from some forms of activity. Training interpreted in a broad sense to include technical, managerial, and entrepreneurial capacity created as a by-product of investment and production activity creates a social gain exceeding the market value of products produced. In one form this is the foundation of the infant industry argument, and its attendant conclusion that protection to permit reaching a competitive level of efficiency and skill is warranted.

Clearly, then, the issue of externalities needs to be assessed so that total gains and costs are included in project and plan development. Gains beyond those directly related to a specific activity can be important. Increasingly, the negative factors such as pollution, effects on rural-urban structure, and so forth, are and should be receiving attention.

Furthermore, plans need to be assessed within the constraints of a broad range of market imperfections, rigidities, and inadequacies in the adjustment mechanisms within less developed countries. Markets fail to transmit knowledge of demand trends and are inefficient in the production of time, form, and space utility. They do not provide an adequate guide for capital investment, fail to stimulate the generation and distribution of new technology, and fail to allocate resources effectively, with the result that unemployment and underemployment of

resources occur, particularly labor. In this framework, resource allocation for short-term adjustment is inadequate, and markets fail to stimulate adjustment necessary for long-term growth and development.
Planning is needed that takes account of future prospective changes in
demand and technical conditions, some of which may be foreseen, but
some of which can be predicted only with a great deal of uncertainty.
Predictability of economic structure in itself carries some premium, as
does achieving flexibility through diversity in production pattern.
Theoretical concepts can represent only a limited guide to planning
and can be used only within the context of the environment within
which planning must be done.

The Importance of Transfer Costs

The theory of comparative advantage generally has abstracted
from the question of transfer costs, yet in the dynamic framework of
planning these can become an important variable in determining
economic returns, profitability, and the justification for stimulating
import substituting versus export industries. The nature of the problem is indicated in Figure 14.

Price P_1 indicates the import parity price of a commodity CIF port
of entry. P_0 indicates the export price for the same commodity FOB
port of departure. The gap between import and export parity price
represents transfer costs to and from overseas markets. The demand
curve facing the industry in a closed economy is $D'D'$, while demand in
an open economy is the segmented line $D_1D_2D_3D_4$. At price P_1 imports
will prevent further price rises, and at price P_0 exports will prevent
further price declines. Between P_1 and P_0 domestic demand and supply
will interact to determine price. The price spread $P_2 - P_1$ represents
the range within which protection may occur before high cost domestic
surpluses arise if supply is as represented by S_1. With supply curve S_2,
equilibrium is at price C. With efficient production, as is the case for
supply curve S_3, exports profitably can be made equal to the difference
along the horizontal axis between the point at which domestic supply
and demand intersect (f) and the intersection of S_3 with the export
demand curve at point e.

The spread between import and export parity will vary depending
upon the bulk of the commodity in relation to value, location in relation
to export markets, and to sources of supply for imports. For many of
the commodities involved in developing nations' trade the spread is

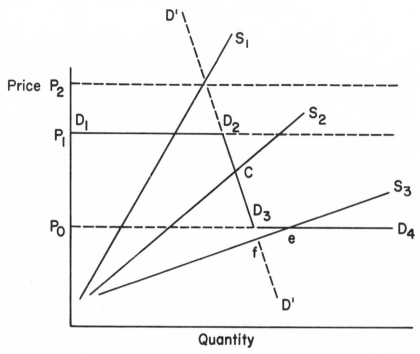

Figure 14. Illustration of Supply and Demand for a Commodity in an Open and Closed Economy

substantial. A recent calculation for maize in Kenya showed, for example, that on a given day the import parity price CIF port of entry was approximately 70s per 200-pound bag. Export price on that same day was approximately 37s. Translated into farm price, an additional 17s was required to move maize from interior points to the port; hence, the export parity price of maize to farmers was approximately 20s. On the other hand, imported maize, if moved to consumers at interior points, increased in price to approximately 85s per bag. These figures illustrate one extremely important problem in applying static comparative advantage analysis to trade policy problems of the less developed, namely, that a major discontinuity in price exists between import and export price, and marginal analysis for decisions on import substitution versus export promotion is meaningless. Marginal analysis is meaningful in determining the mix of commodities to produce for domestic use and the mix to produce for export. It cannot, however, be used to allocate resources between imports and exports.

A dual price structure exists, and a discontinuous price applies in determining resource allocation and output planning. This situation has particularly important applications in agriculture, where allocating resources to export crop production versus domestic food production often is a crucial issue.

In this framework a range of public policy choices can be made. If adequate basic resources exist, investment programs can be established to create supply and move the supply curve outward sufficiently to enter export markets. On the other hand, policy can call for diverting resources into domestic markets at some equilibrium point along the sloping section of the internal demand curve. If output is maintained at a point along the upper horizontal section, $D_1 - D_2$ imports will occur unless protection exists. Import substitution occurs only when monetary policy or specific protective devices are used to raise domestic price above import parity levels. If supply is highly elastic, expanded output resulting from import substitution can be substantial. With appropriate linkages to other sectors of the economy, the development effect can be considerable. Inelastic supply and inadequate linkage to other economic sectors rapidly increase costs of protection, and developmental impacts will be limited. Prices to producers can be reduced below export parity through export taxes, and the implications of this for production are closely related to the supply elasticities. The development impact will be greatest where supply is elastic.

The same kind of distinction which applies at the national or sector level in planning imports or exports is of relevance to individual farmers planning production programs to move from a subsistence to a more commercialized type of agriculture. The opportunity cost of not producing sufficient food for consumption on the farm is the retail price at which it can be purchased. On the other hand, if farmers expand the use of fertilizer inputs, make capital investments, or otherwise take action to increase output to achieve a saleable surplus, the apparent returns to resources are reduced considerably. Given the high marketing cost in many less developed countries, this differential can be substantial. The demand curve facing the individual producer has a horizontal segment at a very high level and drops sharply to a second horizontal segment that may be at a very low level. Beyond subsistence production, the marginal return to additional resource use drops sharply and represents a strong disincentive to expanded output, particularly if achieving the additional output requires purchasing inputs.

Diversification to new crops aimed at increased commercialization should be judged on the same criteria. High resource productivity will be required if small farmers are expected to reduce basic food crop production below their own subsistence level and divert resources into commercial crops for domestic urban use or for export. Output for domestic commercial use can be priced in the market in relationship to import parity price, whereas production for export must be priced in relationship to export parity. The significance of these price differentials is that there is a strong incentive with economic validity to avoid specialization and export as opposed to diversification and self-sufficiency in the case of food commodities. A similar general kind of price pressure exists on industrial commodities. But because of higher ratios of unit values to bulk and marketing costs, the effect is probably of less consequence and often can be far more than offset by differentials in technology, human skills, and scale economies. Domestic production costs also can be very high relative to import parity. Extreme levels of protection will be required in this case, and import substitution becomes very costly.

Strategies for Trade Sector Planning

Economic plans generally are drawn in the context of long-range aggregate change with a view toward achieving increased GNP, increasing employment, maintaining a balance-of-payments position, or other aggregate or macro objectives. Plans are implemented, however, in terms of specific projects and sector programs that hopefully will add up to achievement of aggregate economic goals.[24] In practice, both macro level planning and micro level project selection and implementation often are undertaken with gross inadequacies in data and analysis of potential outcomes. Planning often is done without serious concern about the kinds of decision rules or statements of objective needed to select priorities for specific activities.

All too often individual projects are analyzed in isolation and in terms of the specific immediate results achieved. At least two major questions tend to be overlooked: (1) the nature of interaction among sectors and the kind of direct and indirect effects any specific activity has on other sectors, and (2) the extent to which sequential time effects can be induced as a result of initiating a specific project. The exclusion of either of these factors from project analysis can result either in over- or undervaluing project results.

Another problem in selecting projects is achieving a balance between investment in specific output-increasing activity and in establishing the optimum kinds of rules and procedures that most effectively will implement specific activity yet at the same time contribute to general development through establishing mechanisms to promote improvement in technology, market and institutional systems, and other factors that lead to continuous and spontaneous economic development.

The process of developing guidelines for optimum trade sector planning is not unique in accounting for these kinds of questions. The aggregate guideline that is used or at least counted as a primary decision criterion is the overall balance of payments. Within this framework, decisions concerning the promotion of export commodities, the degree of specialization or diversification, and input substitution become crucial in evaluating specific projects. The role of trade in development will vary greatly among countries depending upon export capacity and the effect any given level of trade has upon development. As pointed out by Gerald Meier,[25] two fundamental elements determine simultaneously the export capacity of developing countries and the effect any given level of trade has upon development. The starting point for assessment of trade position is the export base including resource endowment and the nature of the production function for different commodities and the nature of market conditions broadly defined that provide the environment for production and trade. He concludes that "the strength of stimulus among countries will tend to be stronger, the higher is the growth rate of the export sector; the greater is the direct effect of the export sector on employment and personal income; the less the distribution of export income favors those with higher marginal propensity to import; the more productive is the investment resulting from any saving from export income; the more exports expand through change in production function, rather than simply by a widening process; the more externalities and linkages connected with the export sector; and the more stable are the export receipts retained at home."[26]

When considering both export expansion and import substitutions, trade sector planning is analytically complex. Several economists have suggested that linear programming, wherein objective functions include social costs and wherein constraints are stated in terms of balance-of-payments effects, employment considerations, and other macro level goals, represents a reasonably effective approach to trade sector analysis. As suggested by Chenery, "the linear programming approach provides a convenient link to the principle of comparative advantage because the optimal pattern of trade is determined simultaneously with the optimum allocation of investment."[27] Models, however, can be more general than implied by comparative advantage in that various kinds of constraints can be imposed, and costs and benefits other than those measured in the market can be included in the analysis.

One such system has been made operational in Israel, where the principal objective of the programming is to compute the resource cost of one dollar gained in foreign exchange through alternative export promoting or import substituting activities.[28] Two problems arise in such an approach. One is achieving adequate data to make interproject and intersector comparisons, including specification of the numerous input-output coefficients required. Second, while in theory some secondary and induced effects can be incorporated into the analysis, these largely will reflect static cross-sectional perspectives and will not account for dynamically induced changes that occur in the future as a result of actions taken at any given time. This approach nonetheless represents a step forward from ad hoc planning, and under appropriate circumstances it can provide substantial additional information that may be incorporated into planning by policy makers whose vision hopefully has both broad scope and future perspective.

Export Specialization versus Diversification

The specific options in sectoral planning fall broadly into three categories: (1) those where comparative advantage and production possibilities at cost levels competitive on world markets exist; (2) those where self-sufficiency can be achieved at a cost below import parity price levels but above export parity; and (3) those where production costs exceed import parity.

One approach often put forward as a method for expanding low cost and potentially competitive export production is to exploit unemployed or underemployed land and labor resources more effectively. Where surplus-producing capacity and production above domestic needs can be sold, "vented," on international markets, exports can be expanded at a low or even zero opportunity cost for the resources employed. The vent-for-surplus approach relies on expansion of capacity through increased use of existing resources with a given level of technology. Emphasis is placed on the need for supportive infrastructure, and, as pointed out by Paul Streeten and Diane Elson, "provision of transport, communications and market facilities" is not required.[29] No improvement in resource productivity necessarily is assumed.

For most developing countries, however, the prime source of output expansion is improved land and labor productivity. This requires investment in new technology, education, information services, and production capital as well as supporting infrastructure.

But investment to expand productivity above domestic requirements is a route to development increasingly hampered by slow market growth and uncertainty for many products for which developing counties have or can develop comparative advantage. This raises the question of the degree to which specialization through export-led policies should be pursued and the extent to which diversification should be sought for both domestic requirements and export.

Diversification may take a number of directions. A recent IBRD-IMF staff study indicates that most of that which has taken place in less developed countries in recent years has been aimed at agricultural production, with movement away from sugar, rubber, bananas, wine, hard fibers, and oil seeds, and principal movement toward livestock, grains, and fruits and vegetables (for some countries, toward oil seeds, cotton, and tea).[30] In some cases the trend has been toward import substitution, and in others toward generating a wider range of export commodities. Diversification requires a choice among products; given that major capital investment often is required, extensive analysis of future demand trends, both within the economy and on world markets, is crucial. In general, diversification into domestic foods, particularly grains in highly populated countries, is of high priority and carries the least amount of risk. Other commodities, such as meat, for which income elasticities of demand are high, both within most individual countries where urbanization has begun and on world markets, represent a second order of priority. But this route is available only to countries that have extensive land resources and where expanded employment is not a primary objective of diversification programs.

The employment effect of diversification programs can be major. This fact is illustrated by the following data on manpower labor requirements for coffee in Brazil in relationship to requirements in alternative production possibilities included in its diversification program.

Production activity	Man-hours per hectare
Coffee	600
Pasture	10–20
Maize	277
Rice	430
Beans	240
Sugarcane	336–359
Groundnuts	467
Castor beans	271
Soybeans	260
Cassava	484

Livestock is one of the most promising alternatives in terms of demand trends, but the transfer of coffee land to livestock and pasture results in substantial displacement of labor. On the other hand, diversification into fruits and vegetables normally will absorb large quantities of labor, and demand trends for these products are favorable in many developing countries and on world markets.

A second potential route for diversification is vertical, into processing and refinement of agricultural commodities. This step has been looked upon as an important possibility for increasing value added to agricultural exports. Two approaches are relevant. First, processing simply can be added to the traditional commodity exports. In this way resource use and the value of exports are increased, with the result that foreign exchange earnings will be enhanced, and a developmental effect, even if modest, will occur. Second, processing could develop in conjunction with import substitution. Joint development of sugar production and processing or oilseed production and processing are cases in point. But when looked at in this light, import substitution in agriculture assumes a different dimension. Very often processing facilities are subject to economies of scale, and a large investment is required to achieve adequate size. Unless the domestic market is large enough to permit these scale economies, diversification may not be warranted even at the level of import parity prices.

In general, the same kinds of considerations apply to processing for exports. Normally it can be assumed that world markets will absorb sufficient quantities to fulfill scale requirements in the processing of most agricultural products if a country is at all successful in exporting. For some commodities, providing the production- marketing system to supply products acceptable on world markets requires integrated activities. Tomatoes in Portugal, for example, became a major export

industry, but this was made feasible only through integrated processing and production and joint efforts by government, investors, and
producers.[31] The extent to which this kind of development can be
increased for export purposes in developing nations is unclear. Very
few country studies have been made, and, as indicated previously, this
is an area where tariff discrimination by industrial nations is most
severe; hence, estimates of potential are difficult to make.

The final and most sophisticated form of diversification is industrialization. Questions of import protection, import substitution, export development, export subsidization, and the effect of change on
the general structure of the economy become most pronounced. Scale
economies and the need for expanded markets often are crucial issues,
and industrial diversification normally requires considerable mobility
of resources, particularly labor. Also implied is a rapid upgrading of
the labor force and of techniques to an industrial technology oriented
production pattern. The scope for this kind of change often represents
the crux of planning and development issues. As indicated in the
previous chapter, much of the diversification into manufacturing by
developing nations, particularly for export purposes, still is based on
agricultural raw materials. On the other hand, examples of countries
that recently have followed the industrialization pattern of the
nineteenth century include Korea, Taiwan, and, to a lesser degree,
some communist countries. While the entire question of general industrialization is somewhat beyond the scope of this volume, it remains one of the central issues of long-range development planning
for most countries.

The case for and scope within which planning for diversification
should be considered by less developed countries is presented effectively by Streeten and Elson. They state that "while it is broadly true
both that countries are poor because they are not diversified (and
therefore particularly vulnerable to changes in technology and demand) and that they are not diversified because they are poor, the
more fundamental of the two relations is the second. Diversification is
not so much the condition of successful development, it is its result."[32]
Within this context these authors define *diversification* as the ability to
respond quickly and at low cost to changes in world demand. This is a
precondition to seizing new production and export opportunities efficiently.

It follows, Streeten and Elson argue, "that a discussion of diversification in the context of the alternatives to which actual land and people
can be employed in the production of problem commodities, or in

agriculture generally, is of limited interest. Identification of this as a primary focus of diversification, however valid it may be as a strategy within agriculture, would obscure the primacy of general development. . . . Just as possibilities for action and investment within the entire agricultural sector must be examined, so too must activities outside of agriculture be considered."[33]

Policy Options

In large part, a discussion of policy options available to the less developed becomes an analysis of the arguments for protection. It is also a discussion of the applicability of the idea of free trade and the concept of comparative advantage to these countries.

As a constraint on accepting or rejecting any policy arguments too quickly, it is perhaps important to recognize the concept of "second best." This theorem states that if any one of the optimum conditions of general equilibrium cannot be fulfilled, a second best optimum situation may be achieved only by departing from some or all of the other optimum conditions. The constraint implied by the theory is that there is no *a priori* way of accepting or rejecting policy options which seem to move the circumstances of a country closer to meeting the assumptions of perfect competition. The evaluation of various policy options, then, must be on the basis of their appropriateness or inappropriateness to specific problems or situations.

Import Protection

To planners in most less developed countries, the arguments for protection are pervasive; very often these are based on a domestic disequilibrium criterion. One argument is that a large discrepancy exists between actual money costs and the opportunity costs of expanding production. Because of the wide differential in industrial wage rates and labor returns in traditional sectors, particularly argiculture, money costs are a great deal higher than real costs to the economy. Hence, protection is justified for industrial expansion.

Another disequilibrium approach is the infant industry argument, which seeks protection on a sector-by-sector basis. It is postulated that a neglected or new industry may enjoy decreasing costs as it expands output and gains experience, and it thus is a particular case of divergence between social and private costs. High costs may arise out of premiums required to induce labor into industrial employment, from general lack of skill and know-how that will be acquired only through experience, or because demand is inadequate to permit scale economies. The general approach is consistent with the unbalanced growth position since selective protection of specific growth industries is implied.

In order to make a valid case for protection of an infant industry with potential decreasing costs, the free trade theorists argue that two conditions must be fulfilled. (1) The economies of scale leading to decreasing costs should be external to the firm. If they are internal, output will expand automatically, and there is no need for protection. (2) The economies should be internal to the industry. If the industry is not the true source, there is no case for protecting that particular industry.[34] This argument tends to ignore the existence of externalities and dynamics of sectoral interaction and, to this extent, is somewhat sterile.

In contrast is the import substitution argument for protection. Emphasis is placed on enlargement and exploitation of the domestic market and the gains that accrue to broadly based development through dynamic interaction among industries and sectors. If selected properly, industries create markets for one another; as the size of the market increases, under protection each industry obtains markets in relationship to elasticities of demand for its product. Reciprocal demand is generated by the growth and income created in each industry. Protection for import substitution thus implicitly or explicitly accepts the economic doctrine of balanced growth. Furthermore, it is sometimes asserted that if the package of industries to be promoted is chosen correctly — especially light manufactures — comparative advantage can be developed that will permit exports and achievement of gains from international specialization.

As growth occurs, economies develop much as postulated in the infant industry argument: through provision of "a growing pool of skilled labor,"[35] economies of scale, and certain infrastructures, such as transport and communications. The import substitution approach differs from the infant industry concept in its lack of specificity; it implies not only that selected industries must be protected, but also that "it may be necessary to protect . . . a fairly large group of industries which would form a sort of 'infant' manufacturing sector."[36]

The problems inherent in import protection are numerous. Most often mentioned is the distortion in resource use that ensues. In general, less developed countries try to discourage imports of luxury consumer goods, which automatically leads to the use of domestic resources for their production. In theory, this tendency can be offset if comparable excise taxes are placed on goods produced at home, but from the perspective of the internal politics of many less developed countries, this may be very difficult. Domestic industries may produce luxury goods with concentrated ownership, and more complete internal dualism may arise than that which exists between the traditional and the export economy of many countries. Distortions in income distribution, consumption patterns, and resource use follow.

Another important negative impact is the shift that usually arises in the terms of trade between the industrial and the agricultural sector. Because most less developed countries rely on agricultural products or manufactures based on agriculture for exports, a bias is created against exports, and external terms of trade deteriorate. Protection clearly has a tendency to lock industry into its own small market, and balanced economic growth, in a full sense, rarely can be achieved. Some imports simply cannot be replaced easily by domestic production, and, as pointed out in chapter 9, a clear tendency exists for a policy of import substitution to increase the total need for imports. This condition, coupled with a policy of protection, not only fails to generate export competitive production, but also is biased against expansion of traditional exports. Balance-of-payments difficulties follow. These consequences of broadly based import protection policies for many countries have been stated clearly in UNCTAD documentation.[37] A more appropriate perspective for most developing countries is summarized by I. M. Little, Tibor Scitovsky, and Maurice Scott. In discussing industrial protection in seven major developing countries, they state: "Given the disadvantages of present policies, including the distortions caused by import restrictions, the inefficiencies of government intervention and controls, and the bias against agriculture and exports, we believe that developing countries would benefit from adopting, in general, a more decentralized approach with greater use of the price mechanism; and, in particular given that there are good prospects for exports, a more open approach to foreign trade with less protection and use of controls."[38] This kind of approach would need to be supplemented with internal fiscal and tax policies that restrict certain kinds of imports and with exchange rate policies that do not distort international and domestic price relationships.

Agricultural Policy

Agricultural development policy complemented by a rational system of support and subsidy measures also can have an important effect on trade position. At least three major dimensions should be considered in devising agricultural policy: (1) stabilization policy and provision of incentives for producers; (2) market systems and commercial services available to agriculture; and (3) infrastructure and public services.

The need for stabilization results, in part, from conditions of demand, but more frequently it is related to questions of supply. Variation in output due to weather can cause random price fluctuations for most crops, and cyclical supply response by large numbers of farmers characterize many commodities. For a number of specialized export commodities, supply variation can create large swings in world market prices. For a wider range of domestic products, price variability can be extreme even where potential for export and import exists. Stabilization policy is justified largely as being necessary for producers, who require incentive and a degree of predictability in returns, especially where cash expenditures for purchased inputs are needed to expand output. Stabilization policy must deal with questions of price relations among commodities and the structure of incentives for commitment of resources to various output mixes.

Effective stabilization by individual countries is relevant largely in the range between import and export parity. Stabilization of these boundaries normally requires international action. Thus, a strong linkage exists between a country's ability to manage domestice price and income programs in agriculture and price behavior on world markets.

While stabilization can be justified on welfare grounds, programs need to be developed in light of their longer term effect on resource allocation. Resource use shifts among commodities will occur if price structures that distort resource earning potentials are established. Investment usually will respond relatively quickly to an increase in expected average value of income, and it also may occur as a result of changes in expected annual returns. Variability of returns can produce both internal and external capital rationings. Producers may retain liquidity and be reluctant to borrow to meet unfavorable price periods. Lenders may tend to be conservative when a borrower's income is uncertain. Hedging against uncertainty can cause producers to emphasize short-term investment and diversified and flexible production at the expense of specialized commercial production and lower levels of cost. Stabilization programs can serve broader nonmonetary objectives, such as reducing rural to urban migration and generally stabilizing rural economic systems. Thus, while positive goals can be sought through such a policy, efforts to maintain excessively high prices can create distortions detrimental to development and trade objectives. Proper management of stabilization policy for agriculture, therefore, often is a vital ingredient in trade sector and development planning.

For an internal income-smoothing scheme to work, A. I. MacBean suggests the following: (1) Producers should be small farmers who are unwilling or unable to accumulate reserves against bad seasons, unable to borrow on reasonable terms, and who specialize in a crop; (2) the ability to vary output should be slight; (3) producers should be a substantial portion of the population, and they should be politically sensitive; and (4) the government should be capable of accumulating budget surpluses without allowing this to lead to increased expenditures, and should be able to tolerate deficits in years of poor returns.[39]

While stabilization and incentive programs should have primary importance in agricultural development efforts, these alone usually will not suffice. When considering large numbers of small farmers, market systems designed to handle outputs as well as inputs (including credit) of the right kind in the right amounts at the right time, along with information on their use, often must become an important component of agricultural development planning and policy.

Achieving progress in agriculture also normally requires broadly based training and education programs for farmers at public expense. Providing incentive along with public programs to achieve more efficient production and adequate supportive market systems, physical infrastructure, and sufficient educational sophistication clearly would seem to be warranted if natural conditions are such that production for domestic use can be brought within the limits of import parity prices, or if production for exports easily can be brought below the level of export parity prices. In general, these potentials can be measured with known analytical techniques, and farmers the world over have shown a capacity to respond to incentives in improving production. As with protection in other areas, the danger exists that technological infancy will continue, or that efforts will be made to stimulate production of the kinds not warranted by natural conditions and potential comparative advantage.

Export Promotion

The arguments for export promotion are largely the same as those for import protection, the difference being that a greater degree of efficiency and lower costs of production normally are required. As just suggested, for agriculture, technologically inefficient industries may require assistance in reaching an export competitive position. In addition, the kind of market structure needed for developing and maintaining export markets may be considerably more sophisticated than that required for domestic commodities. Governments in most major advanced agricultural exporting countries have developed various kinds of export marketing assistance, and this approach would seem to be warranted for less developed countries, particularly those that seek diversification in their agricultural sector and must develop new and varied market outlets.

For industry, the scale economy argument and the argument that major externalities may arise from development for export have been used as justification for export subsidization programs. These arguments seek to recognize the benefits that arise in addition to those that are reflected in the value of the commodity produced, and they suggest that the social gain warrants a reduction in prices of commodities on world markets if required to permit sectoral development.

Internal disequilibrium as reflected in high urban industrial wage rates also is relevant. As suggested by Little and others, "in most developing countries the level of wages would justify the calculation of an alternative shadow wage rate which would measure the true cost to the economy employing labor in industry. On this basis and including an allowance for external economies of training labor the equivalent of a labor subsidy of up to 50 percent might be justifiable in the least developed countries. Depending on the labor intensity of the industry concerned, this could justify promotion equivalent of roughly 0–20 percent of value added."[40] These estimates clearly are rough, but nonetheless they indicate an order of magnitude and provide an intellectual justification for export promotion activities that have been developed on a general basis by at least a number of developing countries that have sought to achieve rapid expansion of industrial exports.[41]

As is import protection, export promotion should be designed to give special encouragement to selected kinds of production. In both cases effective and long-range programs will have an important effect on the structure of the economy through encouragement of long-term fixed investment, relocation of labor, and generation of infrastructure. The problem of determining the correct industry or industries to promote is crucial because of uncertainty in world market trends and is difficult to judge in the case of export industries.

Choice of instruments and decisions on a level at which to promote also become crucial. Promotion is a broader concept than protection and can incorporate such policies as subsidization of inputs and improvement of the financial and market institutions that serve industry and agriculture, training for labor and managerial capacity, and direct measures as well. Promotion should be developmental in focus and not merely protective. It should become an integral part of the policy framework that supports planning in an open economy, and both its direction and level should be constrained by considerations related to the objectives of development, efficiency in resource use, and other determinants of development.

Summary

In the dynamic setting of development planning, a number of questions must be dealt with that are not a part of static comparative advantage theory. It is necessary to move into growth or development theory and be concerned with processes of change, the implications of a multiplicity of market imperfections, and varying kinds of development objectives such as economic growth, employment, the balance of payments, and income distribution. Trade analysis as a component of planning needs to examine the role of exports and imports and trade policy, including import substitution and export promotion, as integral components of total development planning.

In general, no single criterion for trade sector planning is adequate, nor will any given set of criteria necessarily endure through time. The pragmatic decisions made by planners require the insights provided by arguments related to balanced and unbalanced growth and the various forms of marginal investment criteria, as well as the vent-for-surplus and growth theories associated with the free trade-comparative advantage focus of the nineteenth century. Strategies and appropriate policies for trade sector planning must be arrived at in the light of a number of economic and institutional variables, including trends in domestic and international demand for relevant commodities; the resource base available to the country; the nature of the production function and the technological base for increasing production and reducing costs; the externalities and linkages — backward, forward, and horizontal — that influence the "development effect" achieved from any project or investment; and the nature of the internal and external market constraints that affect both the rate at which output can be expanded and the distribution of gains from growth.

11

Conclusions

Assessment of problems and issues in international trade policy involves a much broader scope than can be covered in one volume. Policy issues related to industrial trade among advanced countries have not been dealt with, nor have international monetary matters or the issue of aid and international investments. My concern is with the more limited areas of agriculture and development, with a view toward adding a dimension to the literature on trade policy. These two issues have grown in importance throughout the postwar period. The volume of agricultural trade has risen greatly, and, as a result, international interdependence has increased. Problems of export expansion by and the general trade policy of less developed countries have become more critical as the easy limits of import substitution have been reached by more nations and as levels of aid have plateaued and in some cases decreased. These changes have been combined with increased intensity in the drive for development and, hence, require workable trade policy.

Trade Policy in Perspective

Nineteenth-century guidelines, namely, that the ultimate objective is to provide free international movement of goods and services, have been reflected partially in postwar trade policy. Leadership by the United States resulted in establishment of GATT, with principles clearly aimed at freeing impediments to trade in a broad multilateral framework. Through six negotiations, major progress has been achieved in industrial trade, but, in general, the impediments to free trade in agricultural products remain. Major shifts in international relationships, in particular formation of the European Economic Community, have resulted in greater restrictions on agricultural trade than existed during the immediate postwar period. These limitations flow from domestic policies designed to improve farm income and promote other ends. Such policies have resulted in a variety of programs and actions that constrain and distort trade in agricultural products. The extent of this protection is difficult to measure, and the welfare and income transfer effects are not easily defined. Import substitution has resulted, as well as production of unmarketable export surpluses, both of which distort international trade and create disequilibrium in world markets. Problems in international trade policy for agriculture clearly remain a central issue, and they have not been amenable to solution under the philosophical perspective and international arrangements established under GATT.

GATT has not been useful to developing countries for three main reasons. First, it is argued that the free play of market forces inherently works to the disadvantage of developing countries and that multilateral liberalization of trade is not acceptable as an objective when there are major structural differences among economies. The result of this kind of policy is an inevitable deterioration in the trade position of the less developed. Because of the nature of demand for the products they have for export, and because of structural differences among economies, the less developed suffer long-term deterioration in trade. They cannot earn enough to pay for import requirements and must seek international policy that deviates from free exchange in order to improve their trade position.

Second, so many exceptions have been granted covering products of export interest to underdeveloped countries that their inherent disadvantage is further aggravated by policies sanctioned in GATT. A number of preference systems, including the United Kingdom's arrangements with Commonwealth countries and the European Economic Community's special preference for former French colonies, are cases in point. These systems generally have not been beneficial to less developed countries.

Third, it is argued that the bargaining process itself is implemented largely by advanced nations and has concentrated on commodities of interest to them. On a worldwide basis, both economic structure and policy processes have worked against developing countries, and special arrangements are needed to offset the accumulated disadvantages.

Economic Theory and Trade Policy

Bargaining in the GATT format, strongly guided by classical and neoclassical economic thought, has been questioned both on a theoretical-philosophical and on a structural basis. At the theoretical level, the theorem of second best as an approach to policy formation is relevant. It was first discussed by J. E. Meade in relation to trade policies, and he states that "there are strong theoretical reasons why in many cases one particular tariff or trade control should not be removed so long as some other particular tariff or trade control or domestic duty or other divergence between marginal values and costs remain in operation. The maintenance of one particular divergence between marginal value and costs may help to offset the evil effects of another divergence. Welfare might be improved if both were removed; but if one is going to be kept, it may be better that both should be kept."[1]

Within this second-best framework, although he does not necessarily endorse a broad range of managed international trading relationships, Meade points out a number of justifications for deviating from a policy aimed at completely free and liberalized international trading arrangements.

1. That the imposition of trade barriers may affect the international terms of trade and thus help to redistribute income from richer to poorer countries.

2. A protective policy may be used by one country in order to redistribute income inside that country in favor of the factors of production which are especially suited for employment in the protected industries, and

3. Because of the existence of the important economies of large scale production . . . it may be that if the structures of industries in a country were quite different from what it now is the change would represent a true increase in world economic efficiency.[2]

The direct empirical counterpart to this conceptual framework is reflected in much of what has been done to create exceptions to GATT principles and in the structural arguments being presented for change in trade policy.

Historically, the goals of agricultural policy have been aimed at an internal redistribution of income within countries; this has led to a conflict with GATT principles, which call for liberalized trading arrangements. In the Kennedy Round the basic format for negotiations presented by the United States was to achieve a multilateral reduction in trade barriers, including agriculture, with specifically agreed upon exceptions. The European Common Market, on the other hand, entered those negotiations with a different perspective. It refused to participate in the search for lower trade barriers as such and argued that if progress were to be made in normalizing international agricultural markets it would have to be done through broad-ranging, worldwide commodity organization.

This approach was based on arguments related to structural differences among countries and their implications for world trade in agricultural commodities. An EEC analysis asserted that the world economy can be separated into five structurally different categories of countries.[3] One category includes developing countries, whose economies are relatively static, largely self-contained, and have little contact through external markets. A second category includes dynamic, developing economies where industrialization has begun, agricultural development is underway, and a substantial interest in import and export trade has developed. Two categories of advanced countries include those that are primarily agricultural export nations, such as Australia and New Zealand, and developed industrial countries, some of which are major importers of agricultural commodities and others major exporters. In addition to these categories, the world is also separated in part by the existence of a communist bloc.

Among these groups there are major structural differences that create problems in international agricultural markets. Some countries hardly participate in world trade, and others among the less developed countries depend largely on commodity exports for foreign exchange. Some industrial nations protect high cost domestic production, and, in some cases, efforts are made to expand exports on a subsidized basis from protected agricultural production. In the case of communist countries, political restraints influence their participation in international markets. These factors have resulted in basic imbalances in supply and demand, created different rates of technological change among countries in agriculture, affected production cost levels, and in general disrupted the development of orderly exchange in international trade. A free market cannot operate under such conditions, and the only basis for creating orderly international markets is to organize and guide commodity trade. The details of implementing such a move, however, have not been spelled out. The general approach is clearly a move away from multilateral reduction in trade barriers and increased reliance on free markets toward more highly organized international trading procedures.

A second basic point of departure from GATT principles has emanated from UNCTAD. Developing countries argue that structural factors assure a deterioration in their terms of trade, that wealthy nations have characteristics that lead to slow growth in their volume of imports, and that developed countries maintain policies that prevent rapid expansion of exports from the less developed countries. Furthermore, it is argued that a free market cannot be tolerated as the basis for determining imports into less developed countries because investments from outside sources result in economic dualism. Under these circumstances, trade does not become a vehicle of development; rather, it creates high technology export industries with little linkage to basic peasant economies. From the viewpoint of developing nations, international arrangements are necessary to create preferences by industrial countries toward them and among them to increase the use of commodity programs that reduce uncertainty and increase transfer of income from industrial to less developed countries and to increase direct financial assistance in the form of compensatory financing and transfers through aid. The thrust of policy by developing countries as it has emanated from UNCTAD is toward market intervention on a multilateral basis and increased organization of international markets.

A New Focus on Trade Policy

To achieve genuine multilateral free trade, a number of conditions are needed.[4] One is that major trading nations would have to devise and implement internal policies that are reasonably successful in achieving internal stability and eliminating recurrent periods of inflation and deflation that become reflected in balance-of-payments flows and create international disequilibrium. This is particularly crucial for dominant countries, where corrections for this effect, namely, devaluation or imposition of trade restrictions, have a worldwide impact. Policies that provide internal adjustments among sectors so that one sector does not overproduce relative to domestic and international market potentials or underproduce relative to technological potential also would be needed. Stability in the aggregate and flexibility for internal adjustment become prerequisites to multilateral free trade.

There must be a reasonable degree of price flexibility so that production increases and decreases as prices rise and decline. Prices become an important vehicle for shifting resources among commodities, and output is guided by available market opportunities. A third major component needed to maintain free trade is that exchange rates and commodity flows must be free to fluctuate and adjust to varying prices and market requirements. If national policies are aimed at creating an internal balance and overall economic stability, foreign exchange rates must be free to adjust to maintain external balance and prevent accumulation of foreign exchange by some countries and deficits by others. If exchange rates adjust, markets must react readily to changing volumes of imports and exports in order to provide trading response to shifts in current values and eliminate the need to resort to controls, tariffs, and subsidies.

These conditions are far from being fulfilled in today's world. The classical nineteenth-century approach to policy, that internal disequilibrium in individual countries is an acceptable price to pay for international equilibrium, no longer exists. All countries seek various domestic ends, including stability, full employment, economic growth, and development. Policies to achieve these ends vary among nations, as does their effectiveness, but most countries feel the need for trade restraints to achieve various domestic objectives.

In the case of agriculture, an inherent tendency toward imbalanced production in some countries and a tendency to commit excess resources have resulted in low agricultural incomes and have brought forth major programs of income protection. Domestic policies seeking income redistribution conflict with international equilibrium, and these programs are not likely to be abandoned by many countries. They will become inoperative only if substantial world food shortages continue and market prices are high enough to achieve redistribution.

All countries maintain policies to promote economic growth, employment, and structural change. These issues are particularly sensitive in less developed nations, and in most countries are implemented without great concern for international consequences. Policies for protection, import substitution, or export promotion are developed in the light of internal objectives, not with a view toward maintaining external equilibrium. Objectives related to growth and structural change are complemented by trade policies that interfere with the free play of market forces.

Achieving a workable international economic order requires instruments and institutions that extend beyond those prescribed by classical trade theorists. This conclusion rests upon the assumption, which at present appears entirely valid, that governments in general will not sacrifice domestic policy objectives for the sole purpose of achieving international equilibrium and upon the fact that a successful return to more liberal trade through the elimination of restrictions can be achieved only if governments avoid certain well-entrenched domestic policies and submit their economies to the vagaries of international supply, demand, and market forces.

Given these assumptions, a number of specific questions concerning international trading arrangements become important. First, can international commodity arrangements work, and what role can they play in trade policy? The difficulties in formulating and implementing international commodity arrangements are numerous, and there are distinct limitations stemming from technical and market conditions. Yet, if countries accept the policy objectives of creating international income transfers or of stabilizing international markets, and if they are willing to accept a degree of constraint on internal flexibility in developing policy, improved international order may be possible for a number of commodities. Commodity arrangements can vary from those that establish specific prices and quantities to those that seek to coordinate production and storage policy aimed at market stabilization. They provide no panacea nor are they a basis for defining a complete economic order in commodity markets, but their use should not be rejected simply on philosophical or theoretical grounds.

A second question is whether the conflict between domestic agricultural policy and trade policy can be reduced or eliminated. In part this can be done by changing the instruments of agricultural protection. Deficiency payments are less disruptive of markets than are direct price supports. A more fundamental approach, however, can be sought through policies that restructure agriculture. Some specialization in production should be possible, and resource use in agriculture should change in response to market changes and shifts in comparative advantage. Domestic policies are needed that alter the input mix, expand the resource base of individual farmers, and increase resource productivity so that lower levels of support are required to maintain a reasonable income to individual farmers. Providing farmers with the technology and scale of operation that permit adjustments to changing market forces would result in a greater equalization of production costs among countries and reduce the relative need for protection in individual nations.

A third question is whether preference systems for less developed countries can fulfill a legitimate international policy objective and whether or not they will work. If markets are enlarged through exports, will this permit growth, specialization, and technological change which reduce costs so that genuine economic development is stimulated? The answer ultimately lies in whether less developed countries achieve sufficient competitive advantage to increase exports to industrial nations, even when their entry is not inhibited by artificial restrictions. The competitive position of developing countries is strongest in those areas where economies of scale are relatively less important, where technology is less sophisticated, and where the production system is not dependent upon broadly based and sophisticated education and management techniques. While some growth might develop as a result of preferences, it would likely fall far short of that required for general industrialization. Preferences can be one of a number of policy approaches required to fulfill the objective of using trade policy to further growth in developing countries, but they alone will not be adequate.

A fourth issue is whether preference systems or customs unions among less developed countries can be used to promote economic development. Economic integration may take several forms and involve varying degrees of interaction and policy coordination. The short-run effects will depend upon a variety of conditions, such as the height of initial trade restraints among countries, the nature of structural characteristics, the resource bases of the economies involved, and the extent to which specialization might develop. Longer term implications will be determined by the degree to which economies of size can be realized and the extent to which coordinated development planning can be enhanced through joint action (compared with that which would occur in individual countries). Coordinated regional development can be achieved for such things as transportation and communication, educational facilities, industry, and agriculture. A major roadblock to past efforts at coordinated development planning appears to have been the inability of less advanced countries to develop the political will and establish the institutions needed to effectuate workable regional cooperation, either through loosely coordinated functional arrangements or through more comprehensive customs unions or common markets. In the long run, this form of international arrangement may provide the greatest potential for solving the trade development problems of the less developed.

A fifth issue concerns the kind of internal adjustment needed to promote trade interests in developing countries. Trade sector planning involves assessing a number of interrelated conditions. One is the analysis of demand for commodities either being produced or those that have production potential. Growth trends in international markets for some commodities important in developing nations' exports have been slow relative to growth in supply, and prices have declined. On the other hand, demand for certain livestock products, feed, petroleum, and other raw materials is sustained by industrial growth, and long-term continued expansion can be expected. International demand must be interrelated to domestic demand in order to arrive at a composite of domestic and foreign demand for project and development planning.

These estimates should be considered along with assessment of a wide range of production and marketing questions. The available resource base and the nature of production functions vary widely among countries, and they define differences in comparative advantage among nations and among sectors within them. Comparative advantage also should be assessed within the constraints of externalities and complementarities among industries and a broad range of market imperfections, rigidities, and inadequacies in the adjustment mechanism in most developing countries.

Trade sector planning should become an integral part of overall development planning, and trade policy should complement general development policy. The correct policy format has been the subject of considerable discussion among economists and political representatives of both industrial and developing countries. One of the important conclusions of this study, however, is that no single criterion for trade policy or trade sector planning is adequate, nor will any given set of criteria necessarily endure through time.

Widely varying conditions among countries suggest that few guidelines have general and equal applicability. Great differences in income levels, resource bases, and economic structures mean that universal free trade is not acceptable to most nations. Excessive protection, on the other hand, ultimately results in intolerable inefficiency for individual countries or the world as a whole. Planning leads to questions of how resources should be allocated to fulfill development objectives most adequately, including choices related to imports, exports, and import substitution. It also requires choices as to appropriate instrumentation and criteria for policy that most effectively will integrate trade into overall development plans. While there are areas of commonality among countries, there is also great diversity. Each nation must plan in the context of its own situation and avoid being misled by theoretical or politically induced generalities that suggest a single "best" method of trade sector or development planning.

Formulating Trade Policy

A final consideration in assessing trade policy is the process of policy formulation, particularly as reflected by agricultural trade policy in industrial countries. Despite the pervasive effect of international trade policy upon groups within an economy, it is not of particular interest to a large number of people. Since trade policy's effect on consumers and export industries often is indirect and delayed, these groups tend to be inactive in its formulation. Pressure arises from those industries seeking protection and is not offset by those who will be damaged by it. These positions, in turn, are reflected directly in negotiations between countries. Bargaining becomes a process of trading off special interests, resulting in laborious commodity-by-commodity negotiation which has not succeeded in reducing import barriers on or export aids for agricultural products.

In order to change this process and to achieve progress, at least three concepts should be introduced into trade policy formulation. First, objectives should seek to stress national rather than group interests. This emphasis involves decisions both about which trade barriers to retain and which to reduce or eliminate. While the objective of trade liberalization should be of central importance, it is also true that in today's world of mixed and interdependent economic systems, where governments seek to maintain domestic economic stability and assure economic growth and full employment, some barriers to trade represent responsible government action. Where barriers are retained, they should be designed to serve a broad national interest and not simply to protect special interest groups.

In the case of policy changes to expand exports, there is little conflict with group interests, and plans to serve export objectives are not difficult to implement. The national interest in many countries also could be served by liberalizing imports of agricultural products and raw materials both because of their impact on consumer prices and raw material costs and the effect on less developed countries. Larger imports from these nations would increase foreign exchange earnings and enable the less developed to increase imports needed for development. But changes in trade policies that liberalize imports inevitably are damaging to domestic groups and are difficult to implement.

This fact leads directly to the second concept important to trade policy, namely, that individual groups should not be expected to bear the entire cost of change in trade policy. Adjustments to serve the national interest should be paid for by society. To do this, compensation and meaningful public assistance are needed as a part of the trade liberalization package. The principle of adjustment assistance has broad application both within and outside agriculture, and it should come into play if trade barriers are reduced and serious market disruption and injury occur.

Trade policy could be improved if the basis for adjustment assistance were expanded to industries that no longer can compete. The U.S. textile industry, for example, has sought protection because of strong competition from Japan and other countries where lower input prices, especially labor, provide a cost advantage. Economists long have recognized the infant industry concept and accepted it as justification for protection to achieve faster economic growth. It also should be recognized that economic development in other countries and basic differences in available resources among nations, along with the international transfer of technology, can shift comparative advantage and create conditions in which industries that were competitive can be maintained only through continuous protection. In these cases, and where the basic ingredients for competitive survival do not exist, assistance in moving resources to other uses makes as much sense as protection for infant industries.

As a final point, it would appear there is a need to devise more effective techniques for trade negotiation. The format of bargaining heretofore used in GATT has not worked for agriculture nor for reducing a wide range of nontariff barriers in nonagricultural industries. The recent report of the U.S. Presidential Commission on Trade and Investment Policy states: "The necessity to negotiate the techniques and levels of domestic price support systems makes a sectoral approach on agriculture a necessary preliminary step. . . . This approach does not require a self-balancing package. Because agricultural trade flows are not balanced between major nations, equivalency of concessions will be achieved only through broader negotiations involving both agricultural and nonagricultural trade and possibly other international economic matters as well."[5] A number of agricultural economists have argued that the dilemma in trade negotiations for agriculture can be overcome only through broadly based international discussions that deal with issues of price support, import protection, export subsidization, and the orientation of domestic farm policy and agreement by individual countries, both exporters and importers, to cooperate in programs of supply adjustments and production reorganization.

Devising mechanisms for more fruitful international negotiation in agriculture will not be easy. But past efforts built around commodity-by-commodity bargaining based on a trade-off of concessions have led to little progress. Change is needed.

Notes

Chapter 1

[1]From P. von Hornick (1638–1712), quoted in Daniel Fusfeld, *The Age of the Economist* (Chicago: Scott, Foresman and Co., 1966), p. 9.

[2]The three major assumptions of classical trade theory were that (1) labor and capital were fully mobile among uses within a country, (2) they did not move at all between countries, and (3) the supply of money consisted of precious metals and moved freely between countries.

[3]For a comprehensive analysis of the foundations of the classical theory of international trade, see J. B. Condliffe, *The Commerce of Nations* (New York: W. W. Norton & Co., Inc., 1950), chapter 7.

[4]For an insightful and detailed discussion of these developments, see Condliffe, *Commerce*, chapters 10, 11, and 12. For specific developments in agricultural trade, including estimates of major sources of exports of grain and livestock products as early as 1854–1858, see R. M. Stern, "A Century of Food Exports," in Robert Tontz, ed., *Foreign Agricultural Trade, Selected Readings* (Ames: The Iowa State University Press, 1966), pp. 127–42.

[5]Michael Tracy, *Agriculture in Western Europe: Crisis and Adaptation Since 1880* (London: Jonathan Cape, 1964), p. 27.

[6]Condliffe, *Commerce*, pp. 273–81.

[7]Dudley Dillard, *Economic Development of the North Atlantic Community* (Englewood Cliffs: Prentice-Hall, Inc., 1967), pp. 541–42.

[8]J. M. Keynes, *Essays in Persuasion* (New York: Harcourt, Brace and World, Inc., 1932), p. 312. Quoted in Dillard, *Economic Development*, pp. 541–42.

[9]For a more detailed discussion of this point, see Harry G. Johnson, *The World Economy at the Crossroads* (Fair Lawn: Oxford University Press, 1965).

Chapter 2

[1]P. Lamartine Yates, *Forty Years of Foreign Trade* (New York: The Macmillan Co., 1959). *Food* is defined as 0 and 1 of the SITC, to which is added oilseeds in Section 4, but excluding tobacco. This is not fully comparable with other trade and agricultural data presented in this chapter.

[2]Erik Thorbeck and J. B. Condliffe, "The Pattern of World Trade in Foodstuffs: Past and Present," in *Food: One Tool for Economic Development* (Ames: The Iowa State University Press, 1962).

[3]Alfred Maizels, *Industrial Growth and World Trade* (Cambridge: the University Press, 1963).

[4]Food and Agriculture Organization (hereafter FAO), *The State of Food and Agriculture 1970* (Rome: 1971), p. 15.

[5]Thorbeck and Condliffe, "Pattern of World Trade," pp. 177–218.

[6]Organization for Economic Cooperation and Development (hereafter OECD), *Agricultural Policies in 1966: Europe, North America and Japan* (Paris: 1967).

[7]This discussion of Europe is drawn from previous statements by the author. See Vernon Sorenson, "Trade Policies and Prospects in Western Europe," *Journal of Farm Economics* 48 (December 1966): 1348–58; and Lawrence Witt and Vernon Sorenson, "Problems of Agricultural Products in Foreign Trade," in *Issues and Objectives of U.S. Foreign Trade Policy*, Joint Economic Committee, 90th Cong., 1st sess. (Washington, D.C.: U.S. Government Printing Office, 1967), pp. 145–88.

[8]OECD, *Agriculture and Economic Growth* (Paris: 1965).

[9]United Nations Conference on Trade and Development (hereafter UN-CTAD), *Towards a New Trade Policy for Development*, Report by the Secretary-General of UNCTAD (E/Conf. 46/3) (New York: 1964).

[10]Ibid., p. 7.

[11]FAO, "Synthetics and Their Effects on Agricultural Trade," *Commodity Bulletin Series 38* (Rome: 1964), p. 1.

[12]Witt and Sorenson, "Trade Policies," p. 158.

[13]Barend A. DeVries, *The Export Experience of Developing Countries*, World Bank Staff Occasional Papers, no. 3 (Baltimore: The Johns Hopkins Press, 1967).

Chapter 3

[1]T. W. Schultz, "U.S. Malinvestment in Food for the World," in *Balancing Future World Food Production and Needs* (Ames: The Iowa State University Press, 1967).

[2]See, for example, Jacob Viner, "International Trade Theory and Its Present Day Relevance," and Gottfried Haberler, "The Theory of International Trade Policy," in Tontz, ed., *Foreign Agricultural Trade*. See also Gottfried Haberler, "An Assessment of the Current Relevance of the Theory of Comparative Advantage to Agricultural Production and Trade," in *Proceedings of the International Conference of Agricultural Economists* (London: Oxford University Press, 1966).

[3]For an elaboration of demand in international trade theory, see Charles P. Kindleberger, *International Economics*, 3d ed. (Homewood: Richard D. Irwin, Inc., 1963), chapter 6.

[4]These arguments were developed by a number of writers. For a concise review, see Richard Caves, *Trade and Economic Structure* (Cambridge, Mass.: Harvard University Press, 1963), chapter 2.

[5]For a simplified explanation, see Kindleberger, *International Economics*, chapter 5 and Appendix 5. For a complete but concise statement of factor endowment analysis, see Subimal Mookerjee, *Factor Endowment and International Trade* (Bombay: Asia Publishing House, 1958).

[6]Harry G. Johnson, *Trade and Economic Growth* (Cambridge, Mass.: Harvard University Press, 1965).

[7]I borrow this terminology from Charles P. Kindleberger. See his *Foreign Trade and the National Economy* (New Haven: Yale University Press, 1962), chapter 6.

Chapter 4

[1]See, for example, Viner, "International Trade Theory"; Gottfried Haberler, "The Theory of International Trade Policy," in *A Survey of International Trade Theory* (Princeton: Princeton University Press, 1961); and Haberler, "An Assessment,"

[2]For an historical assessment of the range of specific arguments that have been used, see L. W. Towle, *International Trade and Commercial Policy* (New York: Harper and Brothers, 1947), chapters 12 and 13.

[3]For a comprehensive discussion of these issues, see J. E. Meade, *The Theory of International Economic Policy*, volume 2, *Trade and Welfare* (New York: Oxford University Press, 1955).

[4]This categorization builds on a somewhat different classification suggested in a landmark study completed under the auspices of the General Agreement on Tariffs and Trade (hereafter GATT), *Trends in International Trade*, A Report by a Panel of Experts (Geneva: October 1958).

[5]Helen B. Junz, "The Border Tax Issue," in *Issues and Objectives of U.S. Foreign Trade Policy*, Joint Economic Committee, 90th Cong., 1st sess. (Washington, D.C.: U.S. Government Printing Office, 1967), p. 35.

[6]*United States International Policy in an Interdependent World*, Report to the President Submitted by the Commission on International Trade and Investment Policy (Washington, D.C.: U.S. Government Printing Office, July 1971).

[7]Rachel Dardis and Elmer Learn, *Measuring the Degree and Cost of Economic Protection of Agriculture in Selected Countries*, ERS Technical Bulletin #1384, U.S. Department of Agriculture (Washington, D.C.: U.S. Government Printing Office, 1967).

[8]They do, however, state a number of qualifications that must apply to any such measurement. One of these, price quotations for import and export, is generally given at the country border. This means that imports are valued CIF, while exports are valued FOB, and a degree of bias exists in measuring protection by importing and exporting countries. In addition, their study assumes no difference exists in the quality of domestic or international traded commodities, and, very important, where marketing margins are used, these are difficult to measure precisely and are subject to estimating error.

[9]W. M. Corden, "The Structure of a Tariff System and the Effective Protective Rate," *Journal of Political Economy* 74 (June 1966): 222.

[10]J. B. Bridgen et al., *The Australian Tariff: An Economic Inquiry*, 2d ed. (Melbourne: Melbourne University Press, 1929); and J. B. Young, *Canadian Commercial Policy* (Ottawa: Queens Printers, 1957).

[11]T. E. Josling, *The United Kingdom Grains Agreement (1964): An Economic Analysis* (East Lansing: Institute of International Agriculture, Michigan State University, 1967). A previous analysis by Rachel Dardis, "The Welfare Cost of Grain Protection in the United Kingdom," *Journal of Farm Economics* 49 (August 1967): 597–609, estimated the production cost ("economic cost of added output" in Josling's terminology) of the United Kingdom deficiency payment program for the year 1959–1960.

[12]T. E. Josling, "A Formal Approach to Agricultural Policy," *Journal of Agricultural Economics* (British) 20 (May 1969): 175–96.

[13]D. Gale Johnson, "The Role of Trade in Improving the Welfare of the World Community or What Difference Does Trade Make?" Agricultural Economics Paper No. 71:6 (Chicago: Department of Economics, University of Chicago, 3 May 1971). Estimates of the magnitude of the transfers made by consumers and taxpayers to farmers have been made for the EEC and the United States. For the EEC in 1968 the estimates in real costs imposed on consumers and taxpayers ranged from $11 to $14 billion. Johnson has estimated that in 1968 the cost imposed on U.S. consumers amounted to 3.4 billion and that an additional 6.2 billion came from taxpayers. Thus, in the EEC and the United States the total transfer amounted to more than $20 billion and represented approximately $1,330 per worker in agriculture (p. 25).

[14]Dale Hathaway, "Trade Restrictions and U.S. Consumers," in *U.S. Trade and Agricultural Export Conference* (Ames: The Iowa State University Press, 1973).

Chapter 5

[1]Discussion of policies in Western Europe are based substantially on research completed at Michigan State University during the past several years and published by the Institute of International Agriculture.

[2]Brice M. Meeker, "U.S. Feed Grain Markets in the Netherlands," in *USDA Foreign Agriculture,* 24 August 1970.

[3]See Donald Epp, *Changes in Regional Grain and Livestock Prices Under the European Economic Community Prices,* Research Report No. 4 (East Lansing: Institute of International Agriculture, Michigan State University, 1968).

[4]Tracy, *Agriculture in Western Europe,* p. 154.

[5]Consisting originally of the United Kingdom, Denmark, Sweden, Norway, Portugal, Switzerland, Austria, and later Finland.

[6]Special arrangements in the EEC already existed with eighteen North African countries.

[7]In July 1971 imports of fresh chilled and frozen beef and veal and of fat cattle became subject to a system of general variable levies to support minimum import prices. For mutton and lamb, specific duties were instituted. Imports from the Irish Republic are exempted in both cases. Also beginning in July 1971, minimum import prices and levies when necessary were established on fresh cream, canned cream, skim-milk powder, whole milk powder, and con-

densed milk. Increases in minimum import prices on shell eggs and egg products took effect on 29 March 1971, and on grains increases on 1 July 1971. See David P. Evans, "U.K. Sets New Farm Price Guarantees, Moves Toward Variable Levies — Part II," *Foreign Agriculture,* 10 May 1971.
  [8]John Ferris et al., *The Impact on U.S. Agricultural Trade of the Accession of the United Kingdom, Ireland, Denmark and Norway to the European Economic Community,* Research Report no. 11 (East Lansing: Institute of International Agriculture, Michigan State University, 1971.
  [9]In some cases, such as for dairy products and sugar, these changes will be delayed because of special arrangements with preexisting Commonwealth suppliers to the United Kingdom.
  [10]Oscar Zaglitz, "Agricultural Trade and Trade Policy," in *Foreign Trade and Agricultural Policy,* Technical Papers, vol. 6 (Washington, D.C.: National Advisory Commission on Food and Fiber, August 1967), p. 154.
  [11]Except rice, peanuts, sugar, tobacco, or extra long staple cotton. This exception list includes those that remain heavily protected but in composite represent a very small proportion of total acreage.

Chapter 6

  [1]Dale Hathaway, *Government and Agriculture: Public Policy in a Democratic Society* (New York: The Macmillan Co., 1963), p. 241.
  [2]John Wetmore et al., *Policies for Expanding the Demand for Farm Products in the United States,* Part 1, "History and Potentials," University of Minnesota Technical Bulletin 231 (St. Paul: April 1959); and Martin Abel, Willard Cochrane, and John Wetmore, *Policies for Expanding the Demand for Farm Products,* Part II, *Programs and Results,* University of Minnesota Technical Bulletin 238 (St. Paul: April 1961).
  [3]OECD, *Agricultural Policies in 1966.*
  [4]The argument that, as prices decline, farmers need to expand output to maintain an acceptable level of total income and a positive return to land, owned capital, and family labor.
  [5]U.S. export payments totaled $162.9 million in 1970. A total of $4,893.7 million in export payments was made during the 1960s, with variation from a high of $821.7 million in 1964 to a low of $62.9 million in 1969.
  [6]U.S. Department of Agriculture, Economic Research Service, *Foreign Agricultural Trade of the United States,* November 1969; and U.S. Department of Agriculture, *Agricultural Statistics 1971* (Washington, D.C.: U.S. Government Printing Office, 1972). This total value is based on pricing at Commodity Credit Corporation (CCC) support levels, a concept that has been questioned on the ground that the actual aid granted is seriously overstated.
  [7]See Lawrence Witt and Carl Eicher, *The Effects of United States Agricultural Surplus Disposal Programs on Recipient Countries,* Research Bulletin No. 2 (East Lansing: Agricultural Experiment Station, Michigan State University, 1964).
  [8]Zaglitz, "Agricultural Trade," p. 205.

[9] For a comprehensive review of exceptions and special regulations in GATT, see ibid., pp. 205–15. See also Gerald Curzon, *Multilateral Commercial Diplomacy: The General Agreement on Tariffs and Trade and Its Impact on National Commercial Policies and Techniques* (London: Michael Joseph, 1965), chapters 3 and 7.

[10] See ibid., chapter 7.

[11] GATT, *Trends in International Trade* (Geneva: October 1958).

[12] Irwin Hedges, "Kennedy Round Agricultural Negotiations and the World Grains Agreement," *Journal of Farm Economics* 49 (December 1967): 1333–34.

[13] For greater detail, see U.S. Department of Agriculture, *International Grains Arrangement, 1967*, FAS-M-195 (Washington, D.C.: U.S. Government Printing Office, November 1967).

[14] U.S. Department of Agriculture, *Report on Agricultural Trade Negotiations of the Kennedy Round*, FAS-M-193 (Washington, D.C.: U.S. Government Printing Office, September 1967).

Chapter 7

[1] For a brief accounting of nineteenth-century export-led growth, see Kindleberger, *Foreign Trade*, chapter 12.

[2] Hla Myint, "The 'Classical Theory' of International Trade and the Underdeveloped Countries," *Economic Journal* 68 (June 1958): 318–19.

[3] Gerald Meier, *International Trade and Development* (New York: Harper and Row, 1963), pp. 153–54.

[4] Ibid., pp. 156–58.

[5] Hla Myint, *Economic Theory and the Underdeveloped Countries* (New York: Oxford University Press, 1971), p. 126.

[6] For an historical description of this process, see Condliffe, *Commerce*, chapters 10 and 11.

[7] Harry Johnson, *Trade Policies Toward Less Developed Countries* (Washington, D.C.: The Brookings Institution, 1967), pp. 49–52.

[8] Principal among these critics are the following: Hans Singer, "The Distribution of Gains Between Investing and Borrowing Countries," *American Economic Review* 60 (May 1950): 473–85; Raul Prebisch, *The Economic Development of Latin America and Its Problems* (New York: United Nations Economic Commission for Latin America, 1950); and Gunnar Myrdal, *Rich Lands and Poor Lands* (New York: Harper and Brothers, 1957).

[9] Singer, "Distribution of Gains," p. 478.

[10] This theory is largely the product of Glenn L. Johnson and is elaborated in a number of writings, including the following: Glenn L. Johnson and Lowell Hardin, *The Economics of Forage Evaluation*, Purdue Agricultural Experiment Station Bulletin No. 623 (Lafayette: 1955); Clark Edwards, "Resource Fixity

and Farm Organization," *Journal of Farm Economics* 41 (November 1959): 747–59; and three publications of Glenn L. Johnson, "Supply Functions — Some Facts and Notions," in *Agricultural Adjustment Problems in a Growing Economy* (Ames: The Iowa State University Press, 1956), "The State of Agricultural Supply Analysis," *Journal of Farm Economics* 42 (May 1960): 435–52, and "Implications of the IMS for Study of Responses to Price," in Glenn L. Johnson et al., eds., *A Study of Managerial Processes of Midwestern Farmers* (Ames: The Iowa State University Press, 1961).

[11] Glenn L. Johnson and Vernon L. Sorenson, "The World Food Situation: Challenge and Opportunities Facing North America," in *A North American Common Market* (Ames: The Iowa State University Press, 1969).

[12] S. B. Linder, *Trade and Trade Policy for Development* (New York: Praeger and Sons, 1967).

[13] Linder does not attempt to define or analyze factors that will influence the level of noninput or consumption imports. The crucial part of his analysis is that, in their trade with industrial nations, developing countries face both an import minimum and an export maximum.

[14] Linder, *Trade,* p. 13.

[15] Ian Little et al., *Industry and Trade in Some Developing Countries: A Comparative Analysis* (New York: Oxford University Press, 1971), pp. 59, 63.

[16] DeVries, *Export Experience.*

[17] Willard W. Cochrane, "Agriculture and Trade Development in the LDCs," in *U.S. Trade Policy and Agricultural Exports* (Ames: The Iowa State University Press, 1973).

[18] Little et al., *Industry and Trade.*

[19] For a review of these studies, see John Pincus, *Economic Aid and International Cost Sharing* (Baltimore: Johns Hopkins Press, 1965), pp. 25–39.

[20] Both a GATT and UN projection for the 1970s assumed an import propensity above one, or that imports will increase faster than income.

[21] UNCTAD, *Financial Resources for Development: Trade Prospects and Capital Needs of Developing Countries during the Second United Nations Development Decade.* TD/118/Supp. 3 (New York: 22 December 1971).

[22] It should be noted that the trade gap does not include capital flows from industrial countries. The proposal was advanced at the first UNCTAD conference that a target level of one percent of the GNP of industrial countries should be a goal for these transfers. If this proposed level is reached and certain other conditions concerning the grant component of aid and financial terms are met, net capital flows could expand to $29 billion by 1980. The unclosed gap then would be reduced to about $8 billion for Variant 1 and to about $14 billion for Variant 2.

[23] In Geneva, Switzerland, in 1964; in New Delhi, India, in 1968; and in Santiago, Chile, in 1972.

[24] For a more detailed discussion of these problems see Raul Prebisch, "Toward a New Trade Policy for Development," in John Pincus, ed., *Reshaping the World Economy: Rich and Poor Countries* (Englewood Cliffs: Prentice-Hall, Inc., 1968), pp. 109–28.

[25] OECD, *Summary Recommendations Adopted by the U.N. Conference on Trade and Development,* TC(64)15 (Paris: 17 August 1964).

[26] Primarily the EEC and Japan.

Chapter 8

[1]A. I. MacBean, *Export Instability and Economic Development* (Cambridge, Mass.: Harvard University Press, 1966).

[2]Theodore Morgan, "Trends in Terms of Trade and Their Repercussions on Primary Producers," in R. F. Harrod and D. C. Hague, eds., *International Trade Theory in a Developing World* (New York: St. Martins Press, Inc., 1963).

[3]Charles P. Kindleberger, "Terms of Trade for Primary Products," in Marion Clawson, ed., *Natural Resources and International Development* (Baltimore: Johns Hopkins Press, 1964).

[4]E. M. Ojala, "Some Current Issues of International Commodity Policy," *Journal of Agricultural Economics* (British) 18 (January 1967): 38.

[5]Ibid., p. 40.

[6]This leads to the "theorem of second best" developed by Meade in *International Economic Policy.*

[7]Irving B. Kravis, "International Commodity Agreements to Promote Aid and Efficiency: The Case of Coffee," *Canadian Journal of Economics* 1 (May 1968): 297.

[8]For a more comprehensive discussion of these and other agreements, see MacBean, *Export Instability;* or IBRD-IMF Joint Staff Study, *The Problem of Stabilization of Prices of Primary Products,* Part 1 (Washington, D.C.: 1969).

[9]Kravis, "International Commodity Agreements," p. 317.

[10]John Pincus, "Commodity Agreements: Bonanza or Illusion?" *Columbia Journal of World Business* 2 (January 1967): 41–50.

[11]Gerda Blau, "International Commodity Contracts," *Proceedings and Reports, International Conference of Agricultural Economists* (Minsk: 1970), pp. 301–302.

[12]Including the Organization of American States, the United Nations, and the International Monetary Fund.

[13]This section is based in part on an unpublished paper by Earl Kellogg.

[14]IMF, *Compensatory Financing of Export Fluctuations* (Washington, D.C.: September 1966).

[15]Ibid., p. 23.

[16]Ibid., p. 25.

[17]Actually the IMF requires countries to furnish evidence of self-help in offsetting export fluctuations.

[18]Marcus Fleming et al., "Export Norms and Their Role in Compensatory Financing," *International Monetary Fund Staff Papers*, volume 10 (March 1963), pp. 97–149.

[19]The deviation ratio measures the change in variation of export earnings around the export norm relative to that which occurred without a compensatory financing program. A deviation ratio greater than one means that the program increased year-to-year fluctuations in export earnings.

Chapter 9

[1]International comparison of degrees of protection is further complicated by the existence of nonequilibrium exchange rates in many countries. For a

discussion of this question see Benjamin I. Cohen, "The Use of Effective Tariffs," *Journal of Political Economy* 79 (January-February 1971): 128–41.

[2]L. J. Wipf, "Tariffs, Non-Tariff Distortion, and Effective Protection in U.S. Agriculture," *American Journal of Agricultural Economcs* 53 (August 1971): 423–30.

[3]For an assessment of the impact of food aid on several specific recipient countries, see Witt and Eicher, *Agricultural Surplus Disposal Programs.* For a more generalized assessment of the impact of U.S. food aid, see Per Pinstrup-Anderson and Luther G. Tweeten, "The Value, Cost, and Efficiency of American Food Aid," *American Journal of Agricultural Economics* 53 (August 1971): 431–40.

[4]F. O. Grogan, *International Trade in Temperate Zone Products* (Edinburgh: Oliver and Boyd, 1972), p. 101.

[5]UNCTAD, *Commodity Problems and Policies: Pricing Policy Including International Price Stabilization Measures and Mechanisms,* TD/127, 7 February 1972.

[6]UNCTAD, *Commodity Problems and Policies: Access to Markets,* TD/115, 27 January 1972.

[7]J. E. Meade, "International Commodity Agreements," in *Proceedings of the United Nations Conference on Trade and Development,* volume 3 (1964), p. 451.

[8]UNCTAD, *Review of Trade in Manufactures of Developing Countries,* TD/111, 10 December 1971, p. 8. Manufactures include SITC groups 5 to 8 less 68.

[9]Ibid., p. 19.

[10]Quoted in Harry Johnson, *Economic Policies Toward Less Developed Countries* (Washington, D.C.: The Brookings Institution, 1967), pp. 104–105.

[11]John W. Evans, *The Kennedy Round in American Trade Policy: The Twilight of the GATT* (Cambridge, Mass.: Harvard University Press, 1971), pp. 230–31.

[12]The special problems of less developed countries in GATT were not unnoticed. A 1963 program of action was established to deal specifically with their problems. The program included the following major substantive points: standstill provisions on tariff barriers; elimination of quantitative restrictions; duty-free entry for tropical products; elimination of tariffs on primary products; reduction and elimination of tariff barriers to exports of semiprocessed products from developing countries; and progressive reduction of internal fiscal charges and revenue duties. Little action followed, however.

[13]UNCTAD E/Conf. 46/36 Geneva, 3 March 1964, cited in Curzon, *Multilateral Commercial Diplomacy,* p. 332.

[14]Johnson, *Economic Policies,* pp. 22–23.

[15]See Prebisch, "Toward a New Trade Policy"; and UNCTAD, *Towards a New Policy.*

[16]For a discussion of this point, see Sidney Weintraub, *Trade Preferences for Less Developed Countries* (New York: Praeger Publishers, 1967), p. 56.

[17]As of 9 March 1972, some 18 countries had entered into some form of preference arrangement with developing countries. In principle, preferences apply to certain classes of manufactures and semimanufactures as designated in standard tariff nomenclature. The arrangements, however, include exception lists designated by individual preference-giving nations. The depth of tariff cuts the method of calculating ceilings, and tariff quotas (safeguard mechanisms) vary among countries. For an assessment, see UNCTAD, *The Generalized System of Preferences,* TD/124, 12 November 1971, and TD/124, 9

March 1972. UNCTAD reports with detailed accounting of a number of individual country preference systems also are available.

[18] For a full discussion of this agreement, see Josling, *United Kingdom Grains Agreement.*

[19] Weintraub, *Trade Preferences,* p. 148.

[20] The argument sometimes presented that the U.S. sugar program benefits developing nations because of its high import price hardly seems valid. These high prices have been accompanied by gradually reduced quotas. Furthermore, it fails to recognize the employment and other dynamic effects of expanded output of developing countries' commodities for which there is a cost advantage. If measured against a program, as in Europe, where protection exists and import prices are low, the U.S. program is a gain to developing nations, but probably not if measured against a condition of no protection.

[21] As implied by this, economic integration can take several forms and encompasses varying degrees of interaction and policy coordination. As stated by Bela Balassa: "These are a free-trade area, a customs union, a common market, an economic union and complete economic integration. In a free-trade area, tariffs (and quantitative restrictions)between the participating countries are abolished, but each country retains its own tariffs against nonmembers. Establishing a customs union involves, besides the suppression of discrimination in the field of commodity movements within the union, the equalization of tariffs in trade with nonmember countries. A higher form of economic integration is attained in a common market, where not only trade restrictions but also restrictions on factor movements are abolished. An economic union, as distinct from a common market, combines the suppression of restrictions on commodity and factor movements with some degree of harmonization of national economic policies, in order to remove discrimination that was due to disparities in these policies. Finally, total economic integration presupposes the unification of monetary, fiscal, social and countercyclical policies and requires the setting-up of a supranational authority whose decisions are binding for the member states." Bela Balassa, *The Theory of Economic Integration* (Homewood: Richard D. Irwin, Inc., 1961), p. 2.

[22] See, for example, Jacob Viner, *The Customs Union Issue* (New York: Carnegie Endowment for International Peace, 1950); and J. E. Meade, *The Theory of Customs Unions* (Amsterdam: North Holland Publishing Co., 1955).

[23] Bela Balassa, *Lectures: Economic Development and Integration* (Mexico: Centro de Estudios Monetarios Latino Americanos, 1965), p. 28.

[24] In LAFTA, efforts to coordinate trade and regional development have been sought through a series of complementation agreements. As summarized by J. N. Behrman, "these agreements may merely include tariff reductions or extend to the elimination of all duties and allocation of production among members. The agreements must be open to all LAFTA members, and concessions must be automatically extended to the lesser-developed countries (Bolivia, Ecuador, and Paraguay). The agreements are also supposed to include means of harmonizing the members' treatment of imports from third countries (both inside and outside LAFTA) of similar products or materials and components; treatment of capital inflows and related services is likewise to be harmonized." J. N. Behrman, *The Role of International Companies in Latin*

American Integration (New York: Committee for Economic Development, 1972), p. 23.

[25]S. S. Dell, *Trade Blocs and Common Markets* (New York: Alfred A. Knopf, 1963), p. 239.

[26]B. F. Massell, *The Distribution of Gains in a Common Market: The East African Case* (Santa Monica: The RAND Corporation, 1964).

[27]Dell, *Trade Blocs,* p. 227.

[28]Ernst B. Hass and Philippe C. Schmitter, *The Politics of Economics in Latin American Free Trade Association After Four Years of Operation,* Monograph No. 2 (Denver: University of Denver, 1965–1966), p. 64.

[29]UNCTAD, *Towards a New Trade Policy for Development,* p. 65.

Chapter 10

[1]This chapter has benefited from unpublished material prepared by George McDowell for classroom purposes.

[2]George L. Hicks and Geoffrey McNicol, *Trade and Growth in the Philippines* (Ithaca: Cornell University Press, 1971), p. 6.

[3]Gerald Meier, *The International Economics of Development* (New York: Harper and Row, 1968), p. 240.

[4]For a review of this contemporary theory, see H. B. Chenery, "Comparative Advantage and Development Policy," *American Economic Review* 51 (March 1961): 18–51; or John Pincus, *Trade, Aid and Development* (Hightstown: McGraw-Hill Book Co., 1967), chapter 4. I base the summary presented here more directly on the article by Chenery.

[5]Chenery, "Comparative Advantage," p. 28.

[6]Proposed originally by Walter Galenson and Harvey Liebenstein in "Investment Criteria, Productivity and Economic Development," *Quarterly Journal of Economics* 69 (August 1955): 343–70.

[7]Chenery, "Comparative Advantage," p. 30.

[8]Otto Eckstein, "Investment Criteria for Economic Development and the Theory of Intertemporal Welfare Economics," *Quarterly Journal of Economics* 71 (February 1957): 56–85; or see Chenery, "Comparative Advantage."

[9]Other leading writers who support the concept of balanced growth include C. S. Lewis and P. N. Rosenstein-Rodan. Leading proponents of unbalanced growth are A. O. Hirschman and Paul Streeten.

[10]Ragnar Nurske, "The Conflict Between Balanced Growth and International Specialization," in Gerald Meier, ed., *Leading Issues in Economic Development, Selected Materials and Commentary* (New York: Oxford University Press, 1964), pp. 251, 254.

[11]A. O. Hirschman, *The Strategy of Economic Development* (New Haven: Yale University Press, 1958).

[12]Ibid., p. 65.

[13]Ibid., p. 66.

[14]Ibid., p. 121

[15]Myint, *Economic Theory,* p. 164.

[16]Ibid., p. 166.

[17]Paul Streeten, "Balanced Versus Unbalanced Growth," in Meier, ed., *Leading Issues,* pp. 259–63.

[18]UNCTAD, *Commodity Problems and Policies: Diversification,* TD/119, February 1972.

[19]This general concept has been formalized through the theory of representative demand. "According to this theory, a country is most efficient in the manufacture of goods that fit into the economic structure of the domestic market. Inventors, innovators, and entrepreneurs are stimulated by home demand." See Linder, *Trade,* p. 36.

[20]Based on recent observation in Kenya by the author.

[21]Unfortunately, marketing boards are more frequently used as mechanisms of control than as tools of development.

[22]Maurice Byé, "Internal Structural Changes Required by Growth and Changes in International Trade," in R. F. Harrod and D. C. Hague, eds., *International Trade Theory in a Developing World* (New York: St. Martin's Press, Inc., 1963, p. 151.

[23]This is an important component in the discussion of balanced versus unbalanced growth. A concise statement of the concept and possible implications of dynamic externalities is presented in Haberler, "Assessment of the Current Relevance," p. 30.

[24]Johnson, *Economic Policies,* p. 53. Johnson uses the terms *macro level* and *micro level dynamics* to distinguish these two approaches.

[25]Meier, *International Economics* (New York: Harper and Row, 1968), p. 240.

[26]Ibid., p. 245.

[27]Chenery, "Comparative Advantage," p. 39.

[28]Michael Bruno, "The Optimal Selection of Export-Promoting and Import-Substituting Projects," in United Nations, *Planning the External Sector: Techniques, Problems and Policies,* Report on the First Interregional Seminar on Development Planning, Ankara, Turkey, 6–17 September 1965 (New York: United Nations, 1967), pp. 88–135.

[29]Paul Streeten and Diane Elson, *Diversification and Development: The Case of Coffee* (New York: Praeger Publishers, 1971), p. 28.

[30]IMF-IBRD, *Stabilization of Prices,* chapter 7.

[31]U.S. Department of Agriculture, *Portugal's Tomato Processing Industry,* FAS M-196 (Washington, D.C.: U.S. Government Printing Office, January 1968).

[32]Streeten and Elson, *Diversification and Development,* p. 31.

[33]Ibid.

[34]Myint, *Economic Theory,* p. 49.

[35]Ibid., p. 164.

[36]Ibid.

[37]UNCTAD, *Towards a New Trade Policy.*

[38]Little et al., *Industry and Trade,* p. 21.

[39]MacBean, *Export Instability,* p. 227.

[40]Little et al., *Industry and Trade,* p. 15.

[41]For an accounting of one rather extensive program see Park Pil Soo, "Government Export Promotion Policy," report at a seminar, "Korea, Foreign Trade and Balance of Payments," Academy House, Seoul, 28–29 January 1971.

Chapter 11

[1]Meade, *Theory*, vol. 2, p. 565.
[2]Ibid., pp. 566–68.
[3]EEC, *Organization of World Markets for Agricultural Commodities*, Agricultural Series 15 (Brussels: 1964).
[4]These arguments are based on Meade, *Theory*.
[5]Report to the President, *United States International Policy*.

Bibliography

Books

Adler, J. H., and Kuznets, D. W. *Capital Movements and Economic Development.* New York: The Macmillan Co., 1967.

Aliber, Robert Z. "A Theory of Direct Foreign Investment." In *The International Corporation,* edited by Charles P. Kindleberger. Cambridge, Mass.: The MIT Press, 1970.

Balassa, Bela. *Lectures: Economic Development and Integration.* Mexico: Centro de Estudios Monetarios Latino Americanos, 1965.

———. *The Theory of Economic Integration.* Homewood: Richard D. Irwin, Inc., 1961.

———.*Trade Prospects for Developing Countries.* Homewood: Richard D. Irwin, Inc., 1964.

Baran, Paul A. *The Political Economy of Growth.* New York: Monthly Review Press, Inc., 1968.

Bhagwati, Jagdish. "Immiserizing Growth: A Geometrical Note." In *AEA Readings in International Economics.* Homewood: Richard D. Irwin, Inc., 1968.

Black, Lloyd D. *The Strategy of Foreign Aid.* New York: Van Nostrand Reinhold Co., 1968.

Brandis, R. Buford. "The National Need for an Integrated Trade Policy: The Textile Example." In *U.S. Trade Policy.* Ames: The Iowa State University Press, 1973.

Brigden, J. B., et. al. *The Australian Tariff; An Economic Inquiry.* 2d ed. Melbourne: Melbourne University Press, 1929.

Byé, Maurice. "Internal Structural Changes quired by Growth and Changes in International Trade." In *International Trade Theory in a Developing World,* edited by R. F. Harrod and D. C. Hague. New York: St. Martin's Press, Inc., 1963.

Caves, Richard E. *Trade and Economic Structure.* Cambridge, Mass.: Harvard University Press, 1963.

Chenery, H. B., and Tinbergen, Jan, et al. *Towards a Strategy for Development Cooperation.* Rotterdam: Universitaire Pers Rotterdam, 1967.

Cochrane, Willard W. "Agriculture and Trade Development in the LDCs." In *U.S. Trade Policy and Agricultural Exports.* Ames: The Iowa State University Press, 1973.

Condliffe, John B. *The Commerce of Nations.* New York: W. W. Norton and Company, 1950.

Curzon, Gerald. *Multilateral Commercial Diplomacy: The General Agreement on Tariffs and Trade and Its Impact on National Commercial Policies and Techniques.* London: Michael Joseph Publishers, 1965.

Daniels, John D. *Recent Foreign Direct Manufacturing Investment in the U.S.* New York: Praeger Publishers, 1971.

Dell, S. S. *Trade Blocs and Common Markets.* New York: Alfred A. Knopf, 1963.

268   Bibliography

DeVries, Barend A. *The Export Experience of Developing Countries*. Baltimore: The Johns Hopkins Press, 1967.

Dillard, Dudley. *Economic Development of the North Atlantic Community*. Englewood Cliffs: Prentice-Hall, Inc., 1967.

Dunning, J. H. *Studies in International Investment*. New York: Humanities Press, Inc., 1970.

Evans, John W. *The Kennedy Round in American Trade Policy: The Twilight of the GATT*. Cambridge, Mass.: Harvard University Press, 1971.

Freeman, A. M. *International Trade: An Introduction to Method and Theory*. New York: Harper and Row, 1971.

Friedman, Wolfgang G.; Kalmanoff, George; and Meagher, Robert F. *International Financial Aid*. New York: Columbia University Press, 1966.

Furtado, Celso. *Obstacles to Development in Latin America*. New York: Anchor Books, 1970.

Fusfeld, Daniel R. *The Age of the Economist*. Glenview: Scott, Foresman and Company, 1966.

Galbraith, John Kenneth. *Economic Development*. Cambridge, Mass.: Harvard University Press, 1968.

Grogan, F. O. *International Trade in Temperate Zone Products*. Edinburgh: Oliver and Boyd, 1972.

Haberler, Gottfried. *A Survey of International Trade Theory*. Princeton: Princeton University Press, 1961.

————. *The Theory of International Trade with Its Applications to Commercial Policy*. New York: The Macmillan Co., 1936.

Hagen, Everett E. *The Economics of Development*. Homewood: Richard D. Irwin, Inc., 1968.

Hallet, Graham. *The Economics of Agricultural Policy*. Oxford: Basil Blackwell, 1958.

Hathaway, Dale. *Government and Agriculture: Public Policy in a Democratic Society*. New York: The Macmillan Co., 1963.

————. "Trade Restrictions and U.S. Consumers." In *U.S. Trade Policy*. Ames: The Iowa State University Press, 1973.

————. *Problems of Progress in the Agricultural Economy*. Glenview: Scott, Foresman and Company, 1964.

Heller, H. Robert. *International Trade Theory and Empirical Evidence*. Englewood Cliffs: Prentice-Hall, Inc., 1968.

Hicks, George L., and McNicol, Geoffrey. *Trade and Growth in the Philippines*. Ithaca: Cornell University Press, 1971.

Hirschman, A. O. *The Strategy of Economic Development*. New Haven: Yale University Press, 1958.

Jalee, Pierre. *The Third World in World Economy*. New York: Monthly Review Press, Inc., 1969.

Johnson, Glenn L. "Implications of the IMS for Study of Responses to Price." In *A Study of Managerial Processes of Midwestern Farmers*, by Glenn L. Johnson et al. Ames: The Iowa State University Press, 1961.

————. "Supply Functions — Some Facts and Notions." In *Agricultural Adjustment Problems in a Growing Economy*. Ames: The Iowa State University Press, 1956.

———— and Sorenson, Vernon L. "The World Food Situation: Challenge and Opportunities Facing North America." In *A North American Common Market.* Ames: The Iowa State University Press, 1973.

Johnson, Harry G. "Economic Development and International Trade." In *AEA Readings in International Economics.* Homewood: Richard D. Irwin, Inc., 1968.

————. *Economic Policies Toward Less Developed Countries.* Washington, D.C.: The Brookings Institution, 1967.

————. "Effects of Change in Comparative Costs as Influenced by Technical Change." In *International Trade Theory in a Developing World,* edited by R. F. Harrod and D. C. Hague. New York: St. Martin's Press, Inc., 1963.

————. *Trade and Economic Growth.* Cambridge, Mass.: Harvard University Press, 1965.

————. *Trade Policies Toward Less Developed Countries.* Washington, D.C.: The Brookings Institution, 1967.

————. *The World Economy at the Crossroads.* New York: Oxford University Press, 1965.

Johnstone, Allan W. *United States Direct Investment in France: An Investigation of the French Charges.* Cambridge, Mass.: The MIT Press, 1965.

Kaplan, Jacob J. *The Challenge of Foreign Aid.* New York: Praeger Publishers, 1967.

Keynes, J. M. *Essays in Persuasion.* New York: Harcourt, Brace and World, Inc., 1932.

Kindleberger, Charles P. *American Business Abroad: Six Lectures on Direct Investment.* New Haven: Yale University Press, 1969.

————. *Foreign Trade and the National Economy.* New Haven: Yale University Press, 1962.

————. *International Economics.* 3d ed. Homewood: Richard D. Irwin, Inc., 1963.

————. "Terms of Trade for Primary Products." In *Natural Resources and International Development,* edited by Marion Clawson. Baltimore: Johns Hopkins Press, 1964.

Krause, L.B. *European Economic Integration and the United States.* Washington, D.C.: The Brookings Institution, 1968.

Kumar, Dharma. *India and the European Economic Community.* New York: Asia Publishing House, 1966.

Lakdawala, D. T. "Commercial Policy and Economic Growth." In *Trade Theory and Commercial Policy in Relation to Underdeveloped Countries,* edited by A. K. Dasgupta. New York: Asia Publishing House, 1963.

Lewis, S. R., Jr. "Agricultural Taxation in a Developing Economy." In *Agricultural Development and Economic Growth,* edited by H. M. Southworth and B. F. Johnston. Ithaca: Cornell University Press, 1967.

Linder, S. B. *Trade and Trade Policy for Development.* New York: Praeger Publishers, 1967.

Little, I. M. D.; Scitovsky, Tibor; and Scott, Maurice. *Industry and Trade in Some Developing Countries: A Comparative Analysis.* New York: Oxford University Press, 1971.

Little, I. M. D., and Clifford, J. M. *International Aid.* Chicago: Aldine Publishing Company, 1966.

Litvak, Isaiah A., and Maule, C. J. "The Issues of Direct Foreign Investment." In *Foreign Investment: The Experience of Host Countries*, edited by I. A. Litvak and C. J. Maule. New York: Praeger Publishers, 1970.

MacBean, A. I. *Export Instability and Economic Development.* Cambridge, Mass.: Harvard University Press, 1966.

Mackie, Arthur B. "Patterns of World Agricultural Trade." In *U.S. Trade Policy.* Ames: The Iowa State University Press, 1973.

Mandez, Ernest. *Europe versus America: Contradictions of Imperialism.* New York: Monthly Review Press, 1970.

Mason, Edward S. *Economic Concentration and the Monopoly Problem.* Cambridge, Mass.: Harvard University Press, 1959.

Massell, B. F. *The Distribution of Gains in a Common Market: The East African Case.* Santa Monica: The RAND Corporation, 1964.

Maizels, Alfred. *Industrial Growth and World Trade.* Cambridge: the University Press, 1963.

Meade, J. E. *The Theory of Customs Unions.* Amsterdam: North-Holland Publishers, 1955.

————. *The Theory of International Economic Policy.* New York: Oxford University Press, 1955.

Meier, Gerald. *International Economics of Development.* New York: Harper and Row, 1968.

————. *International Trade and Development.* New York: Harper and Row, 1963.

————, ed. *Leading Issues in Economic Development, Selected Materials and Commentary.* New York: Oxford University Press, 1964.

Mikesell, R. F. *The Economics of Foreign Aid.* Chicago: Aldine Publishing Company, 1968.

Morgan, Theodore. "Trends in Terms of Trade and Their Repercussions on Primary Producers." In *International Trade Theory in a Developing World,* edited by R. F. Harrod and D. C. Hague. New York: St. Martin's Press, Inc., 1963.

Mookerjee, Subimal. *Factor Endowment and International Trade.* Bombay: Asia Publishing House, 1958.

Myint, Hla. *Economic Theory and the Underdeveloped Countries.* New York: Oxford University Press, 1971.

Myrdal, Gunnar. *Rich Lands and Poor Lands.* New York: Harper and Brothers, 1957.

Nurske, Ragnar. "The Conflict Between Balanced Growth and International Specialization." In *Leading Issues in Economic Development, Selected Materials and Commentary,* edited by Gerald Meier. New York: Oxford University Press, 1964.

————. "Growth — Balanced or Unbalanced?" In *Leading Issues in Economic Development,* edited by Gerald Meier. New York: Oxford University Press, 1964.

Okigbo, Pius. *Africa and the Common Market.* Evanston: Northwestern University Press, 1967.

Papanek, Gustav F. "Changes in Aid Strategy: A Note to Some Less Developed Countries and Their Friends." In *The First U.N. Development Decade and Its Lessons for the 1970s,* edited by Colin Legum. New York: Praeger Publishers, 1970.

Pincus, John. "Commodity Agreements: Bonanza or Illusion?" In *Reshaping the World Economy: Rich and Poor Countries,* edited by John Pincus. Englewood Cliffs: Prentice-Hall, Inc., 1968.

————. *Economic Aid and International Cost Sharing.* Baltimore: Johns Hopkins Press, 1965.

————. *Trade, Aid and Development.* New York: McGraw-Hill Book Company, 1967.

Powelson, J. P. *Latin America – Today's Economic and Social Revaluation.* New York: McGraw-Hill Book Company, 1964.

————. "Toward a New Policy for Trade and Development." In *Reshaping the World Economy: Rich and Poor Countries,* edited by John Pincus. Englewood Cliffs: Prentice-Hall, Inc., 1968.

Prebisch, Raul. "Toward a New Trade Policy for Development." In *Reshaping the World Economy: Rich and Poor Countries,* edited by John Pincus. Englewood Cliffs: Prentice-Hall, Inc., 1968.

Ramazani, Rouhollah K. *The Middle East and the European Common Market.* Charlottesville: The University Press of Virginia, 1964.

Rowthorn, Robert. *International Big Business 1957–1967.* New York: Cambridge University Press, 1971.

Schultz, T. W. "U.S. Malinvestment in Food for the World." In *Balancing Future World Food Production and Needs.* Ames: The Iowa State University Press, 1967.

Singer, H. W. "The Distribution of Gains Between Investing and Borrowing Countries." In *AEA Readings in International Economics.* Homewood: Richard D. Irwin, Inc., 1968.

Sorenson, Vernon. "Contradictions in U.S. Trade Polcy." In *U.S. Trade Policy.* Ames: The Iowa State University Press, 1973.

Stern, R. M. "A Century of Food Exports." In *Foreign Agricultural Trade: Selected Readings,* edited by Robert L. Tontz. Ames: The Iowa State University Press, 1966.

Streeten, Paul P. "Balanced Versus Unbalanced Growth." In *Leading Issues in Development Economics,* edited by Gerald Meier. New York: Oxford University Press, 1964.

———— and Elson, Diane. *Diversification and Development: The Case of Coffee.* New York: Praeger Publishers, 1971.

Swann, Dennis. *The Economics of the Common Market.* 2d ed. Baltimore: Penguin Books, 1972.

Sweezy, Paul M., and Magdoff, Harry. *The Dynamics of U.S. Capitalism: Corporate Structure, Credit, Gold and the Dollar.* New York: Monthly Review Press, 1972.

Talbot, Ross B. "Effects of Domestic Political Groups and Forces on U.S. Trade Policy." In *U.S. Trade Policy.* Ames: The Iowa State University Press, 1973.

Tausig, F. W. *Tariff History of the United States,* 8th ed. New York: G. P. Putnam's Sons, 1964.

Thorbeck, Erik, and Condliffe, J. B. "The Pattern of World Trade in Foodstuffs: Past and Present." In *Food – One Tool for Economic Development.* Ames: The Iowa State University Press, 1962.

Tontz, Robert L., ed. *Foreign Agricultural Trade: Selected Readings.* Ames: The Iowa State University Press, 1966.

———. "U.S. Trade Policy: Background and Historical Trends," In *U.S. Trade Policy.* Ames: The Iowa State University Press, 1973.

Towle, L. W. *International Trade and Commercial Policy.* New York: Harper and Brothers, 1957.

Tracy, Michael. *Agriculture in Western Europe: Crisis and Adaptation Since 1880.* London: Jonathan Cape, 1964.

Tugendhat, Christopher. *The Multinationals.* London: Eyre and Spottiswoode, 1971.

Urquidy, Victor L. "The Common Market as a Tool for Economic Development." In *Latin American Issues: Essays and Comments,* edited by A. O. Hirschman. New York: Twentieth Century Fund, 1961.

Vernon, Raymond. *Sovereignty at Bay: The Multinational Spread of U.S. Enterprises.* New York: Zanic Books, 1971.

Viner, Jacob. *The Customs Union Issue.* New York: Carnegie Endowment for International Peace, 1950.

———. "International Trade Theory and Its Present Day Relevance." In *Foreign Agricultural Trade: Selected Readings,* edited by Robert L. Tontz. Ames: The Iowa State University Press, 1966.

Walter, Ingo. *The European Common Market.* New York: Praeger Publishers, 1967.

Ward, Barbara, et al. *The Widening Gap: Development in the 1970s.* New York: Columbia University Press, 1971.

Wharton, C. R., Jr. "Rubber Supply Conditions: Some Policy Implications." In *The Political Economy of Independent Malaya,* edited by T. H. Silcock and E. K. Fisk. Berkeley: University of California Press, 1963.

Weintraub, Sidney. *Trade Preferences for Less Developed Countries.* New York: Praeger Publishers, 1966.

Wilkins, Mira. *The Emergence of Multinational Enterprise: American Business Abroad from the Colonial Era to 1914.* Cambridge, Mass.: Harvard University Press, 1970.

Williams, D. B., ed. *Agriculture in the Australian Economy.* Sidney: Sidney University Press, 1967.

Yates, P. Lamartine. *Forty Years of Foreign Trade.* New York: The Macmillan Co., 1959.

Young, J. B. *Canadian Commercial Policy.* Ottawa: Queens Printers, 1957.

Journal Articles

Abel, Martin E. "Price Discrimination in the World Trade of Agricultural Commodities." *Journal of Farm Economics* 48 (May 1966): 194–208.

Allen, Robert L., and Walter, Ingo. "The Formation of United States Trade Policy: Retrospect and Prospect." *The Bulletin,* no. 70–71 (February 1971).

Bastanchuri, Carlos. "Latin American Agricultural Trade with the European Common Market." *International Journal of Agrarian Affairs* 4 (April 1964): 78–98.

Brunthaver, C. G. "U.K. Grain Agreement: Format for an International Grain Agreement?" *Journal of Farm Economics* 47 (February 1965): 51–59.

Chenery, H. B. "Comparative Advantage and Development Policy." *American Economic Review* 51 (March 1961): 18–51.

Cochrane, Willard W. "Public Law 480 and Related Programs." *Annals of the American Academy of Political and Social Science* (September 1960): 14–19.

Cohen, Benjamin I. "The Use of Effective Tariffs." *Journal of Political Economy* 79 (January-February 1971): 128–41.

Cordon, W. M. "The Structure of a Tariff System and the Effective Protective Rate." *Journal of Political Economy* 74 (June 1966): 221–37.

Eckstein, Otto. "Investment Criteria for Economic Development and the Theory of Intertemporal Welfare Economics." *Quarterly Journal of Economics* 71 (February 1957): 56–85.

Edwards, Clark. "Resource Fixity and Farm Organization." *Journal of Farm Economics* 41 (November 1959): 747–59.

Ellsworth, P. T. "The Structure of American Foreign Trade." *Review of Economics and Statistics* 54 (August 1954): 267–85.

Evans, David P. "U.K. Sets New Farm Price Guarantees, Moves Toward Variable Levies — Part II." *Foreign Agriculture*, 10 May 1970.

Fleming, Marcus; Rhomberg, R. R.; and Boisonneault, Lorette. "Export Norms and Their Role in Compensatory Financing." *International Monetary Fund Staff Papers* 10 (March 1963): 97–149.

Fuller, Varden, and Menzie, Elmer L. "Trade Liberalization, U.S. Agricultural Import Restriction." *Journal of Farm Economics* 46 (February 1964): 20–38.

Galenson, Walter, and Liebenstein, Harvey. "Investment Criteria, Productivity and Economic Development." *Quarterly Journal of Economics* 69 (August 1955): 343–70.

Haberler, Gottfried. "An Assessment of the Current Relevance of the Theory of Comparative Advantage to Agricultural Production and Trade." *International Journal of Agrarian Affairs* 4 (May 1964): 130–49.

―――. "Some Problems in the Pure Theory of International Trade." *Economic Journal* 60 (June 1950): 223–40.

Hedges, Irwin. "Kennedy Round Agricultural Negotiations and the World Grains Agreement." *Journal of FRM Economins* 49 (December 1967):41.

Hillman, Jimmye S. "The Peril Point and Section 22 Provisions — Asset or Liability?" *Proceedings, Western Farm Economics Association*, 23–26 August 1960, pp. 10–24.

Houthakker, H. S. "Domestic Farm Policy and International Trade." *American Journal of Agricultural Economics* 53 (December 1971): 762–66.

International Monetary Fund. *International Financial Statistics* 23 (September 1970).

Josling, T. E. "A Formal Approach to Agricultural Policy." *Journal of Agricultural Economics* (British) 20 (May 1969): 175–96.

Johnson, D. Gale. "Trade Policies and U.S. Agriculture." *Journal of Farm Economics* 48 (May 1966): 339–50.

Johnson, Glenn L. "The State of Agricultural Supply Analysis." *Journal of Farm Economics* 42 (May 1960): 435–52.

Johnson, Harry G. "Tariffs and Economic Development: Some Theoretical Issues." *Journal of Development Studies* 1 (October 1964): 3–30.

Kessel, Dudley. "Effective Protection of Industry in Tanzania." *East African Economic Review* 4 (June 1968): 1–18.

Kravis, Irving B. "International Commodity Agreements to Promote Aid and Efficiency: The Case of Coffee." *Canadian Journal of Economics* 1 (May 1968): 295–317.

Lewis, S. R., Jr. "Effects of Trade Policy on Domestic Relative Prices: Pakistan, 1951–64." *American Economic Review* 58 (March 1968): 60–78.

Lim, Chong-Yah. "Export Taxes on Rubber in Malaya — A Survey of Post-War Development." *Malayan Economic Review* 5 (October 1960): 46–58.

Longworth, John W. "The Stabilization and Distribution Effects of Australian Wheat Industry Stabilization Schemes." *Australian Journal of Agricultural Economics* 2 (June 1967): 20–35.

MacGougall, G. A. D. "British and American Exports." *Economic Journal* 61 (December 1951): 697–724.

Mansholt, Sicco L. "Answer to Farm Reform Critics." *European Community*, no. 138 (September 1970): 6–9.

McCalla, Alex F. "A Duopoly Model of World Wheat Pricing." *Journal of Farm Economics* 48 (August 1966): 711–27.

Mead, D. C. "Effective Protection and Investment Criteria." *East African Economic Review* 2 (June 1970): 65–69.

Meeker, Brice M. "U.S. Feed Grain Markets in the Netherlands." *USDA Foreign Agriculture*, 24 August 1970.

Meier, Gerald. "Export Stimulation, Import Substitutions and Latin American Development." *Social and Economic Studies* 10 (March 1961): 42–62.

Mendelsohn, Chaim. "Approaches to International Trade Under Nonprice Competition." *Journal of Farm Economics* 39 (December 1957): 1724–31.

Mikesell, Raymond F. "International Commodity Stabilization Schemes and the Export Problems of Developing Countries." *American Economic Review* 53 (May 1963): 75–92.

Myint, Hla. "The 'Classical Theory' of International Trade and the Underdeveloped Countries." *Economic Journal* 68 (June 1958): 317–37.

Nurske, Ragnar. "Trade Fluctuations and Buffer Policies of Low-Income Countries." *Kyklos* 11 (Fasc. 2, 1958): 145–54.

Ojala, E. M. "Some Current Issues of International Commodity Policy." *Journal of Agricultural Economics* (British) 18 (January 1967): 27–51.

Perlmutter, H. V. "Super-Giant Firms in the Future." *Wharton Quarterly* 3–4 (Winter 1968): 8–14.

Pinstrup-Anderson, Per, and Tweeten, Luther G. "The Value, Cost, and Efficiency of American Food Aid." *American Journal of Agricultural Economics* 53 (August 1971): 431–40.

Robson, Peter. "East Africa and the European Economic Community." *International Journal of Agrarian Affairs* 4 (April 1965): 114–27.

Schmidt, Stephen C. "Regional Distribution of EEC Food, Beverages, Tobacco, Oils and Fats Imports: The Formative Years 1951–59." *International Journal of Agrarian Affairs* 4 (April 1965): 315–34.

Sinclair, Sol. "EEC's Trade in Agricultural Products with Non-member Countries." *International Journal of Agrarian Affairs* 4 (April 1965): 287–99.

Sorenson, Vernon L. "Trade Policies and Prospects in Western Europe." *Journal of Farm Economics* 48 (December 1966): 1348–58.

Vanek, Jaroslav. "Variable Factor Proportions and Interindustry Flows in
     Trade Theory." *Quarterly Journal of Economics* 77 (February 1963): 129–42.
Wehrwein, Carl F. "Government Grain Programs of Canada, Australia, and
     the United Kingdom." *Journal of Farm Economics* 47 (November 1965):
     993–1008.
Wipf, L. J. "Tariffs, Non-Tariff Distortion, and Effective Protection in U.S.
     Agriculture." *American Journal of Agricultural Economics* 53 (August 1971):
     423–30.
Witt, Lawrence. "Trade and Agricultural Policy." *Annals of the American
     Academy of Political and Social Science* (September 1960): 1–7.

Public Documents

EEC Commission. *Fourth General Report on the Activities of the Communities, 1970.*
     Brussels: February 1971.
Great Britain. Ministry of Agriculture, Fisheries and Food. *Annual Review and
     Determination of Guarantees, 1971.* Command 4623. London: H.M.S.O.,
     March 1971.
International Monetary Fund. *Compensatory Financing of Export Fluctuations.*
     Washington, D.C.: 1966.
────── and International Bank for Reconstruction and Development. *The
     Problem of Stabilization of Prices of Primary Products.* Washington, D.C.: 1969.
Junz, Helen B. "The Border Tax Issue." In *Issues and Objectives of U.S. Foreign
     Trade Policy.* Joint Economic Committee, 90th Cong., 1st sess. Washington,
     D.C.: U.S. Government Printing Office, 1967.
Malaya. *Policies and Measures Leading Toward Greater Diversification of the Agricul-
     tural Economy,* by K. Brandt, J. N. Efferson, and D. Pearlberg. Report
     submitted to the Government of Malaya by the Survey Team Provided by
     the Ford Foundation. Kuala Lumpur: February 1963.
──────. *Report of the Mission of Inquiry into the Rubber Industry of Malaya* (F. Mudie,
     Chairman). Kuala Lumpur: 1954.
Netherlands. Agricultural Ministry. *Selected Agri-figures of the EEC.* The Hague:
     August 1967.
Organization for Economic Cooperation and Development. *Agriculture and
     Economic Growth.* Paris: 1965.
──────. *Agricultural Policies in 1966: Europe, North America and Japan.* Paris:
     1967.
──────. *Agricultural Statistics, 1968.* Paris: 1969.
──────. *Foreign Aid Policies Reconsidered,* by Goran Ohlin. Paris: 1966.
──────. *National Accounts of OECD Countries from 1950–1969.* Paris: 1970.
──────. *Policy Perspectives for International Trade and Economic Relations.* Paris:
     1972.
──────. *Resources for the Developing World.* Paris: 1970.
──────. *Summary Recommendation Adopted by the U.N. Conference on Trade and
     Development.* Paris: 1964.

United Nations. Conference on Trade and Development. *Commodity Problems and Policies.* Proceedings of the United Nations Conference on Trade and Development, Second Session, New Delhi, India, 1968. TD/97 v.2.

———. *Commodity Problems and Policies: Access to Markets.* TD/115. 27 January 1972.

———. *Commodity Problems and Policies: Diversification.* TD/119. February 1972.

———. *Commodity Problems and Policies: Pricing Policy Including International Price Stabilization Measures and Mechanisms.* TD/127. 7 February 1972.

———. *The Costs of Aid-Tying to Recipient Countries.* TD/7/Supp. 8. 1967.

———. *Economic Survey of Latin America.* E/CN. 12/E20su. 1970.

———. *Financial Resources for Development: Trade Prospects and Capital Needs of Developing Countries during the Second United Nations Development Decade.* TD/118/Supp. 3. 22 December 1971.

———. *The Generalized System of Preferences.* TD/124. 12 November 1971 and 9 March 1972.

———. *Generalized System of Preferences – EEC, U.K.* TD/B/373 Add. 8/Annex III, Add. 1, Annex III.

———. *Generalized System of Preferences, Scheme of EEC.* TD/B/396. 1972.

———. *Growth, Development and Aid: Issues and Proposals.* TD/7. 1967.

———. *Growth and External Development Finance.* TD/7/Supp. 1. 1967.

———. "International Commodity Agreements," by J. E. Meade. In *Proceedings of the United Nations Conference on Trade and Development.* E/Conf. 46/v. 3. 1964.

———. *Problems and Policies of Trade in Manufactures and Semi-Manufactures.* TD/97, v. III. 1968.

———. *Report of the Permanent Group on Synthetics and Substitutes.* TD/B/201/Rev. 1. Geneva: April 1969.

———. *Review of Trade in Manufactures of Developing Countries.* TD/111. 10 December 1971.

———. *Special Measures in Favour of the Least Developed Among the Developing Countries: Identification of the Least Developed Among the Developing Countries.* Report by the UNCTAD Secretariat. TD/B/269. 11 July 1969.

———. *A System of Preferences for Exports of Manufactures and Semi-Manufactures from Developing to Developed Countries.* TD/12. 1 November 1967.

———. *Towards a New Trade Policy and Development.* Report by the Secretary General of UNCTAD. E/Conf. 46/3. New York: 1964.

———. *Trade Prospects and Capital Needs of Developing Countries.* TD/34/Rev. 1. New York: 1968.

———. *The Tying of Aid,* by J. N. Bhagwati. TD/7/Supp. 14. New York: 1967.

United Nations. Economic Commission for Latin America. *The Economic Development of Latin America and Its Problems,* by Raul Prebisch. New York: 1950.

United Nations. Food and Agriculture Organization. "Commodity Problems and Policies. Review of International Trade and Development 1970." In *FAO Commodity Review and Outlook.* TD/97 v. 2, TD/B/309 rev. 1. Rome: 1970.

———. *National Grain Policies.* (An annual publication of FAO that provides information on production, trade, and policy for a large number of countries.)

——. "A Reconsideration of the Economics of the International Wheat Agreement," by Nicholas Kaldor. In *FAO Commodity Review and Outlook*, no. 1, 1952.

——. *FAO Production Yearbook*. (Available in annual editions.)

——. *The State of Food and Agriculture 1970*. (An annual publication.)

——. "Synthetics and Their Effects on Agricultural Trade." In *Commodity Bulletin*, Series 38. Rome: 1964.

United Nations. *Planning the External Sector: Techniques, Problems and Policies*, Report on the First Interregional Seminar on Development Planning, Ankara, Turkey, 6–17 September 1965. "The Optimal Selection of Export-Promoting and Import-Substituting Projects," by Michael Bruno. New York: United Nations, 1967.

United States. Department of Agriculture. *Agricultural Statistics, 1972*. Washington, D.C.: U.S. Government Printing Office, 1972.

——. Economic Research Service. *Agriculture in the European Economic Community: An Annotated Bibliography, 1958–66*, by Brian D. Hedges and Reed E. Friend. ERS-Foreign No. 213. Washington, D.C.: U.S. Government Printing Office, 1968.

——. Economic Research Service. *Foreign Agricultural Trade of the United States*. Issued monthly by the Foreign Agricultural Service. Washington, D.C.: U.S. Government Printing Office.

——. Economic Research Service. *Measuring the Degree and Cost of Economic Protection of Agriculture in Selected Countries*, by Rachel Dardis and Elmer W. Learn. ERS Technical Bulletin #1384. Washington, D.C.: U.S. Government Printing Office, 1967.

——. Economic Research Service. *World Trade in Selected Agricultural Commodities, 1951–65*. Foreign Agricultural Economic Report No. 42–45, 47. Washington, D.C.: U.S. Government Printing Office, 1968.

——. Foreign Agricultural Service. *International Grains Arrangement, 1967*. FAS-M-195. Washington, D.C.: U.S. Government Printing Office, November 1967.

——. Foreign Agricultural Service. *Portugal's Tomato Processing Industry*. FAS-M-196. Washington, D.C.: U.S.Government Printing Office, January 1968.

——. Foreign Agricultural Service. *Report on Agricultural Trade Negotiations of the Kennedy Round*. FAS-M-193. Washington, D.C.: U.S. Government Printing Office, September 1967.

United States. President's Commission on International Trade and Investment Policy. "Agricultural Policies of the European Community," by Raymond A. Ioanes. In *United States International Economic Policy in an Interdependent World*, vol. 2. Washington D.C.: U.S. Government Printing Office, 1971. Pp. 59–70.

——. "The Competitive Position of U.S. Agriculture," by Vernon Sorenson and Dale Hathaway. In *United States International Economic Policy in an Interdependent World*, vol. 1. Washington, D.C.: U.S. Government Printing Office, 1971. Pp. 811–32.

——. "Special Trade Negotiating Problems for Agriculture," by Howard Worthington. In *United States International Economic Policy in an Interdependent World*, vol. 1. Washington, D.C.: U.S. Government Printing Office, 1971. Pp. 859–72.

———. "Trade, A Look Ahead — Policy Recommendations," by D. Gale Johnson. In *United States International Economic Policy in an Interdependent World*, vol. 1. Washington, D.C.: U.S. Government Printing Office, 1971. Pp. 873–96.

United States. President's National Advisory Commission on Food and Fiber. "Agricultural Trade and Foreign Economic Policy," by D. Gale Johnson. In *Foreign Trade and Agricultural Policy*. Technical Papers, vol. 6. Washington, D.C.: U.S. Government Printing Office, 1971. Pp. 1–34.

———. "Agricultural Trade and Trade Policy," by Oscar Zaglitz. In *Foreign Trade and Agricultural Policy*. Technical Papers, vol. 6. Washington, D.C.: U.S. Government Printing Office, 1971. Pp. 125–269.

Witt, Lawrence, and Sorenson, Vernon. "Problems of Agricultural Products in Foreign Trade." In *Issues and Objectives of U.S. Foreign Trade Policy*. Joint Economic Committee, 90th Cong., 1st sess. Washington, D.C.: U.S. Government Printing Office, 1967.

Miscellaneous

Abel, Martin E.; Cochrane, Willard; and Wetmore, John. *Policies for Expanding the Demand for Farm Products*, Part II, *Program and Results*. University of Minnesota Technical Bulletin 238. St. Paul: April 1961.

Barnes, William Gorell. *Europe and the Developing World: Association Under Part IV of the Treaty of Rome*. Chatham House and P.E.P. European Series no. 2. London: February 1967.

Bhagwati, J. N. *Amount and Sharing of Aid*. Overseas Development Council Monograph no. 2. Washington, D.C.: 1970.

Blau, Gerda. "International Commodity Contracts." In *Proceedings and Reports, International Conference of Agricultural Economists*. Minsk: 1970.

Campbell, Donald R. "Alternatives and Opportunities for Canada in International Trade in Agricultural Products." In *Proceedings of Conference on International Trade and Canadian Agriculture*. Publication no. 5. Ottawa: Agricultural Economics Research Council of Canada, 1966.

Committee for Economic Development. *Regional Integration and Trade of Latin America*. Supplementary Paper #22. New York: CED, January 1968.

———. *The Role of International Companies in Latin American Integration*, by J. N. Behrman. New York: CED, 1972.

———. *Trade Policy Toward Low-Income Countries*. A Statement by the Research and Policy Committee. New York: CED, June 1967.

Epp, Donald J. *Changes in Regional Grain and Livestock Prices Under the European Economic Community Prices*. Research Report no. 4. East Lansing: Institute of International Agriculture, Michigan State University, 1968.

Farnsworth, Helen C. *American Wheat Exports, Policies and Prospects*. Food Research Institute, vol. 1, no. 1. Stanford: Stanford University, February 1960.

Ferris, John, et al. *The Impact on U.S. Agricultural Trade of the Accession of the United Kingdom, Ireland, Denmark and Norway to the European Economic Community.* Research Report no. 11. East Lansing: Institute of International Agriculture, Michigan State University, 1971.

Haberler, Gottfried. "An Assessment of the Current Relevance of the Theory of Comparative Advantage to Agricultural Production and Trade." In *Proceedings of the International Conference of Agricultural Economists.* London: Oxford University Press, 1966.

Hass, Ernst B., and Schmitter, Philippe C. *The Politics of Economics in Latin American Free Trade Association After Four Years of Operation.* Monograph no. 2. Denver: University of Denver, 1965–66.

Hedley, Douglas D., and Peacock, David Lewis. *Food for Peace, PL 480 and American Agriculture.* Agricultural Economics Report no. 156. East Lansing: Department of Agricultural Economics, Michigan State University, February 1970.

Johnson, D. Gale. *The Role of Trade in Improving the Welfare of the World Community or What Difference Does Trade Make?* Agricultural Economics Paper no. 71–6. Chicago: Department of Economics, University of Chicago, 3 May 1971.

Johnson, Glenn L., and Hardin, Lowell. *The Economics of Forage Evaluation.* Bulletin no. 623, Purdue Agricultural Experiment Station. Lafayette: Purdue University, 1955.

Josling, Timothy Edward. *The United Kingdom Grains Agreement (1964): An Economic Analysis.* Misc. Report no. 1. East Lansing: Institute of International Agriculture, Michigan State University, 1967.

Kiene, Werner. *Welfare Costs of Alternative Agricultural Policies in Austria.* East Lansing: Department of Agricultural Economics, Michigan State University, 1971.

Leontieff, Wassily. "Domestic Production and Foreign Trade: The American Capital Position Reexamined." In American Economic Association, *Readings in International Economics,* pp. 503–507. Homewood, Ill.: Richard D. Irwin, 1968.

Malve, Pierre, "For the Development of Dynamic Agricultural Cooperation Between the United States and Europe Through Negotiation of a New Type of International Commodity Agreement." Address before the National Association of Wheat Growers, Denver, Colorado, January 1972.

MacEachern, Gordon A., and McFarlane, David L. "The Relative Position of Canadian Agriculture in World Trade." In *Proceedings of Conference on International Trade and Canadian Agriculture.* Publication no. 5. Ottawa: Agricultural Economics Research Council of Canada, 1966.

Pee, Teck-Yew. "Agricultural Diversification in West Malaysia: Problems and Prospects." M.A. thesis, University of Hawaii, 1968.

Rivkin, Arnold. *Africa and the European Common Market: A Perspective.* Monograph Series in World Affairs. Denver: The Social Science Foundation and Graduate School of International Studies, University of Denver.

Sekhar, B. C. "Natural Rubber in the 70s." Seminar on Industrialization. Kuala Lumpur: 1971.

Seventh Flemish Economic Conference. "The Market Economy of Western Europe." Reports of Committees 3.1, 3.4, 3.5, and 4.1. Louvain: May 1965.

Shefrin, Frank. "World Agricultural Production and Trade." In *Proceedings of Conference on International Trade and Canadian Agriculture*. Publication no. 5. Ottawa: Agricultural Economics Research Council of Canada, 1966.

Soo, Park Pil. "Government Export Promotion Policy." Report at a seminar, "Korea: Foreign Trade and Balance of Payments." Seoul: Academy House, 28–29 January 1971.

Tan, Augustine H. H. "Natural Rubber: Problems and Techniques of Stabilization." M.A. prospectus, University of Malaya, 1962.

Treaty for East African Cooperation, The. Nairobi: East African Common Service Organization, 1967.

Trends in International Trade. A Report by a Panel of Experts. Geneva: GATT, October 1958.

Triantias, S. G. *Common Market and Economic Development: The EEC and Greece.* Research Monograph Series 14. Athens: Center of Planning and Economic Research, 1965.

Wetmore, John; Abel, Martin; Learn, Elmer; and Cochrane, Willard W. *Policies for Expanding the Demand for Farm Products in the United States.* Part I, "History and Potentials." Technical Bulletin no. 231. St. Paul: University of Minnesota, April 1959.

Witt, Lawrence, and Eicher, Carl K. *The Effect of United States Agricultural Surplus Disposal Programs on Recipient Countries.* Research Bulletin no. 2. East Lansing: Agricultural Experiment Station, Michigan State University, 1964.

Index